Hyperinnovation

HYPERINNOVATION

Multidimensional Enterprise in the Connected Economy

Chris Harris

palgrave
macmillan

Softcover reprint of the hardcover 1st edition 2002 978-0-333-99438-2

First published 2002 by
PALGRAVE MACMILLAN
Houndmills, Basingstoke, Hampshire RG21 6XS and
175 Fifth Avenue, New York, N.Y. 10010
Companies and representatives throughout the world

PALGRAVE MACMILLAN is the global academic imprint of the Palgrave Macmillan division of St. Martin's Press, LLC and of Palgrave Macmillan Ltd. Macmillan® is a registered trademark in the United States, United Kingdom and other countries. Palgrave is a registered trademark in the European Union and other countries.

ISBN 978-1-349-43238-7 ISBN 978-1-4039-0735-6 (eBook)
DOI 10.1057/9781403907356

This book is printed on paper suitable for recycling and made from fully managed and sustained forest sources.

A catalogue record for this book is available from the British Library.

A catalog record for this book is available from the Library of Congress.

10 9 8 7 6 5 4 3 2 1
11 10 09 08 07 06 05 04 03 02

Editing and origination by Aardvark Editorial, Mendham, Suffolk

Transferred to Digital Printing 2012

For Sarah Harris

May you have good ideas

CONTENTS

List of Figures and Tables

Figures

Tables

INTRODUCTION

Hyper: many interconnected dimensions
Innovation: successful implementation of new ideas

As we set off into the twenty-first century, we are suddenly, and quite dramatically, faced with fundamentally different industry structures; configurations and patterns like none we have experienced before.

Specifically, these new structures have begun to interconnect a diversity of ideas, technologies and organisations to emerge as brand new product and service archetypes. Of late, these innovations have been widely viewed as a result of so-called technological convergence. But in truth, if we care to scan the wider business landscape, convergence is not the only driving force at work here. If we open our eyes, we begin to see the collateral *convergence*, *divergence*, *paralleling*, *panning*, *customising*, *real-time* and *accelerated pace* of innovation. Thus these new industry structures, and the innovative products and services that emerge, are not simply a result of convergence, but quite literally *the multidimensional interconnection of ideas*.

The surprise in all of this, however, is that this kind of *hyperinnovation* is not merely confined to the internet, but quite explicitly impacts on the naked marketplace; even hard physical artefacts are being transformed.

Just take a look around: more ideas are being interconnected to the ubiquitous family car than ever before. Initially designed to go from A to B in comfort faster, and recently safer and more efficiently. But emerging now is the MediaCar: evolving as an intelligent road navigator, an interactive entertainment centre, a broadband video-voice-data communicator, a home from home, a playground, a workstation – you can add as your imagination thinks fit. Sony, Motorola, Swatch, Nokia, even Disney's imagineers are beginning to collaborate with the likes of Cadillac, Toyota and Ford to develop a new generation of *infotainment* vehicles; and the advanced concepts smash the mould. Ford's Telematics Group, a global division responsible for the integration of all this diverse technology, will soon be larger, both in terms of value-added and physical infrastructure, than the side of the business that actually make the cars! Cadillac's largest project is a Space Satellite programme. The XM satellite will deliver multiple channels of comedy, news, sport, music and talk via digital radio to the year 2002 Cadillac DeVille and Seville models. So what business are Ford or Cadillac now in?... Cars or infotainment?... The answer: a rapidly growing *multidimensional enterprise*, and this is only the beginning...

Interconnections know no bounds – like cars and infotainment, the world of biotechnology chases the same course. Agriculture now blurs with genetic engineering to conjoin information technology that links with cosmetics that integrate with pharmaceuticals. And this is Monsanto's strategy right now. A world of superfood is being born: yoghurt with anti-depressant, chocolate with cognitive enhancer, vegetables with antibiotic, fruit with a shelf life of months. Next, cosmetics synthesise with medicine (big-time), so shampoo that restores hair, perfumes activated by hormone, face creams that really work, are beginning to flood the shelves. Want to stop your skin ageing by some 64.5 per cent, clinically proven? Try Clarins skin care range: 'Multiregenerant Foundations' and 'Antipollution Complexes' synthesising the artificial molecule with nature's composite chemistry – *n*-innovation if ever there was. So no wonder Procter & Gamble are racing to buy up pharmaceutical and cosmetic businesses, as the promise of youth off the self is here and now. No surprise that IBM's biggest project is a biotech venture called Blue Gene (does IBM now stand for International Biotechnology Machines?...). As technologies conjugate, market boundaries distort, so industries radically transform. The rules of the multidimensional biotech game – as with all technology – are rapidly unfolding as I write...

What of the future of retail banking? If it is possible to obtain a credit card from a supermarket (Safeways), a football club (Manchester United), a car-maker (General Motors), an electronics media innovator (Sony), then what is the future of retail credit? If a 13-year-old, with zero experience, can broker a portfolio over the internet, outplay Wall Street professionals, and make $800,000 profit in less than two years (a true anecdote), then what is the future of brokerage and investment? Answer: as cash and capital become increasingly intertwined with information and knowledge, as distance dies through virtual banking and brokerage, so the role of retail and investment finance will expand towards multi-channel services, providing multiple end-products. Mobile communications devices, as one example, give unheard flexibility, intelligence and immediacy to real-time data and transaction. No longer does the client have to second-guess a personal account, but checks up in real time. Credit cards disappear, transactions go directly one-to-one: that is loyalty points, air-miles, insurance premiums, attention rewards, and all else. The time of cash money is nearly up. In another dimension, Banc One now retails more and different kinds of knowledge intertwined with its financial services. You are a student and need to buy a used car? Banc One lists local approved car dealers, then secures the bank's special discount price, underwrites and packages the financial plan all on one statement – *n*-finance is here...

Even the utilities are in the mix. RWE, not so long ago, was a homogeneous, quite bland electricity supply company; today, RWE is powering up for the *n*-innovation race – they say:

> Multiutility... is a creative leap forward in energy and energy related services... Whether Water, Gas, Oil or Coal – customers expect energy and innovative services; energy and information services, energy and home automation, energy and building services... We know how to combine individual products to create complex, intelligent systems... we will also be forming ever closer networks with our customers, as the partners with innovative all inclusive solutions... At present we are already busy with the necessary preparation such as Powerline Communications, the trend setting technology for data exchange through the power mains.

And of course, communications systems have for sometime now multiplexed in all directions. Over a billion people now communicate via the hypertext transfer protocol, specifically designed for the interconnection of ideas. From the web content itself, to the integration of voice-video-data, through and across countless minds engaged in live dialogue, the internet is intermeshing ideas at warp speed. Even the very way we think on-line has begun to multidimension. Peter Cochrane, BT's former visionary head of research (subsequently cofounder of The Concept Lab), says this can and must go further if we are to realise the full potential of the multidimensional:

> When we move toward the world of the bit we encounter a new world of multiple dimensions. This world is a network of n-dimensional space, of multiple copies, existence, connectivity, locations and form. Information can be simultaneously distributed or clustered, singular or plural, static or dynamic, living or dead, past or present, real-time or warped, accelerate or delayed.

As advanced communications technology converges and bandwidth grows arithmetically, handheld/portable devices shrink towards the invisible and functionality expands and interconnects in all directions towards the multidimensional: pocket-size access to everyone, every byte, every TV station, every media, every transaction on the planet instantaneously becomes a reality sooner than expected. As the big broadband telesatellites go up, so the borders of product, service and nation-states alike, collapse. Integrated portable videophones with hip-hop stereo sub-bass conferencing one-to-one, one-to-all, all-to-all and all-to-one emerge on every street corner from Iceland to Ice-Tea. Take BT's SmartSpace, a high-tech styled seat that integrates voice-activated devices, surround sound, touch-sensitive screens and see-through head-up display allowing simultaneous video-conferencing and face-to-face meets (clever). And this is the state of the art *now*? Tomorrow the cost of holographic view technologies will fall dramatically, so does the teraflop microprocessor, HD-CDD camera, teramemory storage media and all manner of intelligent and customisable software applets. Soon and suddenly everything is endowed with free voice-video-data technology at ever higher bandwidth; that is every room, street and artefact... Go figure...?

None of these examples have single points of convergence, but collocations of many commercial ideas and technologies from disparate origins uniting at several levels and planes. Hence, once narrow and disparate fields and industries have now begun to expand and combine under the context of hyperinnovation.

Towards a New Management Model

Clearly the world has entered a brand new era. And this new epoch is having a profound impact on business strategy, education, society and the global economy at large. The implications for economic regeneration and sustainability are unprecedented. At no other time in the history of commerce have there been such opportunities for innovation and growth. Because as the confines of both traditional and contemporary business context combine, so extraordinary possibilities for new kinds of ideas, products, communities, indeed whole new industries and institutions emerge.

Yet, it is with these new possibilities that come equally great challenges; and it is important to understand what these new challenges mean... To begin with, it means greater complexity in terms of the *design work* and *diversity* of technologies and skills needed to realise such composite invention. It also means effectively managing this new magnitude of complexity at a faster pace... It means that the linear business world we have come to know so well, that unfolds in a fairly predictable manner, quickly falls to new markets that form in discontinuous, sometimes unrecognisable patterns; where technologies that appear overnight bleed into unknown applications, then become obsolete as abruptly as they came; where competitors from remote industries that you thought unlikely to enter your market, totally redefine and take over your most valuable sector… It means that today's events move along so fast they have little bearing on the outcomes of tomorrow; where cumulative and hard-earned experience accounts for less, and where new, quite radical ways of thinking provide for the future… It means a time in which best practice and procedure have not yet been set or written, where rapid learning and expansive knowledge oversee the rules of the game, and where foresight and imagination become the predominant forces for competition… And most significant of all, it means that the kinds of interconnection we make between known and unknown ideas become the engine for economic growth, whether for an individual, local enteprise or global institution… All told, this new era brings with it the utmost sweeping threats, yet the most wide-based opportunities the business world has yet seen.

In the light of these opportunities and corresponding challenge, I present a new kind of management model. The model is designed to capitalise on these opportunities, and successfully navigate the associated risks. Specifically, it has been constructed to enable all manner of enterprises to innovate in many interconnected dimensions at extraordinary speed and magnitude. Consisting of six interrelated parts, covering hyperinnovation (1) strategy, (2), culture (3) organisation, (4) projects, (5) tools, and (6) ignition:

Part I – *Hyperinnovation Strategy:* As the business world interconnects, it becomes a more diverse and interdependent place to compete; as this happens, the rules of the game fundamentally change. In this world, outcomes, and the behaviour of the competitive environment itself, become unpredictable, counterintuitive and contradictory. To thrive, businesses must master the five major paradoxes that sit with such complexity, and begin to *think* and *learn* in many connected dimensions. In turn, enterprises of all shapes and forms, must adjoin with dissimilar concepts, technologies and organisations to create new value, to a point where lines and borders rearrange or disappear altogether.

Part II – *Hyperinnovation Culture:* Innovation depends not only on strategy (as crucial as it is), nor does it merely boil down to organisation or project methodology. It goes much deeper than that, and into the very hearts and minds of the people working within your organisation. Human behaviour and emotion play a lead role in innovation. Mould that behaviour, and tap and direct emotion in the right direction, and whoosh: an

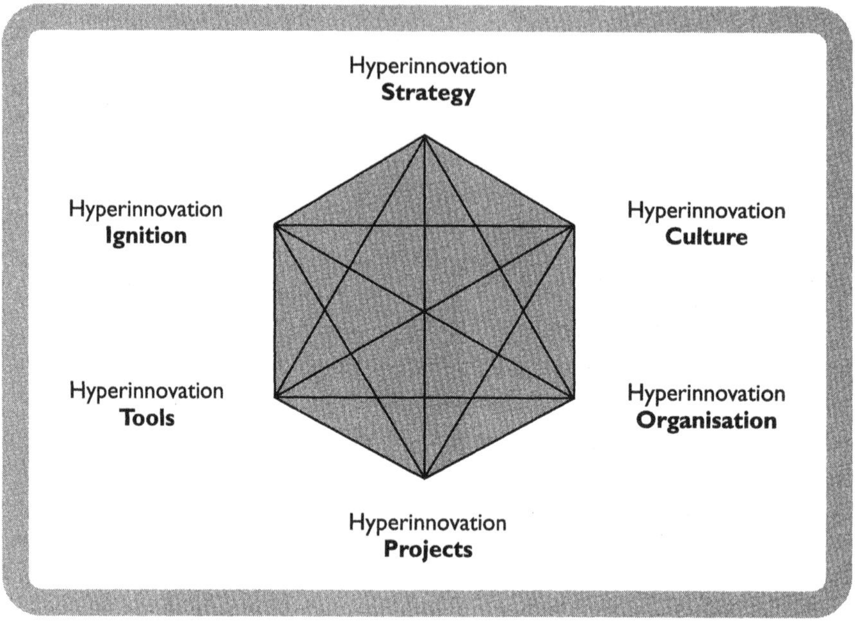

Figure 0.1 Hyperinnovation management model

endless stream of *n*-innovation. This is exactly what the hyperinnovation culture is about: building a work climate that motivates people to search through and interconnect ideas at untold pace.

Part III – *Hyperinnovation Organisation:* To effectively move a complex systems invention through the various stages of technical development and commercial adoption, a particular kind of organisation needs to form. I call it the hyperinnovation organisation, reinventing itself as the dynamic demands arrive.

Part IV – *Hyperinnovation Projects:* Innovation, by its very nature, means going beyond current experience and knowledge pools, and on into the unknown. As a result, uncertainty underlies innovation's every step. Conventional project management crumbles under such conditions, and is reason number one why innovative products and services often arrive late to market, below specification, over budget and, ultimately and most importantly, fail in the market. Here, hyperinnovation projects make use of new management concepts, outlining the necessary project principles and methodologies that support the kind of dynamic project environment needed for hyperinnovation.

Part V – *Hyperinnovation Tools:* All teams involved in all kinds of innovation need so-called structured methodologies. Methodologies are the concrete, actual doing part of innovation. These are formal intellectual tools and techniques that give rhyme and continuity to the capture of information and problem solving throughout a project cycle. The section describes and applies such intellectual tools.

Part VI – *Hyperinnovation Ignition:* Outlines a framework, based on the control theory of complex systems, for orchestrating the necessary move towards multidimensional innovation.

The model is itself *multidimensional.* Each part, and the chapters within, are designed to reinforce one another. For example, without the right kind of organisation; the tools could not be executed with full effect. Without the right kind of culture, strategy will be limited. Without the right kind of performance metrics, the project methods just would not actualise. It is the same around the whole model. Each element interconnects with each other element. The true definition and power of the multidimensional.

The model is also based on contemporary ways of thinking and learning. *Thinking* and *learning* are, of course, the two pre-eminent factors for innovation in a business of any kind. Essentially, the perspective of *hyper* enables accelerated learning within complex business environments; it also allows for breakthrough insight that serial thinking cannot possibly provide. So-called *hyperlearning* and *hyperthinking* are rapidly growing and accepted ways of viewing the world. The logic is, as the business realm and beyond extends across technological, industrial and cultural borders, the most effective and insightful way to innovate must be through *multidimensional enterprise in the connected economy… Enjoy!*

CHRIS HARRIS

ACKNOWLEDGEMENTS

Inspirations and sources of information for this book are as diverse as any subject could be. Hyperinnovation is all encompassing. But I have set out to achieve a simple aim: to show that there are endless possibilities for developing wealthy, fruitful futures for all economies, organisations and individuals. And that hyperinnovation is not only tangible and manageable, but has a centrally important role in the connected economy.

The thesis drinks deep from the cutting-edge of scientific and management thinking and practice, inspired by people working in the foremost innovative institutions and radical commercial ventures. Without doubt the thinking and writings of: Chris Argyris, Brian Arthur, Bruno Bettelheim, the late David Bohm, Fritjof Capra, John Casti, Peter Cochrane, Richard Dawkins, Daniel Dennett, Michael Frye CBE, Charles Handy, Gary Hamel, the late Soichiro Honda, Douglas Hostadter, Fumio Kaodama, Stuart Kauffman, Kevin Kelly, John Naisbitt, Mavin Minsky, the late Akio Morita, Rosabeth Moss-Kanter, Ken Ohmae, Norman Packard, Tom Peters, C.K. Prahalad, Howard Rhiengold, Rudy Ruggles, Michael Schrage, Peter Senge, George Stalk, Jim Taylor, Alvin Toftler, Jim Utterback, and Watts Wacker, penetrate every page of this book. Few other people's memes have affected my thinking with such intensity.

It also draws from the multitude of experiences I have gained working with and learning from some of the most innovative enterprises and institutions the world over: American Airlines, British Airways, BBC, Boeing, Bank of America, Capital One, Cisco Systems, A.P Besson, Concord Lighting, Hewlett-Packard, IBM, McDonnell-Douglas, Matra Satellite Systems, Rockwell-Collins, General Electric Corporation, Raytheon and Toyota.

Many thanks to my mentors and professional colleagues over the years: Terry Andrews, Dave Betts, David Bradford, Andy Clark, Morris Duzelman, Tony Herbert, Tony Lawrence, Geoff Snowman, Derek Smith, Fred Smith, Rob Stuart, Roger Thorpe and Terry Watts.

Cheers to my close friends for all their support while this project was in development: Mark Beacon, Kevin Reeves, Steve Hayward, Mark Jackson, Mark Lawrence, Paul Mazzeros, Simon Nobel, Richard Pither, Dave and Peter Robins.

Last, but by no means least, I am indebted to my publishers Jacky Kippenberger, Nathan Gaw and Steve Rutt in the UK, and Paige Casey in New York whose guidance during the completion and marketing of *Hyper-innovation* has been invaluable. Thank you.

PART I

Hyperinnovation Strategy

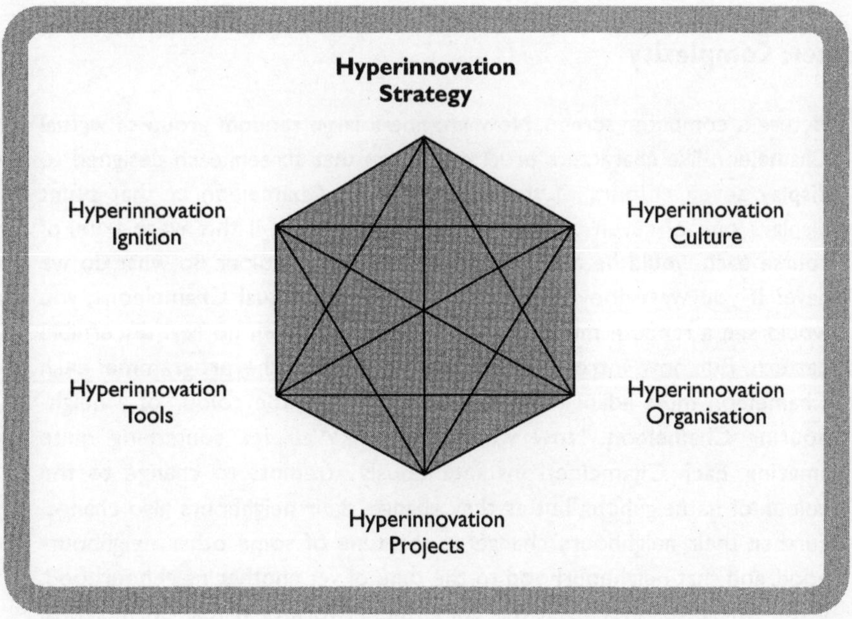

> So how will the telcos – and others – make enough money for profit, R&D, and systems maintenance? By expanding what we consider a telephone to be... This is easy to do in a network economy because the crisscrossing of ideas, the hyperlinking of relationships, the agility of alliance, and the nimbleness of creating nodes, all supports the constant generation of new goods and services where none were before.
>
> KEVIN KELLY

The business world not only operates at a faster pace than ever before; it is increasingly diverse and interdependent. For now change not only arrives without warning, it occurs on multiple fronts. Markets not only disintegrate before maturity, they extend across unknown territory. New technology is not only obsolete within months, in its wake it obliterates long-held economic assumptions. The effect this interdependence and rate of change give is a somewhat ambivalent proposition. On the one hand, a world made of greater opportunities and possibilities for new kinds of enterprise and growth; on the other, a frenetic and deeply perplexing order that demands a complete rethink in terms of the strategies for innovation.

Enter: Complexity

Picture a computer screen. Now imagine a large random group of virtual Chameleon-like characters programmed on that screen, each designed to display seven colours of the rainbow. Each Chameleon at that point displays one of seven colours of their choice, and if this were true, of course each would be a slightly different shade of colour. So what do we have? If you were looking upon this crowd of virtual Chameleons, you would see a random mixture, awash with colour, with no real discernible pattern. But now introduce *one simple rule* into the programme: each Chameleon must adapt – again at random – to the colour of a neighbouring Chameleon. Now what happens? Well, it's something quite amazing. Each Chameleon instantaneously attempts to change to the colour of its neighbour, but as they change, their neighbours also change. Further, their neighbours change to the tune of some other neighbourhood, and that neighbourhood to the tune of yet another neighbourhood. If you where still looking at this colourful network of virtual Chameleons, you would see something quite beautiful, you would see cascading fractals, swirling round and around, continually unfolding in complex patterns. This virtual network would never settle down to one colour, but continually unfold in evermore *novel* arrangements.

A more interdependent world means a more complex world, and what better way to comprehend how this new era functions, than through a science of complexity. Specifically, complexity science is concerned with understanding how a collective of large numbers of interrelated agents behave as *one whole*. Agents can be any independent body; examples are atoms in a molecule, neurones in a brain, virtual chameleons on a computer screen, or here, connected innovations in a marketplace. Under this scheme, agents, in whatever guise, begin to form dynamic linkages, which in turn build up in cascading energetic order. A dynamic order of self-organising patterns.

The great news, however, is that the self-organising dynamic found on a computer screen, is in fact now applied science in disciplines as diverse as traffic control, materials science and artificial intelligence. What has been discovered in such complex systems, both on the computer screen and in the real world, has far-reaching consequences for business. We unequivocally now know that:

- Large numbers of independent agents, interconnecting to the tune of a few simple rules, can give up the most extraordinary and counter-intuitive products; astounding results not found in those many constituent parts.
- O*rder* can emerge for *free* from the inside out, without any top-down planning and control. But no common kind of order, instead patterns more intricate and profound than anything yet devised.
- There is amazing potential for unique combinations among agents, such as ideas, leading to unending possibilities for innovation, whether in business, or in any discipline you care to mention.
- It also begins to give an explanation of how the quite amazing diversity and elaboration we find in the natural world emerge, and now in our rapidly complexifying man-made world as well.

This simple introduction to complexity sets the stage for the first part of this book. In fact, complexity science gives an extraordinary insight into the way the business world is set to work from now on, particularly concerning the dynamics of innovation. The insights are straightforward, yet at the same time profound. When we look at many of the emerging areas of technology, even the markets and wider societies they produce, we not only see levels of complexity, approaching that found in living-breathing-biological ecologies, these man-made systems actually begin to mimic basic architectural structures and behaviours found in nature. By comparison, the markets of the past will appear like barren tundra; the markets of the future will mimic richly intertwined tropical ecologies, chock-full of colourful, interconnected products and services, exhibiting ingenious competitive strategies and proliferation tactics. As we shall explore in this first part, as the business world approaches such elaborate complexity, the whole dynamic and rules of the game for innovation fundamentally transform.

Multidimensional Innovation Strategies

Under this setting, the smartest and most effective way to understand and direct the new dynamics of innovation, is to engage the sciences of complexity. Accordingly, this first part outlines five strategic management concepts based on complexity science, that enable multidimensional innovation:

Chapter 1 – Thriving on Paradox: In the past, when industries were independent and clearly demarcated, we could anticipate the future and its consequences with some degree of confidence. In this linear world, outputs rolled away from inputs in a reasonably consistent fashion. By contrast, in a complex world, whether an ecology found in nature or interconnected markets now found in commerce, outputs and inputs begin to stray, behaving in counterintuitive, sometimes paradoxical ways. And there is no hiding from this. As the links between once disparate business concepts grow, there is a mandate for new management strategies that thrive on the paradox that such complex systems exhibit. This chapter introduces abstractions of complex systems as applied to innovation, describing the key strategies necessary to prosper in interconnected and paradoxical times.

Chapter 2 – Multidimensional Thinking: Serial thinking is the pervasive, perhaps pre-eminent mode of thinking today. Yet serial thinking can lock us in an equally linear context out of touch with the market realities described in the first chapter. In fact, linear thinking can so limit our perceptions that we are utterly blind to the highly novel business contexts emerging now. The second chapter outlines, and arms managers with, the mental capacities for a multidimensional business world. The thinking modes of *contrary perspectives, counterintuition, uncommonsense* and *strategic serendipity* are described.

Chapter 3 – Multidimensional Learning: In a world that changes without warning, and in a multiplicity of ways, there is a need to accelerate market learning at least at pace with the competitive context. Again, lessons from the complexity sciences give us the strategies to learn what the market is selecting for in real time.

Chapter 4 – Multidimensional Enterprise: The past was marked by the specialist enterprise, targeting narrow market segments, with well-defined steady-state technology. Today, we see the emergence of a new kind of polymath: multidimensional enterprise. Marked by diverse competency, technology and market panorama, this is a fresh kind of operation that is already redefining the competitive ground rules. Here, the strategic concepts of such enterprises are described.

Chapter 5 – Collaborative Commerce: To realise multidimensional enterprise, companies will have to work with other, sometimes unusual, organisations normally outside the fold. This chapter describes the basic building blocks for achieving such collaborative commerce.

All told, multidimensional innovation rewires the philosophy and theory of business innovation strategy as we have known it. Hyperinnovation sits as a true breakthrough, serving as the edge of today's strategic practice.

CHAPTER 1

Thriving on Paradox

The unavoidable difficulty with convoluted webs of innovation, is that these systems – like all complex systems – begin to exhibit paradox: behaviour and outcomes that seem absurd or contradictory; yet they are in fact well founded. Specifically, *perpetual novelty, constant surprise, acausality, uncertainty and discontinuity* all sit as unavoidable, yet often desirable, consequences of the kind of complex markets and technology now emerging.

Valuing, indeed thriving on the corollaries of interconnection, may be the business world's most pressing challenge. Because if you think the world is complicated right now, you can only imagine what it is going to be like tomorrow. Thus, the biggest risk for any enterprise, indeed any institution, is to continue with convention, to use the management mindsets and strategies that worked effectively when markets, technology and all else, were considerably more steady-state and autonomous. High risk, because routine linear thinking, and top-down methods of planning and control, unequivocally do not work in the complex breeds of trade looming now. Consequently, it is imperative to seek and develop new and relevant strategies that *thrive on paradox.*

The First Principle of Hyperinnovation

Many moons ago, a tutor of mine gave up the fact that a student studying science at high school has the opportunity to learn more about the laws of physics than the great Sir Isaac Newton ever did, or could have known in his time. Since that day, I have long wondered how knowledge develops, how ignorance can blossom to enlightenment, how seemingly mystical breakthroughs in understanding come from simpler, less structured understandings, but more, how complex innovations originate from much lesser innovations. After much thought and deliberation over the years, it became clear that the answer may lie in the *many potential interconnections of ideas*. To gather a perspective on *how more comes from less, through hyperinnovation*, we can look back to a time when one of today's most ubiquitous consumer products was just about to break through.

The year, 1931; the place, Alexandra Palace; the innovation, the television. And to be sure it captured the public imagination. The police would at last have a medium to transmit pictures of wanted criminals to remote parts of the land. Most exciting of all was the prospect of 'moving picture home entertainment', they thought. Still, much of the press saw it quite another way, as this 'white elephant' simply required far too much sophisticated technology and investment for successful commercialisation. At this time perhaps the very rich and a few critical commercial applications could afford such grand technology. But look at it from a 1930s point of view. Market penetration and ultimate commercial success would take a vast corporation to make the television programmes, with the aid of far-sighted financial investors and sponsors. It would require a body of top minds to develop the physics of the core technologies, and scores of top brains to design the TV sets themselves. Next, a vast network of transmission centres and a multitude of hill-top antenna to transmit the signal to each home (or community centre as first proposed). On top of this, vast sprawling factories would be needed to manufacture the TV sets, with a supernetwork of partners to supply the materials. And then on to the distribution channels, in association with a maintenance force comparable to an army. Oh yes, then there is the power supply from the national grid, it would simply double power demand at peak times... Of course, none of this was so clear, as the 20/20 hindsight we have now.

Let us turn the headlights forward to give a perspective on all this. Holographic television becomes a serious technological proposition when optical transistors, microlasers and the equivalent of today's supercomputing are commoditised. High-quality colour three-dimensional TV pictures that you can wave your hand through. Yet, what technological and commercialisation adventures lie ahead? Again, I hear commentary (much commentary), that such an invention will be far too costly to commercialise. It will take... Well, all of the above and no doubt much more.

And *more* is the point here: it is not a free lunch – technological research, and ultimate innovation, is a saving account born of successive interconnections amid both mature and contemporary technologies and/or discoveries that accumulate a greater whole. In short: it is a synergy among known and novel, diverse and local, but quite often disparate ideas that give the bigger, different, more sophisticated technology... In a word: it is all in the *interconnections*!

In fact, when we observe what emerges from these kinds of complex systems of ideas, we find that the output or whole activity is greater than the sum of individual agents: 1+1+1+1=6? Synergy in fact (the secret: four agents in a network have six possible interconnections). The underlying mechanism here is the space of *innovation possibilities*, the actual number of unique innovations possible from a finite or growing set of agents in a system. In mathematical terms, for every agent that joins a network, so the number of new interconnection possibilities, and thus innovations, goes up dramatically. There is in fact a principle of innovation at work here. I call it *the first principle of hyperinnovation*:

$$Hp \propto Im \cong \tfrac{1}{2} * \Sigma\alpha^2$$

The potential for hyperinnovation (Hp) is proportional ($\propto$) to the number of meaningful interconnections (Im) between agents. Meaningful, as in those interconnections that hold a level of perceived or authentic value.

As an indication of the potential for hyperinnovation, the number of possible (meaningful or otherwise) interconnections, is towards ($\cong$) one-half the square of the sum of agents in a network ($\tfrac{1}{2} * \Sigma\alpha^2$): 10 agents in a network would have 45 possible interconnections. One hundred would have 4950 possible interconnections. One thousand would have 499,500 possible interconnections. One million agents would have over 499 billion possible interconnections.

The payoff: for every new scientific discovery and consequent technology coupled to a network, so the number of innovation possibilities increases dramatically, so driving the synergy among ideas further and faster uphill. And so accordingly, a flourishing variety and correlation among ideas, knowledge, technology and market demands, are the spur for creativity and innovation. The more diverse and interconnected an invention – whether a core technology, a service provision or an entirely new business platform – the greater the inherent value and potential for yet more innovation.

Develop a Passion for Perpetual Novelty

The new is strangely familiar these days. In the consumer arena, we are now witness to the most prolific stream of gadgets and gizmos, flooded by new tools and toys, to a point that almost overwhelms. In medicine, we hear of continuous breakthrough, in science the limits and power of human knowledge now boggle the mind. In every conceivable industry and field the rate of innovation has reached stupendous heights… Only, I do not want to perplex you with examples and facts here, as I am confident that your immediate experiences are testimony to increasing rates of change. The point I want to make is a further fundamental reason for all this innovation, and why in particular this reason is radically transforming the rules of the game.

A dominant, yet not so well-known trait of any sufficiently interconnected system is *perpetual novelty*. Whether it be an immune system, an ecology, or network of ideas, novelties reliably emerge with vigour. As above, the deeper the complexity, the larger the space of potential combinations for novel patterns to emerge. And since markets now organise and behave like a complex system, it follows why novelty is reaching epidemic proportions. Therefore, we must at some rudimentary level, acknowledge that novelty is not only omnipresent in the arcane world of complexity science, but flush in reality too. To give an active insight on the dynamics of perpetual novelty, consider what M. Mitchell Waldrop wrote in his inspiring book *Complexity:*

> it's essentially meaningless to talk about a complex adaptive system being in equilibrium: the system can never get there. It is always unfolding, always in transition. In fact if the system ever does reach *equilibrium*, it isn't just stable. It's dead. And by the same token, there's no point in imagining that the agents in the system can ever 'optimise' their fitness, or their utility, or whatever. The system space of possibilities is too vast: they have no practical ways of finding the *optimum*. The most they can do is to change and improve themselves relative to what the other agents are doing. In short, complex adaptive systems are characterised by *perpetual novelty*.

So what does this cool scientific perspective give?… Evidently, it says that *new stuff* happens. But between the lines, it hints that the all-consuming love affair we have with efficiency (optimisation) and tight control (equilibrium), is not only short-sighted, it leads blindly to extinction. Any so-called efficient organisation (business or otherwise) set in stasis cannot live with the novelty that now surges throughout markets, since frigid, isolated systems can neither anticipate, nor perpetuate, innovation.

The logic is this: in the past, the reflex has been to stamp out novelty; but suppressing novelty only destroys the very mechanisms that keep the system (your business, your technology, your markets, your customers) alive and well. If a system is characterised by little or no change, it means that the system is in equilibrium and near death (as above). And this is a recurrent tale: firms exhibit permanence and homogeneity, where nothing much changes, hence the system at large is at best listless, at worst approaching its demise. What is more, many a good manager considers smooth equilibrium as a clear objective, as equilibrium is innately seen as necessary for normal operation. It means high levels of order, of certainty, of peace of mind. It means that things will change gradually, and therefore controllably. But look at any company that is heading for equilibrium, and that firm will be out of touch with *live* competitive context. They will find it difficult to respond, let alone anticipate new market permutations or competitive eccentricities; and we have to remind ourselves that it is often a curious irregularity or unique combination of technology that kick-starts the next big market wave. And as for being up with the technological and/or market elite, a firm resting in equilibrium will not even be able to identify what is truly current, let alone the direction of market evolution. The inroads for the collection of market and technical information will be somewhat obstructed, its dissemination moderate, and the interpretation shallow.

The reason is that equilibrium, in the form of highly ordered command structures and functions, signifies that a firm has begun to ossify, its agents are stabilising. Which means a firm has become set in its ways, choked by old dogma, blind to what is new and germane to the market. Xerox, back in the 1970s, is one case in point. Xerox endeavoured to outline the major technological breakthroughs (for example lower cost microprocessors), the major shifts in customer demands (for example sophisticated documents), and new competitors' innovations (for example Canon's reliable, easy-to-use copiers), but even after its strategists produced report after report, Xerox was so concerned with tight command and control, so poised in stasis, that it was sapped of the ability to recognise and exploit such major shifts. And shift it did. The pursuit of equilibrium has taken Xerox and others like it (IBM, Chrysler, Kodak and Sears) to near death's door on more than one occasion, and in industries that have developed and burgeoned like no other.

Hand in hand with the pursuit of equilibrium, is the quest for *optimisation*. Ratcheting up productivity, incrementing costs down, polishing quality and honing core service, was how the corporation made great wealth. This wisdom brought with it intensified learning curves and economies of scale; focused learning meant better understanding of the technology and market; scale economies led to lower unit cost, lower unit cost led to greater margins. So the logic went. This is optimisation at its very best, and so ingrained in management mindsets, that anything else is seen as ambiguous and frail.

But optimisation, in the final analysis, will never harvest a constant stream of innovation. First, it is quite impossible to sustain superior value by optimising old ground, as sharpening aged products and practice quickly leads to diminishing returns. Second, optimisation never (ever) leads to any radical innovation, as continuous improvement of prevailing products, services and their processes is always a fast track to bland mediocrity. But most of all, the innocent and well-intended endeavour to become the very best, will quickly fall prey to someone, or something, or some company, that is thinking, tinkering and doing something *different*. Whether in sport (Tiger Woods), or business (Amazon), or war (SAS) or politics (New Labour), someone, somehow, someday (soon) will blow the roof off what is thought possible because they act and perform in distinct and unique ways. It is not enough to seek *excellence* any more (as momentous as this goal used to be), a firm must now be superlative at fundamentally reinventing itself, to be sustainably different. Paradoxically, to be truly the best, an individual, a team, an enterprise, needs to be altogether different. And to be different you have to focus your attention on quite different issues. In short, in a perpetually novel world, you need to be perpetually novel yourself.

Clearly, there is much to learn and do, as the consequence of the dogmatic, ubiquitous pursuit of efficiency (optimisation) and tight order (equilibrium), is that innovation is not only held back, it is stopped in its tracks. In fact, these convictions are so deep-seated in corporate culture and places of learning (I find), that they flagrantly interrupt the aspiration to build new competitive strategies that pre-empt novelties in the market. Therefore, it is essential for leaders to adjust attitudes and priorities in strategy development. To enlighten teams to the shortfalls of *efficiency* and *tight order* when *perpetual novelty* is both the *goal* and *behaviour* of the competitive context. In sum, we must all *develop a passion for perpetual novelty*, if we hold any chance of sustained competitive advantage through hyperinnovation... Here are four strategic goals that may kindle such a passion for innovation:

- *Spend more time on innovation issues.* It is not that the pursuit of optimisation is neither worthy, nor illogical. It is just that management tend to over-direct and value optimisation over innovation. That is, the emphasis on cost-cutting or continuous improvement and the like, is so apparent in benefit, that the idea of creativity and innovation is seen as some second-class activity. But facts are facts, innovation is several orders of magnitude more difficult and time consuming than slicing a penny or two off unit cost. Yet the proportion of time spent on innovation is far far less than cost containment projects. Look at your diary, look at your people's schedules – it is optimisation driven, isn't it? The solution is straightforward, but not easy. Measure time spent on both *optimisation* and *innovation*. If you are not meeting a 20/80 target respectively, you are not in the game.

- *Exceed your best innovations*. As the marketplace, and all within, coalesce, we can only expect to see ever more distinct competing technology concepts and business platforms. Like it or not, many of the finest, most remarkable innovations of the day – your innovations – will end up as mere junk before much later. This is precisely because established domains in complex networks tend to disintegrate suddenly, and then, in turn, are replaced with fresh patterns of connections. Consequently, there can be no sustainable competitive advantage, unless there is a mandate to supersede the established model with a more progressive and germane innovation. The late Akio Morita, co-founder of Sony, often said, 'If we want to sustain value in the market, we have to become our own best competitor'. As tough and as risky as it sounds, the ability to kill your innovation, even at its peak, with a finer, different, more consummate innovation, is the only way to compete with incessant novelty in the market. Set a goal of exceeding 50 per cent of your best-performing innovations, over the next three years.
- *Renew half your business activities over the next five years* (whether IBM or a mid-sized company). We often forget that end-product and services are not the only agents we must supersede on a continuous basis. Enterprises need to execute unaccustomed operational activities too. And that means strange ideas, unfamiliar competency, fresh functions, new people and diverse technology. Embrace this, get used to deeds anew. So, measure how much of your business – core capabilities, skills, tools, knowledge, processes, people – are less than five years old. If well over half of your business activities are more than five years old (five months in e-commerce), novelties in the market will negate your brightest efforts.
- *Equilibrium is death, but too much change will kill with equal effect*. Turbulence and variation are what give rich life in nature's garden, but too much can destroy an ecology outright. Small-scale upheavals make way for new seeds, larger-scale catastrophes uproot and destroy genes and species. So how much or how little? What is the crucial point that causes a system to crash, freeze up or perpetuate? Every complex network (whether biological or technological) is a distributed web of nodes always in flux, always in the process of adapting itself. It is the same for business systems at all levels, whether hypertechnology, multidimensional markets or inter-industrial arenas. The secret is to let the

system emerge in its own particular order for free. Too much innovation will crash the system, too little will freeze it. So keep searching through different levels of complexity to actively make your innovations more diverse and interconnected. Various methodologies are outlined further in Part V, to achieve a suitable level of variety and interconnection.

The business world is now an evolving, unceasingly expanding system of interconnection possibilities: a *perpetual novelty machine* of constantly shifting patterns. Therefore, there is little room for excessive optimisation and equilibrium from a competitive perspective, only a boundless search across vectors of more imaginative orders of innovation. And there is no stopping this, novelties will arise in your markets whether acknowledged or not. So the business manager's first capacity from now on is to seek, expand and exploit this new-found paradox: *perpetual novelty*.

Seize on Constant Surprise

In the mid-1980s, I was tasked with benchmarking, and finally selecting, a computer-assisted design (CAD) system for GTE's European Lighting Products Division (divested as Sylvania Lighting). The proposition was a multi-million dollar investment, panning eight business units, the length and breadth of the continent. As a young engineer, I took on the assignment with verve, embarking on a tour across Europe and the United States. Compiling the system's technical specification was reasonably straightforward, a list of functional performance targets set against a list of tasks performed in each business unit's design process. Remarkably, the processes across each business unit were fairly uniform. This was my first surprise… The next task was more arduous: selling a *single* pan-European system to each business unit's management team. The reasons were just (they thought): *optimisation* and *equilibrium* across divisions! I did not anticipate any of this to be an easy buy-in, but I did expect the technology per se to be welcomed, as it would give at least an order-of-magnitude improvement in R&D productivity. But no! The reactions were quite different, and sometimes indifferent. The Italians were concerned that such tools would lead to cutting headcount (at that time, a sensitive issue due to the national political climate). The French already had a CAD system (a French system), and saw no reason to change. The Dutch claimed they were not ready, that they needed to put their design process in order before such investment could be justified. The British, like the Italians, were also concerned with job losses. All this rebuttal was due to a complex set of indirectly related operational and political issues not, at first, apparent in my analysis, nor in my remit as a young engineer. All this was my second great surprise… Some years later, while actually implementing another CAD system, came a third, but pleasant surprise. That CAD systems create valuable work, not cut work. Computers – from internets to the microprocessors themselves – have led to a quite amazing and unexpected amount of job creation, not a decline as originally predicted back in the heady days of the 1980s.

Another challenge with complex systems is that they are often *irreducible*; the very act of stripping a system down to its component parts, destroys the very essence of what the complex system actually *is*. As Socrates was supposed to have said many times, cut an elephant in half, and you do not educe two elephants, but one great entangled mess. Now consider the mainstay of how management attempt to understand and control complex projects like the one above. They try to break the system down into measurable and manageable parts, then hand out each bit to a problem solver. But in doing so, managers lose sight of what they are attempting to understand in the first place. As day-to-day assignments and tasks become more complex, requiring more hands on deck to give up solutions, the very distributed conclusions themselves often lead to completely unexpected tasks, situations, opinions and so on. In brief, interconnected systems give rise to *continual surprises* too. Even when we break a system down to get to its roots, we cannot see all the surprises, snags, contingencies, spanners in the works, coming. In complex systems, even subtle things can blow up in your face unexpectedly.

Yet, what is the nature of a surprise in the first place? A surprise is merely the end result of a prediction (conscious or otherwise) that has failed. Predictions are made by working out and following a commonsense set of rules of thumb learnt through experience or teaching. But in a complexifying world, identifying the rules of thumb is not always possible, because (a) the rules of the game are always changing (perpetual novelty), (b) the system is always redefining itself (more perpetual novelty), and (c) you cannot always acquire every piece of relevant information (uncertainty below), so events do not always turn out as we project.

John Casti, a fellow of the Santa Fe Institute, New Mexico, has carried out much research into the anatomy of surprise in complex systems; concluding, like my experiences above, that we cannot always anticipate, or deliver outcomes as we like. In his book *Complexification* Casti wrote:

> Complex processes, on the other hand, generate counterintuitive, seemingly acausal behaviour that's full of surprises. Lower taxes and interest rates lead to

higher unemployment; low-cost housing projects gives rise to slums worse than those the 'better' housing replaced; the construction of new freeways results in unprecedented traffic jams and increased commuting times. For many people, such unpredictable, seemingly capricious behaviour is the defining feature of a complex system.

But should we not be seeing less of the unexpected, you may ask? As technology evolves, should the world not get more ordered, and therefore more predictable? Do things not get simpler anyway? Does technology not shrink and become easier to use? Is it not much easier to travel further, faster these days? Can I not talk to people around the planet at the push of a button? Is productivity not way up?

Yes, of course, on the *surface*, things do get ever simpler, easier, faster, better and more productive. But under the skin of any object, inside the structure of any system, lies deeper embedded, more entangled complexity to produce such efficiency and refinement. Think of Intel's microprocessor. Its processing power doubles every 18 months, but the number of transistors per unit square, also doubles in that same time. The television has burgeoned in functionality when compared to models a mere 10 years ago, but to achieve this expanse, ever more and different technology is packaged inside the same or smaller volume of space. Pharmaceuticals embed deeper complexity. The latest drugs are designed via so-called nonrational design techniques, resulting in synthetic chemical molecules approaching the complexity of that found in biology. To be sure, the future of all technology is smaller and more refined towards the nano-scale, with ever greater functionality and interconnectivity. But complexification does not stop at the molecular or core technology level, it also occurs at the system-wide level as well. Because as increasing numbers of interdependent technological systems, such as airports, road systems, and computer networks continue to complexify, they only tend to reinforce and complexify each other further. For instance, if Heathrow airport grows, so Hong Kong and JFK reciprocate. If inner-city road systems swell, so all adjacent urban road systems expand. If one internet file server capacity grows, so all servers have to keep up.

And no wonder surprise is rife. No wonder unexpected events happen more frequently. The business world is now so interdependent, our contraptions so complex, that any attempt to reduce them and understand them in their constituents, is a false and wasted endeavour. Because when the business world and its inventions become interconnected, the old Newtonian model, where each and every event had an equal and predictable outcome, is supplanted with a nonlinear dynamic, where each and every event may have an unequal and unexpected consequence. I am sure the great Sir Isaac would turn in his grave if he knew what was emerging: as our contraptions and markets, and the world in turn, become increasingly interconnected, expect more of the unequal and unexpected. Surprise is a consistent tenet in a multidimensional realm.

So, what is there to do here? How are firms supposed to manage amid such surprise? How can you thrive on this kind of paradox?... Fortune, it is said, often favours the prepared mind. And that means, at least in today's growing reality, galvanising a mindset that accepts surprise as not only a fact of business life, but as real bounty. As a real gift! Here are three basic strategies that begin to attune to surprise in interconnected markets:

- *Time to insight.* There's a principle in rapidly evolving markets, that says, as the *number* of competitors that *recognise* the same opportunity goes up, so the value of that opportunity falls towards a commodity proportionally. Hence, the *time* it takes to *identify* an unexpected opportunity is a key to sustaining value. And remember, it is often the novel eccentricity or unexpected combination of technology that kick-starts the next killer application. To accelerate time to insight, there is a need to perceive the subtle initial condition, the weak signal, no matter how faint, before it begins to swell and amplify. To begin to do this, there is a critical need to relentlessly gather new knowledge and data outside your fold. That is, look outside the normal boundaries of your current technologies, markets and industry. Look for ways to think and learn differently. Look at the edges of life, look at what is new and unfolding. Find underground or emerging culture, such as nascent music, radical books, outspoken people, extraordinary incidents, outlandish issues. Within all of this, search for novel patterns and trends you would not have readily acknowledged before. These are surprising sources of fresh insight. And remember, that a surprise is a boon if a firm is in a position to capitalise on a novelty that the competition is not aware of yet.
- *Time value.* Once an insight has occurred, there is a *time value* attached. Unexpected events in the real world can ignite or extinguish the value of an new idea literally overnight. Sudden incidents, like major disasters, can lead to abrupt economic down-turns, geopolitical rifts, even new legislation that literally washes away value. New technology, we know, can suddenly level a working business model. Digital technologies, for example, have put waves of ideas, knowledge and skills out of work in as little as a few months (XML being a case in point). On the other hand,

an unexpected occurrence can increase and/or give longevity to the value of an insight. Surprise events can also have a positive effect on value. Clearly, the ability to capitalise on insights, in shorter time frames than the competition, is a key strategic issue today. But this is not merely about *speed* per se, it is about developing an ability to anticipate, and to do that, an organisation needs to develop a learning disposition.

- *Learning disposition.* In the wild, many of the most successful species are opportunists lying on trees, in thick undergrowth, hidden under rocks in pools. Yet they are no ordinary opportunists, they are perfectly adapted to the environment to the point of invisibility. And this is exactly why they are so successful: over millions of years they have learned and adapted to shifting competitive conditions. It is the same for an enterprise, learning and adaptation are key to thriving on the paradox of novelty and surprise. Like the network of virtual chameleons in the introduction to this part, as the colour of the market changes, an enterprise must change its colour in synch; as that business's colour changes, the market modifies in response. Yet developing a learning character that can adapt an innovation strategy with such agility, can be fraught with scepticism, even out-and-out cynicism by those of the tight-order (optimisation/equilibrium) school. Only by acknowledging that the market is awash with novelty and surprise, will constant, sometimes naive, learning be seen as a strength. The key factors here are not only in the kinds of market learning strategies you develop, but in the kind of organisational culture you build (Chapter 7).

In sum, *seizing on constant surprise* boils down to learning and adaptation in synch with the real world in real time, outside the normal fold. We shall be revisiting learning and adaptation throughout this text, particularly in Chapter 3, where we will master learning in multidimensional markets.

Leverage on the Certainty of Uncertainty

There are three frustrating paradoxes tied up with forecasting the future. First, firms really only need to predict the future when major shifts occur. That is, if events and scenarios pan out with little or no change, a firm would not need to forecast the future in the first place. Second, forecasters' projections are most likely to *fail* when a firm needs them most; when there are in fact major shifts and surprises in the market. This is because forecasters often base their plans on assumptions gained from past experience, and so, by definition, past experience will always be out of synch with any real shift in the market. Third, the bewildering, and for the most part, quite scary thing about a complexifying business world, is that the interconnections found in these markets often buck linear logic: turbulence may give rise to order, stability disorder. In fact, complex markets may have known and codable inputs, but result in outcomes that do not reflect those few original states. Frustrating in the extreme.

The combined result of such contradiction is that *uncertainty* becomes not merely an occasional, deviation from predictability; it is now a basic feature of the business environment. As complex systems not only deliver perpetual novelty, not only bestow constant surprise, they also give rise to the utmost ambiguous situations. And once uncertainty becomes a certitude in commerce, we have no choice but to develop strategies that thrive on such paradoxes. Rosabeth Moss Kanter, the Harvard Business School professor, attempts to catch the tail of uncertainty, in her book *When Giants Learn to Dance:*

> To some companies, the contest in which they are now entered seems increasingly more like the croquet game in Alice in Wonderland – a game that compels the player to deal with uncertainty. In that fictional game, nothing remains stable for very long, because everything is alive and changing around the player – all-too-real conditions for many managers. The mallet Alice uses is a flamingo, which tends to lift its head and face in another direction just a Alice tries to hit the ball. The ball, in turn, is a hedgehog, another creature with a mind of its own. Instead of lying there waiting for Alice to hit it, the hedgehog unrolls, gets up, moves to another part of the court, and sits down again. The wicket are card soldiers, ordered around by the Queen of Hearts, who changes the structure of the game seemingly at whim by barking out an order to the wickets to reposition themselves around the court... Substitute technology for the flamingo, employees or customers for the hedgehog, and everyone from government regulators to corporate raiders for the Queen of Hearts, and the analogy fits the experience of a growing number of companies.

The list of anecdotes I have gleaned working with senior management teams, attempting in vain to circumvent uncertainty, would fill this book twice over. They employ the best graduates, engage the top strategy consultants, engaging in the most detailed advanced scenario planning methodologies. But whether you believe that such commitment and strategic soothsaying works effectively or otherwise, is not my point here. My point is, a company that is set up for learning and adaptation, that is geared up for shock, surprise and non-stop novelty, can thrive on the certainty of uncertainty, without even a hint of what is going to happen next.

Yet a common business response is to restrain uncertainty: tie the croquet game to a strict set of operating rules and regulation, bringing the game into tight and uniform order, where projection and outcome are fixed and sure. After all, it would be a peaceful life if this were possible. Tomorrow's croquet game would look pretty much like yesterday's. But what a meaningless, and even more nonsensical game it would be without uncertainty. Because it is the very uncertainty that paradoxically gives meaningful order and real sense in this world. Uncertainty brings with it intrigue, dynamism, new challenge, the spur of creativity. Uncertainty *is* disequilibrium, which is, in fact, innovation's vista, it is wild new territory. Thus the only reliable assurance any business has is *leverage on the certainty of uncertainty*.

Clearly, no business can see beyond the looking glass, because the reflection beyond does not exist yet, it has not yet been concocted or found. And the only way to view the future is to walk through the looking glass, explore and invent a new croquet game as and when the uncertainties unfold… Here are three key strategies to scheme when the business world embodies unbroken *terra incognita*:

- *Accept uncertainty*. The more accurate and detailed a prediction of the future is, the more it is merely outlining actuality. All future reality is uncertain, so you have no choice but to make uncertainty an ally. Live off uncertainty, walk in uncertainty, but leverage its properties, its openness to new ideas and concepts. And the first step on the road to levering on the certainty of uncertainty is to accept it as a fact of innovation's life.
- *The greater the novelty, the more uncertainty grows*. Too much uncertainty, and risks begins to compound, and eventually overwhelm. Too little uncertainty, and an enterprise will not be doing much innovation, and eventually heads towards equilibrium. A key skill to innovation is to manage uncertainty at the level where an organisation can thrive. A secret here is to take on the right number of innovation projects, with the right balance of novelty and complexity. The project methods in Chapter 18 explain how to do this.
- *Even though we are conditioned to think in serial terms*, and even though we organise in linear ways, at the end of the day, all innovation results from a nonlinear acausaul process, continuously leading in unexplored domains and outcomes. And by definition, these unexplored outcomes are unfamiliar, and therefore it is impossible to predict their

behaviour either in the lab or in the market before output. After all, if we understood an invention, it would be familiar, and if it is familiar, again by definition, it is not an innovation. So, it is difficult to understand the true nature of any given innovation until will have experienced the trials and tribulations in the real world. Luckily, this enigma can be broken. What drives uncertainly out is learning, and what accelerates learning is experimentation and prototyping to the breaking point in the real world. We shall be exploring advanced strategies and methods for designing rapid experiments and prototyping in Chapter 3.

If a firm can learn to thrive on uncertainty, that firm will be around for a long time to come. Its market value will be sustained, its people self-assured, and its business platforms always fresh. Therefore, thriving on the *certainty of uncertainty* is now a strategic necessity to prosper in such paradoxical times.

Focus beyond Cause

At 2 a.m. on 16 October 1987, black storm clouds and rushing gales gathered about 100 miles off the south coast of England. Almost immediately they began their approach. When they arrived, all of an hour later, they hit with devastating impact, felling trees as if they were matchsticks, flipping cars as if they were toys. It was the most grievous of storms. A kind that England had not endured for at least 200 years. But it is not solely the force of the storm that is noteworthy, but the way it appeared. The Met Office, even with their billion-dollar technological compound eyeball, had no way of knowing it was on the way. In less than half a dozen hours, a dramatic change in local weather conditions, on a scale not recorded before, began to unravel. The chain of causality that led to the storm moved so abruptly, that it was already too late to prepare for by the time the tempest had begun its approach.

This vivid anecdote begins to tell of yet another great facet of complex systems: that small initial events can swell up so fast, into something so vast, that any attempt to determine the causal chain that leads to an outcome, is totally impracticable. As a system grows to a critical point of complexity, the integrity between ordinary cause and effect shatters. Not because the chain of causality disappears, but because by the time we have tracked down all such correlations, the system itself would have moved on.

Attempting to project into the future with any accuracy, or attempting to plan for tomorrow in detail, or merely speculating on what might come next just for fun, becomes increasingly difficult, if not impossible. In an intertwined world, familiar reason and outcome begin to break down. In this world, projects are late, journeys are delayed, ambitions are foiled, predictions are illusive, all due to unforeseeable perturbations starting chain reactions elsewhere and remote in the system. Jim Taylor and Watts Wacker express this in their book *The 500 Year Delta:*

> In a truly reasonable world, you could plan your way to a reasonable end. Cause would be discernible, effect would be predictable. There would be rewards for rules followed, for loyalty given. Social organisation would hold. Economic and political decision would be binding over the long haul, because the ends they were meant to achieve were discernible at their birth. In a truly reasonable world, the concept of a single career pursued over a lifetime would still make sense. That it doesn't – virtually every young person coming out of college today at least senses the need to be prepared to pursue multiple careers in multiple fields – tells us a great deal about how the world is, not as nostalgia wants it to be… Just as cause has come unhinged from effect, experience has come unhinged from outcome. If you are going to succeed in chaos, you must connect with chaos. You must act in concert with chaos. What does that mean? It means you must trust in intuition, trust in self. One of the beauties of the age now forming is that, finally, you will have to make choices on purely arbitrary bases – because they feel right. It is the ultimate democratisation of logic.

The comprehension required to grasp all of the variables that make up a market system of possible outcomes, is too vast and too fast for any single brain to capture in one hit. The number of facts are so many, and the interval amid cause and effect is so tiny, that detailed explanations become irrelevant. And if an enterprise cannot grasp any explanation, with any reliability, how can that firm plan for any reasonable future? The answers:

- *Focus on a single key variable*. As we shall thoroughly explore, you cannot control or optimise each and every variable within a market system, it is far too complex. However, if you can grab hold of any one agent within a system, and direct it in all its proportions, you will have collateral control over the complete system, because all agents will indirectly adapt to that controlled variable (vis-à-vis virtual chameleons). And what are the key agents in any complex market system? *Customers!* By focusing all your innovation efforts on learning and adaptation to the demands (expressed, emerging, unexpressed) of the customer, you will begin to lead all those zillions of variables throughout the market system. We will expand much on this throughout this text.

- *Focus on end-results*. The further one looks into the future, the more it deviates from the present. Hence the only reliable way to understand any given situation is to act in concert with it. As with surprises, you need to learn and adapt new ideas as and when the changes occur. To do this, takes a different mindset. A thought mode that is indifferent to cause and effect, but concerned with outcome and results in real time. All of this means shifting your focus away from lines of causality towards the far end points of outcome. In fact, a quest for ultra-planned innovations is a delusive way to think and learn, because it assumes the application of linear logic in a nonlinear, paradoxical world. When causal relationships are obscured or unforeseen, the intended innovation seldom pans out as expected. Thus, do not plan in the traditional mode, do not plot projects and schemes in fine detail, but focus on end-result. What, at the end of the day, is it that you want in your hand? Part 5 outlines tools and techniques here.

No one knows when the next market storm will hit, the variables are too many and too fleeting to comprehend. So focus beyond the multiplicity of cause and effects, and on to the end-results that you desire. Even with such complexity, a firm can lead and exploit a hurricane to advantage, if it is certain about where to go.

Leap Discontinuity's Break

Greater interconnected innovations deliver not only unexpected storms, faster, but impart immense structural shifts that compromise the current standard. Because of this, we find ourselves suddenly surrounded with new and often strange concepts, schemes, rules, even laws that all but confuse. In turn, what we know best, or are best at, is quickly overtaken by some unexpected novelty. What we have honed to perfection is soon superseded by some other unfamiliar scheme. In short: cumulative learning and knowledge are lost to discontinuous innovation. Rowan Gibson, a business consultant who has a finger on the beat of complexity, begins to thread together the dynamics of discontinuity in his anthology *Rethinking the Future:*

> For a long time we have known deep down that the future will be different from the past. Every science fiction writer, from Jules Verne to William Gibson, has reminded us of that. But what we have stubbornly refused to believe is that the future will be different than we expect it to be. Most of us

still behave as if the future will be a linear extrapolation from the present, like a long straight road that stretches into the horizon... Where A leads to B leads to C lead to D. Chaos theory tells us that the opposite is true. As Michael Crichton writes in *Jurassic Park*: 'Chaos theory teaches us that straight linearity, which we have come to take for granted in everything from physics to fiction, simply does not exist. Linearity is an artificial way of viewing the world. Real life isn't a series of events occurring one after another like beads strung on a necklace. Life is actually a series of encounters in which one event may change those that follow in wholly unpredictable, even devastating ways.' As our world becomes more complex and interdependent, change becomes increasingly non-linear, discontinuous and unpredictable. Therefore the future becomes less like the past. And less like we expected it to be. We find that A might lead to E, then on to K and suddenly Z!... The fact is that the future will not be a continuation of the past. It will be a series of *discontinuities*. And only by accepting these discontinuities and doing something about them will we stand any chance of success and survival in the 21st century. The exciting thing about discontinuity is that it breeds opportunity. It means that nobody owns the 21st century. But in order to grab hold of the future we have to let go of the past. We have to challenge and, in many cases, unlearn the old models, old paradigms, old rules, the old strategies, the old assumptions, the old recipes.

An interconnecting world brings with it a greater number of new possibilities, demanding entirely different ways and means, frequently seeing that old modes die off more rapidly – sometimes catastrophically. Once stable lines of decision and ascension crumble to radically new questions, organisations, concepts, models and orders, that is in economics, markets, technology, education and society as well. What worked yesterday, does not work today, and is all but harmful tomorrow. Tomorrow's innovations from public services to exotic technology will be unlike anything we have known in the past. Thus what we have hard learned and invested in, turns sour sooner than we think.

The message: *all* markets, sooner rather than later, completely disintegrate. Sooner or later an innovation, whether technological, process or conceptual, obliterates established market economics. The television (again), the kind we have known for two or three generations, has beeen transformed out of recognition, and these radical innovations will in short span be superseded by some other bright scheme. Emerging thin-film display technology, for example, means that TVs will one day soon be printed on T-shirts, at discount prices. Sony, Philips and Mitsubishi better take heed: all markets sooner rather than later completely disintegrate. Sooner or later an innovation, whether technological, process or conceptual, obliterates established market economics, whether auto-engines, travel services, fast food, gas turbines, anything you care to imagine. And yes, your markets too.

A foreboding paradox of this kind of discontinuity, is that it seems to happen in proportion to the confidence that it will not actually happen! *That is, when an enterprise is sure that a discontinuity will not happen in its markets, it is in fact quite likely to occur.* For example, what could be more secure than the faithful electric-lamp industry, a $100 billion global market?

Looking back once again: in 1880, gas-lamp technology manufacturers held the market as their own, and so slumbered in near *equilibrium*. But when Victorian entrepreneurs came up with the *novel* and *surprising* idea of electric-lamp technology, the gas-lighting firms sprang to life. Only, what did they do? They went to work – yes – on *optimising* the gas-lamp technologies. And boy, did they come up with some efficient contraptions. At first, the optimisation strategy paid off, many of the electric start-ups went bust. But it was not long before the likes of Thomas Edison made the necessary technological breakthroughs, when the cost of electric-lamp technology dropped significantly. One by one, the gas-lamp manufacturers disappeared.

Now, casting our headlights forward once again. At the beginning of the 21st century, the electric-lamp manufacturers still fare well and hold a panoply on lighting markets. And now, as so-called nanocrystal optics (NCO) entrepreneurs enter the fray, the electric-light manufacturers spark to life, making lamp technology ever more efficient. Even so, NCO may eventually exceed all this clever stuff. NCO may still only be at the embryonic stage, a mere pinprick in the order of things. It is expensive, unreliable, and a one millimetre-square area only pumps out just enough light to see with the naked eye in the dark. But the breakthrough has happened, and the discontinuity will, some time soon, shift in a huge and unpredictable way. Conventional electric-lamp technology, just like the gas-lamp technology of 1880, is on its last legs. Your ceilings, walls, signs, roads, wherever there is an application, may one day soon, emit bright light.

Jim Utterback, the Harvard Professor of Innovation, who studies the discontinuities of innovation, has some deeper concerns here. The overwhelming fact, that even with shock-waving news, such as a new kind of power source, or radically new high performance material, or new management process, most incumbents ignore such novelties. As I have outlined above, optimisation and equilibrium still dominate the management agenda. From Utterback's book *Mastering the Dynamics of Innovation:*

> A pattern emphasised in this study is the degree to which powerful competitors not only resist innovative threats, but actually resist all efforts to understand them, preferring to further entrench their positions in the older products. This results in

a surge of productivity and performance that may take the old technology to unheard-of heights. But in most cases, this is a sign of impending death.

So a message to my friends in lighting land (and all industries for that matter), do not simply polish your best lantern technologies, and wait for a new genie to appear; dive into NCO paint, on ceilings, on walls, on roadways, on shopfronts, on – well you name it? Because whatever technology or process or market gave you triumph in the past, can devastate your chances of success in the future… So strategically, what does this mean?

- *Swim across current.* This is the most difficult of all challenges here. How often do we get caught up in the current of rhetoric and dogma of the market? Look at the internet boom (and mobile phones, personal computers, automobiles, retail banking, and so on), it was going to go on and on for ever, wasn't it? But venture capitalists forgot one of the key principles of complex networks, that established domains tend to disintegrate suddenly, and then are replaced with novel patterns of connections. And all markets now suffer this impasse. Whether telecoms, banking, foods or lighting, we all have to live within increasing interconnections, thus discontinuities. So, when the current of excitement, opinions, investments, media news, even the hard market data you have gathered, is in flowing in one direction, your business must have at least 25 per cent of its mass swimming in several different streams. If not, discontinuities will overwhelm.
- *Perfection is dead, long live perfection!* Sustainable value now comes from exploiting a discontinuous stream of the unknown, not smooth optimisation of the well-known. Of all commercial organisations that have ever existed, '99.99' per cent are now part of the business fossil record. The reason? As their inventions became successful, they all, in earnest, attempted to *perfect* their contraptions further. But as they tirelessly honed and improved, they eventually became world-class experts in dead-end knowledge and technology (re: oil lamps, gas lamps, and one day soon electric lamps). But this does not mean that a new breed of technology should not be robust or reliable. Of course, to compete today, an innovation must be rugged under use and abuse. What *perfection is dead, long live perfection* actually means, is a move towards a strategy of discontinuous experiments, learning and innovation, that creates multiple streams of value, while using the appropriate methodologies to make these new discoveries robust and reliable. This we will expand upon in Chapter 3.

- *Unlearning*. There can be no true competence in discontinuous innovation if there is no expertise in destruction of current ways. In fact, trying to forget and letting go of old ways is often harder than learning new ways. Learning is a key proponent of innovation, but little has been said about *unlearning*. It is difficult to break out of old context for a mix of reasons. First, it is quite natural to become attached to current work, whether it be a product or craft. Second, mediocrity is all too often tolerated, it creeps under the skin without notice. Third, managers tend to limit risk taking as a business matures. Fourth, firms value optimisation, over innovation (above). But the most significant reason why firms cling to old ways, is that they forget to forget! That unlearning is not even on the agenda. Here are some ideas for unlearning: Give up equipment (including capital-intensive kit) more than five years old to local schools and colleges (they will love you for it). Continually develop the roles of everybody in the company to (a) a wider context, (b) ones that pre-empt novelties in the market. Bend over backwards to support people in the strive to be different. Praise risk taking, especially when someone trips up. Lastly, log unlearning on the agenda. Paradoxically, you have to learn how to unlearn.

In the bold words of Gary Hamel and C.K. Prahalad: 'To be a challenger once is enough to challenge the orthodoxies of the incumbents; to be a challenger twice, a firm must be capable challenging its own orthodoxies'. And that means tireless provocation of the discoveries you find, and the new ventures in which you partake. Only then will you learn to let go and leap discontinuity's break.

Thriving on Paradox

It is a different world, is it not? The mild and comfortable divisions of yesteryear are gone. The interconnections are here, and growing at a rate faster than any can count. As markets and technology mimic the network-*like* structure of complexity, we will only become increasingly exposed to the paradoxical behaviours of perpetual novelty, constant surprise, acausality, uncertainty and discontinuity. Therefore, there is little room but to adopt the strategies and mindsets that thrive on such paradoxes. Accordingly, the rest of this book embeds and expands upon the stratagem outlined above. In particular, each is complemented with the multidimensional thinking modes described in the following chapter.

CHAPTER 2

Multidimensional Thinking

The whole book in general, and this chapter in particular, is intended to offer original and appropriate ways of thinking and learning fit for the era we are now entering. Yet in the way sits the obstacle of changing our thought logic towards something we may find hard to perceive in the first place. The challenge of challenges. The principal obstacle for not perceiving new modes of thinking, is something we all too often forget to consider: something known as context.

Context Breakthrough

We are all conditioned to particular, circumscribed context. Context is what gives us bearing in this world. It gives us clear lines and borders that define ourselves, and to settle within. It even contributes to our peace of mind. For a business, it is *all*-important. Without a central business context, the lines and borders of products, markets, whole industries, are unclear. Banking, oil, transport, pharmaceuticals, are all examples of circumscribed and well-known boundaries of business context. Elementary stuff, but with good reason. Because it is with little wonder that enterprises have in the past clung like hell to such robust commercial context. Breaking out of any normal context can give rise to considerable anxieties. But this does not mean that we should avoid looking beyond normal context. Looking beyond normal business context is in fact the precursor to innovation.

Ponder this: comprehension of a given reality, is the ability to grasp an overall *ensemble* of elemental ideas. As a simple example, the carburettor, camshaft, spark plug and sump are a few of the basic components that make up the *context* of the combustion engine. What builds this capacity to contextualise, is knowledge and experience. Generally speaking, the deeper the knowledge base and the broader the experience field, the more ideas we encounter, the more sweeping and powerful our contextualisation capacity becomes. *But – and this is a key point – learning new knowledge, and gaining new experience, are often encumbered by the very context in which we are set.* It is a kind of negative feedback loop. A kind of self-selection and self-organisation of knowledge, where like selects more of like. Thus confined fields of experience and knowledge build so-called *normal context*, which tends to become more and more frozen over time. Essentially, normal context precedes what we think and do next. Like a railway track, normal context guides us on to the next thought or task. Within a normal context we stay inside a narrow range of thought. We all know the football fanatic who can talk of nothing else but his team. That is normal context taking over a mind in the extreme. Dogma, strong opinions and views, form and work in much the same way. Thus normal context can limit new ways and ideas, because the contexture defines the scope of what we can think, see and say. For everyone in general, and for the firm especially, this is not only bad news, it is common news. Firms find it difficult to move away from institutionalised contexture (indigenous ideas and perennial systems), and not merely because of human nature, politics and company culture (although these are authentic reasons why contexture solidifies, as cultural values and norms can subvert rationale and logic. These aspects are addressed in Part II). Specifically, here, the common management intuition is to build experience and knowledge in finely focused areas, so that cumulative learning and expertise can build. But this only works well when markets are considerably more steady-state, where technologies are distinctive, where customer demands are homogeneous, and where the competition is well defined. In a multiplexed world, narrow skill sets cannot cope with a rapidly increasing diversity of ideas, and a continuous unfolding of novelty and surprise. Hence, acute convergence of knowledge and experience, like equilibrium, ultimately leads to a limited end.

The hub of the issue is this. When an incumbent organisation sets out to develop a bright new future, they are all too often restrained by the very experiences and knowledge that got them to their lofty heights in the first place. To grasp, in the abstract, what I am getting at here, think of the common or garden tree. The roots and trunk are mature business thinking (seasoned ideas and systems); the budding leaves, modern business thinking (fresh ideas and systems), but the latter thinking is still very much a development on from past business platforms. Old pathways of thought only reinforce our approach, and therefore events. And that is normal context at work. The reason for this is that any institution is ultimately a *closed system* of ideas, and therefore all change is a continuation from past experience and knowledge. But the context in which any company is to compete, is an *open complex system* of ideas, and therefore change can be sudden and discontinuous. Of course, context within any business modifies over time, but it is a relatively long period compared to the open architecture of the competitive context. And in a era where the competitive context is itself moving from linear progression to a nonlinear system in perpetual novelty, surprise and so on, the closed context of any business is often left wheezing far behind. So the question remains, how does any perennial business achieve a context breakthrough that gives completely new ideas and systems fit for a multidimensional world?

There are two main ways to break normal context. One, pack your bags and start again. In fact, lessons from Darwinian evolution in the natural world tell that it is much easier to destroy an organism and to replace it with a new one, than to change an organism from the inside out. However, in the business world, this can lead to compound risk, as start-up situations have ultra-high levels of mortality, which is only exacerbated by loss of cumulative experience and knowledge. Two, achieve a true and continuous context breakthrough, via mimicking the very behaviour of the new marketplace itself – to think, learn and therefore interconnect in multiple dimensions.

Multidimensional Thinking

How many ways of thinking exist or can exist? How many of all the types of reason have we found? The number of ways to conquer a problem, or prospect a notion, or prove a statement, or give birth to a new idea? It may be vast. It may be tiny. There may even be types of thought we humans cannot understand. We do not know yet, it is an area of brain science and philosophy that has barely left kindergarten. But what we do know, is this: there is certainly more than one way to think. And with this knowledge we open a new thinking space. A way to think fit for a multidimensional world.

Until very recently, business thinking was bound by linear lines of ideas, and so reasoned in very ordered, top-down states. Stability fed prediction, so thought and projection were merely an extrapolation from well-known ways. Nothing much changed, if at all. But all this is quickly passing, as the way we are set to *think*, purely to cope with an immense dislocation and reconnection of ideas, will be very different from now on. To begin with, networked knowledge never (ever) stands still, convoluted webs of ideas continuously morph from something we know into anything that we do not. Multidimensional notions rush together and split more rapidly, they do not arrive in any particular order either, do not turn up when we expect them to, nor behave as we predict. But the real gift here, is that transdimensional viewpoints open a door to an *infinite space of innovation possibilities*. For every new dimension interconnected to a nonlinear perspective, so the portal of value, discovery and invention opens exponentially. The consequence of a world of ideas with fewer divisions and boundaries within and throughout, dramatically opens up the potential for value creation and growth… And this is no mere philosophy lecture I might add, this is hard-nosed business acumen at work. Rosabeth Moss Kanter, the Harvard Business School professor, wrote in the anthology *Management 21C*:

> Trying to create a business while the system itself is being redefined puts pressure on brains – to imagine possibilities outside conventional categories, to envision actions that cross traditional boundaries, to anticipate repercussions and the advantages of interdependencies, to make new connections or invent new combinations… call it business creativity, call it holistic thinking… for business strategy this means *multidimensional* and multilocational *thinking*.

Hyperthinking is not some strange alien intelligence, it is the most natural of all ways to think. It is just that for reasons of primitive history, even latter-day mass-organisation and control, we have been programmed to structure thinking in top-down series. And simply because of this history, we have all but forgotten how to think in *n*-dimensions, and all the power and insight that follow.

Above all its many powers, *hyperthink* enables much needed recontextualisation: a means to reposition our minds, so that distinct perspectives and conceptions occur. Consequently, this kind of recontextualisation enables a firm to play with boundaries, to see ideas in new association with each other, breaking through to insights beyond any normal context.

For our purposes here, we can look to four requisite thought modes that actualise multidimensional thinking: (1) contradigms, (2), uncommonsense, (3) counterintuition, (4) strategic serendipity.

Contradigms

The term *paradigm* was first made famous by philosopher Thomas Kuhn, in his 1962 treatise *The Structure of Scientific Revolution*. Essentially, paradigms are self-reinforcing concepts; dominant ideas that condition the mind, moulding and directing the way we are supposed to think. Unfortunately, paradigms are often adopted because of their popularity. In fact, a paradigm can be a heedless falsehood, yet people often take them on, holding them as some universal truth. Like normal context, paradigms often reinforce ideas, so much so that they eventually begin to solidify states of mind, keeping us from seeing anew. As a consequence, a true *paradigm shift* is a scarce event. Even when new evidence, knowledge and ideas actually break through, new kinds of thinking, even authenticated truths, are held back by some enduring paradigm.

An example I often apply to qualify the dangers of the paradigm and the fixed assumptions it can build, is that of the legend of Christopher Columbus and his discovery of the Americas. I use it not solely because everyone accepts Columbus' triumph as some cultural axiom, but its explicit illustration of how vulnerable we all are to paradigms, whether they are right, wrong, good, bad or totally indifferent. The paradigm is this: it is generally accepted that before Columbus' so-called unparalleled nautical adventure, no human east of the Atlantic had borne witness to American territory. The technology of navigating and sailing across an ocean the size of the Atlantic, had not reached sufficient development until that time. But based on overwhelming new evidence, Columbus did not first spot America. The truth is, the native people we know as Red Indians originally found the big country. Only the controversial question is, how on earth did these people land there in the first place, if technology was not capable of crossing such a vast distance before Columbus? Did they fly, did Scotty beam them up? It may just as well have been the case, because it is just about as fantastic to believe that Columbus did discover America first, when you look at the contradictory scientific evidence.

First, the native Indians (as we call them) of America share a direct genetic lineage with native Africans. Second, the South American continent's tectonic plate broke away from the African continent more than 130 million years ago, and the North American continent began to break away from the European continent 65 million years ago. Third, it was only 2 million years ago, when *Homo habilis* (the ape that we *Homo sapiens* advanced from) evolved around the north-east African plains, what we now call Ethiopia. All people alive today evolved from *Homo habilis*. Whether Japanese, Irish, Austrian or Indian, we all originate from Ethiopia. And with these three exhibits in place, logically, there are only two practical ways the native Indians could have reached that far-off destination: (a) by boat across the ocean, or (b) over the ice-cap through generations of migrating families… . The answer is probably both. But the point I want to make above and beyond this contrary perspective, is that we have known these facts for generations, yet the Columbus paradigm has remained stubbornly in place. This is truly dangerous stuff. What is more, I have non-exhaustive lists of so-called cult-axioms that fog our minds today, that are simply way out of date, or were totally wrong in the first place.

In a business context, clearly an accepted commercial paradigm can jeopardise a firm's capacity to see the world either as it really is, or in new and unique ways. Clearly, there is a genuine need to see the world through a fresh perspective in this new era. So we need a kind of thinking mode that can accelerate context breakthroughs when a conventional and pervasively held paradigm says old facts are still current facts. And one thinking mode that benefits here, I have coined the *contradigm*.

A contradigm is the antithesis of the paradigm. Contradigms are to paradigms what water is to stone. If paradigms are self-reinforcing patterns of thought, then contradigms are *self-repelling* thought patterns that effect *contrary perspectives*. Contradigms break the givens, axioms, the maxims we are conditioned to and take for granted, often blatantly repudiating what we have known to be true. Contradigms challenge principles and fundamentals, facilitating a constant shift of mind towards ever newer fields of ideas. The beauty of the contradigm is that it stops a mind from freezing over, enabling insights to possibilities beyond the what is now and known. A typical contradigm asserts a contradiction or exception to the rule. Exceptions or contrary perspectives are yet more precursors to something new or unforeseen. But a contradigm is much more than this. In its most extreme and powerful form, a contradigm can totally and spontaneously reorientate the mind to not only observe what we could not see, but to comprehend what we thought not possible.

To begin to develop and become adept at generating contradigms, we can turn to so-called axiom antithesis, difference as inspiration, and fuzzy thinking:

Axiom antithesis: This is a simple mode of thinking, that travels a long way in innovation. An axiom is a fundamental principle or premise, and is the most stubborn paradigm of all. Like biological antibodies, axioms fend off new ideas (memes) like viruses, blunting or stopping ideas from replicating and propagating within a cultural system. To break such obstinate axioms, we must relentlessly challenge them through seeking antithesis.

The objective here is to challenge the very givens a business is run by, the rules and fundamental precepts a firm takes for granted. To practise this, start by taking any standard model or accepted idea in a business, then think of an antithesis. Write down a list of phrases that describe the standard model, than next to each phrase write down an antithesis. Here are some examples you may find surprising:

Axiom:	*Antithesis*:
You cannot unscramble an egg	To unscramble an egg, feed it to a hen
Beefsteak is made of meat	Beefsteak is made of nothing but water, air, sunshine and green grass
We need a highly disciplined manager at the top to command and control the innovation process	We need a facilitatory host in the team to nurture hyperinnovation
Cars need wheels to run on roads	Cars need aerofoils to float on cushions of air
Mobile telephones are for one-to-one communication	Mobile telephones are for live professional photography

A route to finding a workable antithesis, is first to look for the *origins* of a given axiom, then second to look at the original idea in the modern context. For example, 'We need a highly disciplined manager at the top to command and control the innovation process'. Where did this axiom come from in the first place? The answer: a direct and dogmatic transfer from the military model. There were few other organisational models around when industrial commerce began, so almost unconsciously, the top-down military model was transplanted into the business realm. And now, after hundreds of years, it is accepted as a commercial axiom, and often without question. So, the first principle here is to think of the origins of an idea, then, second, attempt to validate that idea's integrity or authenticity in a modern technological or competitive context. Once the origin of an axiom has been found and then authenticated or invalidated in a contemporary context, a divergent or contradictory antithesis can be generated. Put 'we need a highly disciplined manager at the top to command and control the innovation process' in the present context of hyperinnovation. Bring in the new context of complex systems, such as self-organisation and emergent patterns (outlined in the introduction to this first part). A strong hand at the top, in absolute command and control, will nullify the processes of emergence and self-organisation. So self-managing teams, with a conciliatory style of leadership, is better placed for *n*-innovation. Hence, the axiom antithesis: 'We need a facilitatory host in the team to nurture hyperinnovation'.

To the point: axiom antithesis is about rebuttal, dispute about the origins of a model or idea set in the latest context. That white is not white, but a phase integration of many colours. That intellectual walls are in themselves illusory, and solely a hangover from times when things were slower and segregated. We will be making the most of the power of axiom antithesis throughout this text.

Difference as inspiration: When two or more distant ideas or disciplines close together, there is a possibility of initial conflict. After all, unique ideas often emerge in schools that have distinct cultures and beliefs. We know, in everyday life, that when two distinct belief systems collide, it can result in monstrous consequences: interdepartmental rows, union walkouts, and in the extreme, sectarian wars. But, and as will become clearer throughout this text, difference is also a source of creativity and eventual innovation. To mediate between two or more conflicting ideas we need a thought arbitrator, a way of thinking that seeks a synergy between the many. This, again, is the role of the *contradigm*.

Essentially, contradigms express difference as an unequivocal source of inspiration, a precursor to unique insights which enables recontextualisation. Here, different perspectives broaden the landscape on innovation, offering up wider options on the future. The goal, then, is not to find what is negative about a discord, but positions that reciprocate. Marguerite Yourcenar, who became the first woman writer elected to the Académie Française, in her novel *Memoirs of Hadrian*, wrote:

> The rules of the game: learn everything, read everything, inquire into everything… When two texts, or two assertions, or perhaps two ideas, are in contradiction, be ready to recognise them rather than cancel one by the other; regard them as two different facets, or two successive stages, of the same reality, a reality convincingly human just because it is complex.

Yourcenar asserts that we must not strive to demolish each other's notions, precepts or values, but find a synergy among them. To begin to do this, to bring out the positive, at what point does each idea complement each other, even if each notion is at loggerheads? I suggest that you consider any one of the following contradigm generation techniques when doing so:

- Pick out three good things about each conflicting idea and three issues that might be seen in a different way.
- Pick out three aspects of conflicting ideas that you have observed to work together elsewhere.

- Pick out three fundamental themes from each conflicting idea that should be incorporated in a hyperinnovation.
- Pick out three attributes of difference that affect internal people positively and directly.
- Pick out three attributes of difference that affect external people positively and directly.
- Pick out three measures of success that are germane to each of the conflicting ideas.

For example, take the archetypal conflict between oil and water molecules, stubborn foes that do not like to mix. *Pick out three aspects of the conflict that work together elsewhere*:

- Emulsion paint.
- Beautiful oily iridescent patterns on the surface of a pond.
- Machine lubricant.

Oil and water living together in harmony, and if it can be done with these two adversaries, it is quite possible to find areas that work in the most controversial conflicts in business, politics and innovation.

Fuzzy thinking: This kind of logic breaks down fixed assumptions, it enables a team, or an individual, to become the master of their thoughts. The Japanese call it *not-this-not-that reasoning*, thought patterns that are fluid and malleable. It also enables a firm to take control and define the lines and borders that bound a given industry context. It can even allow us to see different meanings in the very same issues. To introduce this, think of what Bart Kosko describes in his book *Fuzzy Thinking*:

> Consider this question: can you draw a circle? No one has ever seen a circle. No one has ever seen a square or a triangle or an ellipse or any geometric shape. We have only seen approximations, imperfect greys instead of perfect black and whites. Zoom in close enough and you will see imperfection in the drawing or printing or engraving or assembly of subatomic particles.

Things are not always as they seem. Moreover, for innovation, things do not have to be as they seem. Seeing things differently is the essential spark for invention. Yet we all too often let the current paradigm totally dominate our thinking, ruling out the possibility of seeing things in new and unusual ways.

To think fuzzily, we must loosen up our mind, not take things as literal, to see the meaning we need, want, love to see. I have many a good friend who flies off the handle when engaging in fuzzy thinking. The reason, here, is that we often confuse *ourselves* with the meanings of a situation or object or designation of some description. There's the story of the coal miner, who years after pit closure, still found himself unemployed. He is a bright and amiable man. But he could not get over the fact that miners do not do any other kind of work except to go down the pit. He identified himself as a 'coal miner', it was who he was, so how could he possibly become a factory worker or police officer? The point is, strong association with meanings can lock us in rigid modes of thought. Fuzzy thinking, on the other hand, enables us to detach ourselves from situations, and once we do that, we can blur the lines between ideas and begin to see new meanings in a context.

Approximation of *rules* is a good starting block for fuzzy thinking. To think in terms of loose rules of thumb for what a given situation, or object, or indeed word, actually means. For example: how many teams play in a doubles tennis match? Two? What about several all playing at once? If you look on the court you will see four: the players, the umpires, linesmen, ballboys! What about a final at Wimbledon? What about the groundsman, the camera crew, the commentators, the ticketing organisers, the waiters in the restaurant, and the dozens of other teams that go to making up this kind of tennis match? Or are they all one team? It depends on where the lines and borders of the rules or meanings are drawn; and these boundaries are defined by the fuzziness of our thinking.

The strength of fuzzy thinking is this: do we let the object of our thinking – like a tennis match – take control, do we let it define the lines and borders of our thinking? Or do we control the object of our thinking, do we control the boundaries? If we let the object of our thinking control our thinking, then the situation is in control of us, not the other way around. Think of what the great Lewis Carroll had to say on fuzzy thinking, in *Through the Looking Glass:* 'When I use a word,' Humpty Dumpty said, in a rather scornful tone, 'it means just what I choose it to mean – neither more nor less.' 'The question is,' said Alice, 'whether you can make words mean so many different things.' 'The question is,' said Humpty Dumpty, 'which is to be the master – that's all.' The world, and our innovations, do not have to be that which we have inherited. It does not have to be the way the current paradigm says it should be. If we open up to fuzzy thinking, then we can draw our own lines, and create our own meanings; and if we can do that, then we become the *master*.

Now think of the hard-nosed marketplace. Deadlines to meet, customers to satisfy, value to maintain. What mustard does this seeming woolly thinking cut here? First, fuzzy reasoning can pan across isolated, totally entrenched technologies and industries that seem to have little in common, yet can unlock extensive new business concepts. Again, when we are master of defining boundaries, new kinds of industry definitions emerge. Second, and as a result of the first, fuzzy logic can spur unlimited market value in times when everything seems to be falling towards commodity faster, value in markets today is often multiplied at the intersection of individual network domains (see introduction to Chapter 4). Here are two fuzzy thinking exercises for kick-off:

- *Contrasting concepts*. An effective way to blur the lines between disparate network domains, or distinct business/product/service context, is to think of and integrate contrasting ideas into basic common or garden end-products or services. Think of the car. What is its purpose? A means of transport from A to B. Now think of a contrasting concept that breaks the boundaries of the car. Think of play. Why not a means of *transport to play with*? Why not integrate games, amusements, toys, and so on, in the back seat to entertain passengers, especially children, on long journeys? No more 'Are we there yet…?' echoing from the back. In fact, the whole definition of the car would change if the *transport to play with* concept was developed.
- *Forced meanings*. Look at an object or situation, and force a new meaning upon it. Here, you are the master of new meanings that create new value. For example, what is the point of a night out on the town?… Letting your hair down? Socialising? A good ol' chat? Or are there other meanings that could be coerced to change the definition of a night out? What are kids up to these days? The *techno-rave* is part of youth culture nowadays. Millions of kids go to mass raves every night of the week, the world over. Now force a new meaning – say *learning*? Why not have a *learning rave*? A technologically driven rave, with giant screens, lasers and sound systems pumping out music and visuals, depicting pithy maxims, life lessons, germane facts and figures. Learn while you party! And this is no fiction. Cap Gemini Ernst & Young, hold conferences with top-brained consultants, called 'raves'. The notion is of free-flow emergent learning in the collective. In fact, this kind of learning rave is only set to proliferate as the life events of work, rest and play intermix.

This is fuzzy thinking, practise it, play and toy with it, and you will begin to exploit context boundary crossing and all the value that comes with it.

Develop Uncommon Sense

Common sense is *rational* man's most cherished mode of thought. From an early age we are told that common sense prevails over all, it is how we apply reason to the world, it is an integral part of all rational enquiry. And of course, without question, common sense has much significance in this world. But is it enough?... In particular, is common sense sufficient for innovation?... I think not!

At one level, common sense is the application of experience and knowledge that worked well in the past. In theory, as we grow in experience and gain more knowledge, our common sense improves; does it not?... But facts are facts: good old common sense once told that the sun revolved around the earth. That the world was as flat as a pancake. That the human body would disintegrate if it travelled faster than 30 miles an hour. That humans are not meant to fly, and that man would never go to the moon. All of these statements were once held as axiom, as good common sense, by almost all. But for the sane no longer. Thus, common sense is chiefly a cultural-related phenomenon. Essentially, as breakthroughs in science and technology advance, we are given new conceptual frameworks and intellectual lenses that allow us to see further, deeper, wider; and most important of all, differently, unusually, even rarely. But, adhering to common sense – the sun revolving about the earth – can limit new conceptions and breakthroughs in understanding, stopping innovation in its tracks. As an example; for decades the idea of a meteor impact wiping out the dinosaurs, was seen as utter nonsense. Then, thankfully, the smoking gun of an impact site on the Yucatan peninsula was discovered. What was deemed as nonsense, was gradually (very gradually) accepted as most likely and mutual. But now put this in the competitive context: businesses operating under common sense values and long-held management tradition. Competitive advantage? Little chance. The point is, what is deemed common sense now, may not be (probably will not be) deemed common sense tomorrow, because in a world of discontinuous change, chance and discovery, common sense is perpetually obliterated. And if that is our central and ostensible mode of thought, our business is obliterated with it.

Yet the problem here, it seems, is deeper and more widespread. Karl Teigen, a renowned psychologist, conducts simple experiments that shed further light on the shortfalls of common sense. It involves writing down a handful of well-known pithy maxims, then retrospectively turning each of them into a contrary phrase. For example, 'What goes up, must come down,' becomes 'Success breeds success.' Teigen then gives a set of students a list of genuine proverbs mixed up with those he had concocted via his transposing method. He then asks the students to rate each maxim for integrity. But the scholars never find any discernible difference between one set of maxims and their antitheses. In sum, almost any observation, and its diametric antithesis, can be taken as a maxim of everyday common sense. Consequently, if we take any common-sense maxim as read, it can be a deluding, even a totally disabling, way to think and act.

As if I had not denigrated common sense enough, what happens when put in the context of hyperinnovation? Again, common sense dies on its feet. Multidimensional thinking and invention are about seeing things differently. Seeing what others cannot or will not. Further still, inventions of the interconnected kind, mean extensively cutting across distinct business contexts, something the most agile of minds find difficult. The reason why this is difficult, is that common sense clings to normal-day context as if its life depended on it, locking out contrary ideas as if they were some poor mad dog. I would go so far as to say that *common sense kills innovation*. Hence, firms that hunger for innovation, must develop an uncommon kind of reason. A sensibility to the not so obvious and subtle clue. To whispers of insight and inspirations that others miss, or see as irrelevant or senseless or untrue.

Thankfully, there is much we can do… To begin to master an exceptional kind of reason, we can turn to the pursuits of so-called open play and deep comparison:

Open play: 'You can't be a serious innovator unless and until you are ready, willing and able to seriously play', says Michael Schrage, high priest of innovation. '"Serious Play" is not an oxymoron; it is the essence of innovation.' Yet, *play* is fraught with taboo in business culture. For reasons of religious history, play is still too often seen as the direct opposite of work. And that is a shame. Because all creative work precisely requires a mix of aimless fun-like play and focused work activities. Howard Rheingold (1992), king of the thinking tool, points out, 'If it isn't turned into toil by a relentless instrumental viewpoint, play is our most important thinking tool – particularly when we are learning to think in new ways… It's a mental can-opener for liberating new ideas.'

Play is yet another complex, and therefore poorly understood, activity. Its function as part of human evolution, for example, is still not too well understood, although we have gained some important insights to why and what play might be about. In fact, we find all warm-blooded animals play (birds, rodents, cats, even lower forms like insects too). Wild rats, for example, love to play. When captured on slow-motion film, you can actually hear them in fits of hysterical laughter. Fascinating stuff. But animals play for many of the same reasons as humans. Centrally, play is an unstructured, stress-free way to experiment, to practise and learn in new fields, without demolishing old success patterns. It is about creating new ideas in neutral and stimulating ways, where routine falls short. Think of a new word processing package. A structured training course and work manual will accelerate learning. But you will learn only what everybody else knows (important, but will not get you ahead). Now go off and play, skip your way through the package in areas you are not meant to explore. You trip, blip and blunder, but you will find real diamonds from time to time. In all disciplines it is the same trick. Talk to any professional ballet dancer, and they will tell that they discovered and created some of their best and most original movements while just larking around. The mistakes they made gave them insights no master class could ever provide. Howard Rheingold again:

> Are you the kind of worker, communicator, decision maker, designer, artist, business person, or engineer who builds a detailed plan for each creation, then follows it step-by-step? Or do you just start pottering around with ideas or material until some kind of order begins to emerge? If you are the latter kind of worker, you've probably suffered the jibes and innuendoes of your more analytical minded colleagues, and if you are any good at 'thinking by the seat of your pants,' you also know that you are capable of putting together concoctions on the fly that careful planners will probably never achieve in years of deliberate effort.

In its most abstract, play is about tinkering with our minds, opening new ways of thinking and looking at the world. Play *is* creativity. When at play, we make space for our imagination to roam over notions we would not readily have time or room for. A chance to open up the unexplained, a chance to elucidate the arcane. Play can lead to extraordinarily original thought and ideas, if we actively make merriment a normal part of our work routine. After all, when do you have your best and most creative ideas? At your desk? In a meeting? Or on the golf course or playing with the kids? It is a fact that most people have more brainstorms while out walking than at any other time. Furthermore, play is about preparation for uncertainty (aha!), a way of thinking ahead, a chance to run through mental prototypes. Like physical prototyping (which we will explore later in detail), our imagination during play can de-risk certain situations. By running playful mental simulations we can often see the consequences of our actions before we execute them in reality.

Play is not only the original way we tinker and create ideas, it is our brain's favourite way to learn and generate ideas. In fact, all smart people have an exaggerated and uncommon sense for play. Richard Feynman and Walt Disney, for example, loved to play. They were adamant their best and most creative work came through play. Likewise, the Don himself, Mavin Minsky, is a prankster of the first order, his den looks like a playground for the mind. Last time I saw him, he had a green mechanical hand climbing out of his jacket pocket. And he, one of the smartest people alive, and the father of artificial intelligence to boot. And the one I like most is Albert Einstein's success equation: if A = success, B = work and C = play, then A = B + 2C. Nuts, I know, but if it works for the smartest of the smart, then it might work for us. In fact, maybe play is the most important strategic issue of all.

Open play should not disrupt work, but provide extra avenues for thinking and creating in other dimensions. Therefore, strategically speaking, open play is not merely about enough slack in the system to sit and ponder or 15 per cent off-line time to pursue extracurricular activities, as they do at the likes of Hewlett-Packard and 3M (although this adds to the sauce). It more of an attitude, even a cultural value of seeing play as creative way to solve and create new ways out of normal context. Play, learning, thinking and innovation in turn, are all tied up in a patchwork of interaction. Consequently, to stimulate uncommon breakthroughs, play must be a strategic and culturally manifested work issue. So put game playing into the heart of your business. Call projects *games*, call management teams *games masters*, call project leaders *party hosts*.

Deep comparison: Another good route to an uncommon sense, is the capacity and scope to compare matters at hand for an extended period. Essentially, if one diligently compares even the most *like for like* for long enough, new kinds of sense and insight emerge. In fact, this is another proponent of complexity: the deeper we look the more elaborate the world becomes. And as complexity gains, the world transforms from something we thought we knew well, into something quite unlike anything we have known before.

The world of teaching gives wit here. Harvard University's Louis Agassiz, as one example, was a master of the art of deep comparison. Wave after wave, his scholars emerged as distinguished teachers and practitioners in the life and zoological sciences. Some say Agassiz was the greatest of all teachers (after Socrates), giving up principles on unleashing an all too rare sensibility. I found a passage that captures the essence of Agassiz's teaching, in Jane Copper's book *Louis Agassiz* as *Teacher*. It is a pithy account from one of his original students, that informs us of the power of looking deeper and longer at seemingly simple problems:

> 'I had assigned to me a small pine table with a rusty tin pan upon it. When I sat down before my tin pan, Agassiz brought me a small fish, placing it before me with the rather stern requirement that I should study it, but should on no account talk to anyone concerning it, nor read anything relating to fishes until I had permission to do so. To my inquiry, "What shall I do?" he said in effect: "Find out what you can without damaging the specimen; when I think that you have done the work I will question you." In the course of an hour I thought I had compassed that fish… I was anxious to make a summary report and get on to the next state of the business.' But Agassiz paid no attention to his student that day, the next, or during the following week. So the novice, after suppressing his impatience, took another look, and then another. To his surprise, he learned more: 'I set my wits to work upon the thing, and in the course of 100 hours or so thought I had done much – a hundred times as much as seemed possible at the start.' Agassiz eventually responded: 'On the seventh day came the question, "Well?" and my disgorge of learning to him as he sat on the edge of my table, puffing a cigar. At the end of the hour's telling, he swung off and away, saying "That is not right."' Reluctantly, the student went back to his tin pan. After another week of hard, silent labor, he had results that astonished him and passed muster with his taciturn teacher. Agassiz acknowledged the student's successes by bringing him a big pile of bones, with the order to sort them out. Much more agonised examination was in store, with stupendous results: 'Two months or more went into this [second] task with no other help than an occasional looking over my grouping with the stereotyped remark: "That is not right." Finally the task was done, and I was again set upon a remarkable lot of specimens representing 20 species of the side swimmers… I shall never forget the sense of power… which I felt in beginning the more extended work on a group of animals. I had learned the art of comparing objects, which is the basis of the naturalist's work.'

Again, like play, deep comparison is about the room to prospect the not so ordinary. Taking time to see what others do not, or cannot. It is not easy, and not always possible for reasons of time. But the venture in my experience is always worth the price of entry (the solitude, the frustration, the nagging feeling that you are overlooking something else), as in due time deep comparison ushers our thoughts to the quite *uncommon sense* that the sun does indeed revolve around the earth in a hyperbolic curve once every galaxy cycle…

Nurture Counterintuition

Hyperinnovation, like all complex systems, is not merely different, it can be counterintuitive. When the number and kinds of ideas, technology and demands are rich enough, *n*-concepts rush and coalesce with fervid intensity; and with this zealous interconnection, we not only see the emergence of fundamentally new markets, but the conspicuous breaking and rewiring of trade rules, product givens, and technological maxims. Yet the insights needed to bring together and develop such a diverse and interconnected set of ideas, often go against the grain of what we feel is right and necessary.

Many senior managers rely on their intuition, even in major decision making, especially those with long-held careers. They tend to develop a sixth sense for *how things simply work*. But in times of change, a strong intuition not only stops effective decision making, it destroys any chance of innovation, as intuition under this context often jumps to a conclusion that leads back to where it began. After all, intuition is only an unusually developed and deeper form of common sense, and we know what that ushers in. Thus, there is a distinct need to develop an instinct that clasps on consequences that flow in unlike directions. Here, intuition is prediction of an outcome that comes from a deeper level of thought. Hence, *counterintuition* is a bone-deep feeling about outcomes that behave differently from what we expect, it is the rare capacity to both understand and anticipate effects that go beyond the predictable. It is also an unconscious faculty that discerns beyond the reasonable, even above what is considered legitimate, systemic and orderly – now that is hard. Here are some examples:

Intuition:	*Counterintuition*:
If we take more time and deliberation on a project and introduce it when we have met each performance target, we will achieve a better solution.	Quick-fire projects injected into the market for continuous feedback, give rapid learning, which enables a more germane solution.
We must have fully developed technical/market specifications,	Thumbnail sketches, a morning with the customer, then an

before we move to the design stage.	afternoon in modelshop/lab, will give the design outline.
Our senior management must check each key stage in the design process through an official review procedure.	The team is responsible for coughing up a fully functioning prototype for customer review.

Counterintuition often flies in the face of common sense. But we have no choice. A complex world exhibits paradox, which means perpetual novelty and surprise, which means that learning and innovation are the keys to sustainable value – not the intuition of rigid order.

At its best, a highly developed counterintuition is the ultimate mental adjustment to complexity. It receives perpetual novelty as advantageous. It greets surprise with open arms. It does this by viewing novelty as indication of thriving activity, an indication that the system is growing and unfolding. It knows that when the unexpected is the norm, the future is bright. Equally, counterintuition knows that lack of novelty or surprise means the system is either being suppressed (optimisation) or is expiring (equilibrium). It notes that if strange, weird, quite freakish consequences never appear in the system, the market is in trouble. Thus, counterintuition brings with it an indispensable higher and altogether special level of *rationale* necessary to appreciate paradox as the harbinger to great times ahead.

To accelerate the development of counterintuition, we can look to two quite unconventional thought modes, horizontal causality, and childlike imagination:

Horizontal causality: Which came first: the chicken or the egg? It must have been the egg, because the chicken had to come from somewhere in the first place. Right? Hold on, where did the egg come from? So it must have been chicken first?... Well, all this seems to buck linear logic, as rationality says that *energy* cannot come from nothing. Energy has to *be* in the first place to serve up a second helping. It sounds utterly absurd, quite counterintuitive, to say that something sprang from nothing – does it not? But in this quandary sits a huge treasure of insight. If we could answer such a nagging paradox, we could perhaps apply the model to other complex conundrums. To crack such a paradox we call upon so-called *horizontal causality* (a.k.a. chicken-and-egg logic), a counterintuitive way to think if you are conditioned to the linear set. It starts by thinking of reality not as a serial step-by-step sequence of events, but as a kind of interdimensional loop. In this realm, events are not triggered by a chain of causality with a beginning, but an extensive field of causes and effects impacting on each other concurrently.

Old linear logic directs our thinking, where A=B=C. Although simplified to the abstract, this kind of serial logic gives a myopic outlook, it blinds us to the *whole*, and the complex *interactions* between its variables, and if we cannot see the system's whole, we cannot truly begin to understand the system elements, and how they came to be. Yet, linear thinking is endemic in management circles. We all, in time, *intuitively* conceive that all events will pan out in a neat line, one after another (which it never does). Horizontal causality, on the other hand, gives us a counterintuitive insight, which is embedded in all complex systems, giving sense to a world that is not merely linear, but multidimensional. The statements A=B; B=A are an expression of horizontal causality. Where A leads to B; but B can also lead to A. In other words, the effect of a system can paradoxically become the cause of the system. This happens all the time in complex structures, such as connected economies or ecologies. But if something *can* be its own cause, is common sense not up for grabs? – yes, and that is my point. Reason is out, hyperlogic is in. Markets are interconnecting. Escher's strange, impossible etchings are taking over. No matter where you head, you will always end up in a place you either did not expect or a place you did not know could exist. So what can horizontal causality give us?

All hyperinnovation is the result of multiple sets of horizontal causality, feeding deeper among themselves, yet without this kind of counterintuitive thought mode, *n*-innovation is difficult to conceive in the first place. Like the chicken and egg paradox, ideas need to co-evolve in mutual adaptation, feeding from each other as they develop. For example, walk into any Borders store on a Sunday afternoon and enjoy an extradimensional experience. Buy a magazine or newspaper, sit in the coffee-bar and enjoy a glass of wine, listen to an album, and browse through the book list. Meanwhile, your two toddlers are listening to a story read by, yes, its author, in the children's section. They are being watched by closed-circuit TV, so they are safe as houses. You then decide to check out the Borders computer database for a specialist book and order it on the spot. At last you decide to go browse around the book store that is chock-a-block with every title from Accounting to Zen… And so it can be now seen that Borders experience is a result of horizontal A=B; B=A causality. And is the very reason why each product line complements each other so well.

All innovation, and in particular, new product development, happens through a process of horizontal causality. In fact, as you will see throughout this text, hyperinnovation emerges through a nonlinear, counterintuitive process.

Childlike imagination: There is nothing more luminous, nor counter-intuitive, than a child's imagination. To see the world through a child's eyes is a true gift. Edward de Bono, artisan of lateral thinking, and arguably the world's leading authority on creativity, remarks: 'From time to time every creative person wishes he had the outlook of a child so that he could find his own perceptions and escape from the ones that have been imposed on him'. Only, what does a childlike imagination have to do with serious innovation strategy?... Quite a lot I find.

Like play, a childlike imagination is not only undervalued, it is often read entirely wrong. How many times have we seen talented people passed over, merely because they express a wonderment about the world? Individuals with a brilliant imagination are sometimes considered immature, trouble-some, not focused and often perceived as a risk. Yes, some of these special types often have a highly developed sense of humour, and sound the occa-sional left-field view from time-to-time (don't we all). But, there is a mile of difference between childlike imagination and childish behaviour, yet such characters are often confused. In fact, childish behaviour is exactly the kind of conduct I have encountered in boardrooms the world over: managers guarding turf, playing politics, fiercely arguing over a quite witless point. Now that really is childish behaviour. A childlike imagination on the other hand, is indifferent to all that stuff and nonsense. A childlike imagination detaches from convention, throwing caution at old dogma. It is perpetually curious about the world, and is often unaware of the profound insights it conceives. With such a character, the inevitable, not the rhetorical has to be.

I have had the great fortune to meet and work with such extraordinary people over the years, adding something quite special to my work and life. Yet the experience is all too rare. The real world, the uncompromising world, seems to suppress our imagination from an early age. Back in the early 1940s, a team of distinguished psychologists carried out a study to quantify the level of creative thinking and imagination found in the average 45-year-old. They found that the typical imagination was as bland as bean-curd, less than 5 per cent thought in any creative ways. The shock, however, was that it stayed at 5 per cent all the way down to age 18. At 17 it improved a smidgen, edging towards 10 per cent. So, and as you have probably guessed, the psychologists carried the tests on with children. They discovered that creative thinking steadily increases all the way down to age 6. Then at age 5 – boom – the percentage rockets to 90 per cent. And in the great Sigmund Freud's own words, 'What a distressing contrast we find between the radiant intelligence of a child and the feeble mentality of the average adult'.

Test this: draw a dot on a dry marker board, and ask any adult what you have drawn. They answer, probably, 'It's a dot!' Now ask any five-year-old, and the answer is something like, 'my cat' or 'the noise my mum makes when she's shaving'. To a five-year-old, a little *stick* is Robin Hood's bow and arrow, an old *box* a knight's castle, and a *bottom drawer* in a cabinet a whole magic kingdom. In contrast, to the average veteran manager (am I being harsh?) a beautiful branch of a willow is a *stick*, a million dollar piece of custom test kit is a *box*, and a multibillion customer market a spreadsheet in a *bottom drawer*. Education, by whatever medium, and assimilation by the corporate ideas and values we pick up and give out, can, and too often does build psychological brick walls, which in turn puts up direction signals for the way we are supposed to think, dampening the ability to see and connect ideas in unusual and unique ways.

Another surprise here, is that imagination has little to do with IQ. Imagination is more to do with emotional intelligence and personality. About an attitude to life. The late Richard Feynman disclosed, after winning his Nobel prize, that his IQ was just above average (it was 124). He was adamant that the greatest breakthroughs in science and technology do not come from brute logic, but, in his own words, a 'youthful imagination'. Likewise, Einstein's original insight to the theory of relativity was conceived while imagining what it would be like to sit on a beam of light. He always claimed that imagination is more powerful than knowledge.

Recently I came across an old article in my research notes, from *Esquire* magazine (5/93), that describes the kind of management disposition needed to appreciate and seek such a childlike wonderment:

> He came in and seats himself carefully on the edge of my guest chair. He is staring at the toys on my desk, trying to suppress the realisation that I am an infantile nit whose job he could probably do much better. Of course he does not play with toys. He looks out of my window instead. 'Nice view' he says rather perfunctorily, but he does not say 'Wow!' – which is what my view of the canyons and spires of the high-mercantile capitalism deserves. 'I'm looking for an entry-level position in public relations. Maybe corporate marketing, if I get lucky' he says. 'Really?' I say. 'Like, out of the entire realm of human possibility, that's what you want to be doing?' I'm sorry. He's really starting to tweeze my bumpus. What twenty-four-year-old really and truly wants to be in corporate marketing, for God's sake? I look him over as he burbles on about targeting demos or retrofitting corporate superstructures or some figuring like

> that. The guy makes me want to stand up on my desk and yell, 'booga-booga!' Instead I say 'Didn't you ever want to be a rock musician or a forest ranger or anything?' He looks at me like I have a banana peel on the end of my nose. It's quite clear to me, that since he was in high school, he's been preparing to be a communicator. That's actually what he says. Screw it. There is no poetry in this dude. No soul. No surf or wind or whalebone in his eye... He makes me sad.

If you find an associate who can see the world anew everyday, be surprised with what they've seen a hundred times before, that someone is worth their weight in gold. That individual will hold the ability to respond to problems with animation and illumination, rather than merely habitually. People with a childlike imagination constantly create and recreate images which enable them to represent ideas vividly and originally in – yes – *surprising* and *novel* situations. In fact, to a childlike imagination everything seems new and unexpected. Think of a child, perhaps your little 'un? A dog is real exciting news, a pigeon is some bizarre creature (isn't it?), and a tiger some indescribable monster under the bed. Thus kids and adults alike, with an unwavering imagination, thrive on paradox and uncertainty, where events they do not even understand do not link up in expected ways. Exactly the kind of market dynamic all enterprises face. Further still, a childlike imagination has amazing recontextualisation abilities in unusual environments, it has complex systems sussed, it knows how to instinctively interrogate and draw up counterintuitive strategies.

One of the major characteristics of a childlike imagination, is systematic, almost reflex-like curiosity. A machine-gun-like mind enquiring into idea after idea, in perceptions bound up in fantasy and reality. If such an imagination was put to work in a business context, it would allow that business to escape from the imposed normal context it has, offering fresh perceptions and breakthroughs. Furthermore, individuals or teams that emulate a naive imagination behave like the most creative scientists, concocting experiments, formulating theories, and then testing those hypotheses with even more experiments; exactly what is needed for hyperinnovation.

So, could we not nurture such a disposition? Develop organisations that cherish such values?... Favourably, there is much we can do and address throughout the rest of this book. Culture development in Part II discusses the kinds of values and attitudes needed here. Environmental management in Chapter 13 describes the kinds of physical working environment, suggesting tools and toys to play and create with. All contribute to nurturing a company-wide, childlike imagination.

Strategic Serendipity

Of late, and because of an intense rush and interconnection of innovation, raw ideas have become increasingly more promiscuous, cross-fertilising with different, sometimes unknown ideas to produce unexpected conceptual fruits. Again, surprise is ubiquitous in a complex world. Consequently, innovations now emerge that simply would not, without some unexpected collision: *chance* now plays a greater part in innovation! Here are some supporting facts that indicate that luck, as part of innovation, is on the up.

Mathematicians tell that luck is merely a consequence of the ultimate symmetry of numbers. That is, the law lords of averages always control outcomes in the end. For example, when a coin is flipped a large number of times, the proportion of heads (or tails) is very close to 50 per cent. While the result of any individual toss is totally uncertain, a long series of tosses results in a near certainty of a 50/50 outcome. Thus, in the most simple terms, the probability of any successful outcome through a sheer fluke is result of the number of tries. In the end, if you have enough goes, you must win. But of course, life, the universe, and everything, is none so simple. If you were to attempt to pull the ace of hearts from a full pack of cards, you have a 1 in 52 shot of winning. If you took the card you picked, and put it to one side – assuming it was not the ace of hearts – the next attempt would give you a 1 in 51 shot. If you keep on going the odds become more and more favourable. The probability is that you would have a 25.5 in 51 chances of picking the ace of hearts by the time the stack dwindles to half its original number. But even though the odds become more favourable, the odds are not really so good in the end. But now ponder this? You have an imaginary unlimited stake of cards, with an almost unlimited set of winning card options. Here the odds are amazingly good for everyone. Everyone's a winner!

So, what if the world was like an infinite stack of cards or coins, with almost unlimited tries? What if we lived in a world where there are millions of possibilities among its agents (ideas, people, businesses, whatever) and the interconnections between them? The probability is that an increasing number of people and firms would achieve successful outcomes – in whatever their endeavour – as the world continues to complexify. And the real-world facts, in fact, stack the cards and coins in this favour.

Enter, the fundamental, the quantum world where lady luck resides. A quite weird world of relationships, where things are not things but probabilities of interconnection between other non-things. Physicist Fritjof Capra wrote in his book *The Turning Point*:

> Discovery of the dual aspect of matter (its behaviour as both particle and wave) and of the fundamental role of probability had demolished the classical notion of solid objects... The solid material objects of classical physics dissolves into wave-like patterns of probabilities. These patterns, ultimately, do not represent probabilities of things, but rather probabilities of interconnections. Careful analysis... in atomic physics has shown that the subatomic particles have no meaning as isolated entities, but can be understood only as interconnections... Subatomic particles then are not 'things' but are interconnections between 'things' and these 'things,' in turn, are interconnections between other 'things' and so on... As we penetrate into matter, nature does not show us any building blocks, but rather appears to be a complicated web of relations.

In quantum physics, and all of nature, it seems, it is not the individual parts that determine the whole, but the whole that determines the behaviours of the parts. Reality is a probability of interconnections. Reality is hyperinnovation. Reality is luck itself. The lesson: increase your connections and good fortune will – according to quantum physicists – emerge from nowhere.

And the good news is that the connection possibilities *are* on the up. Go back to the Middle Ages and you'll find no more than two-and-half-million people across the whole planet, just 2.5 million the world over! In mighty contrast, by the year 2020, the World Bank *estimate* (there we go again) that at least 12 billion people will be thriving, 1.7 billion literate Asians will enter the world's workforce, much of the developing world, as we know it, would have transformed into high-tech cultures, more than half the world's population will be linked real time to an ultraband internet, and global consumerism will have increased by some 50-fold or more. And in a world where there are more people, with more affluence, with more connections, consuming more – *serendipity* thrives.

We have all met someone we know from the neighbourhood or workplace, at some far-off holiday resort or business destination. And we still get that freaky feeling when it happens. Well, sorry to spoil the party. It is just that for thousands of years we have lived in small communes, where a mere century ago, a 100-mile journey was a major trek. In the distant past, we would get to know no more than 100 people well in a lifetime. Today, the average person is likely to meet with at least 100,000 people, an executive could meet as many as half a million people in his career. Couple this with international travel and global media, with 24-hour access to everywhere and everything, and the chances of meeting people you know in far-off places, all of the time, becomes commonplace. Again, in a complexifying world more stuff happens: expect the unexpected.

And no wonder the unexpected is rife. Ever asked yourself how big the world *really* is? Not so big, it seems. Mathematically speaking, there are only six levels of separation between every man, woman and child on this planet. Think about it: how many people do you know well? Maybe 150? The average is 150. Now each of those 150 know another 150 people themselves (most of whom you will not know or even meet). Now each of those alternate 150, know yet another 150 people, and so on and so on. If you keep on going, by the time you have reached the sixth level in the chain, you would have run well over the number of people alive on this planet today. Again, how big is the world after all? Just six levels of separation between every man, woman and child on this planet!

And now think of the impact of marketing? Walk down your local high street, or visit any shopping mall, and you are bombarded with a profusion of publicity, propaganda, slogans and catchy ads, all beyond the limit of human tolerance. Before the Second World War, people had little notion of this concept called marketing. Back then, the average person was exposed to no more than 30 very polite advertisements in any given week. Now, we are all open to superstreams of *in-your-face* messages daily. Globally, 12 billion display ads, 2.5 million radio commercials, and 300,000 million television commercials are dumped into our collective consciousness, everyday. That is above nine orders of magnitude increase in under three generations.

Almost all of the 4 million miles of road systems in the United States was paved in the 60 years between 1920 and 1985. The entire world's automobile stockpile is largely replaced every 12 years. Berlin and Tokyo two decades after the Second World War were thriving. In fact, two-thirds of Germany's buildings, highways, powerlines and other infrastructure are less than 25 years old. In the 1700s, the local village market haggled no more than a few hundred kinds of ware (at a stretch). At the dawn of the 1800s industrial production began, but was pretty much the same picture of scarcity. By the mid-1800s through to the mid-1900s, productivity of goods and services increased by several orders of magnitude. By the late twentieth century, local supermarkets stocked some 16,000 different product lines. At the end of the twentieth century it was approaching 50,000 lines, and by the beginning of the twenty-first century the internet provided an almost limitless choice of channels, goods and experience.

All of this is a gauge of what is really going on: in a world of abundance, at the beginning of the age of the plenty, the whole notion and nature of market systems transform. As the stack of cards gets bigger and the number of winning options increases, as strange and surprising as it may seem, *luck* is now a major component in the development of an innovation strategy. Thus, the issue here is how we capitalise on all this widespread happenstance. Are there any principles we can apply to expedite serendipity among ideas? The difficulty, as always, is setting out all of the right circumstances in the right place at the right time. So how do you achieve such congruence? Here are 10 ways:

- *First and last rule:* more tries, goes, attempts, ups the probability of success. If you are not out there in the game, you will never catch the ball. Just because a complex world means more stuff happens, it does not mean that it will beat a path to your door. So get connected. Build relationships. Speak on the conference circuit. Publish or perish. And network like there is no tomorrow.
- *Develop a sound attitude towards luck.* First, like surprise, be *ready* for it, make the most out of it when it appears. Be on your toes. Get kitted up and out. Second, look for luck, do not wait for it to happen, go out and knock on doors. I was offered an unconditional place at the University of Sussex, not by taking exams or panel interviews. I went straight to the Professor of Engineering and Applied Mathematics and told him I was going to turn up in October. He laughed, asked a few pithy questions, got me to solve a simultaneous equation, and then with a big grin, said 'Okay'. The message, a positive attitude can sometimes make luck go your way.
- *Break up the word coincidence.* 'Co'... 'incidence'... Incidences that come together at the same time. So, to increase the rate of coincidence, you have to spend more time at the crossroads in business. And where are the junctions of commerce? At the complex boundaries between *order* and *chaos*: where new industries are conjoining, where new music is emerging, where new food and drink are being created. Metropolitan zones such as San Francisco or Frankfurt. Intercultural places like Goa and Brighton. This is where life is rife, where massive rates of interconnection happen between people and ideas. It is the equivalent of Douglas Adams's infinite improbability drive.
- *Change your patterns frequently.* Go shopping at midnight. Try out five or six different martial arts (I did, and found that *Geet Kendo* out-thinks any of the game strategies I have come across). Visit unusual places: how on earth are you going to interconnect new and unusual ideas, if you go to the same old haunts? What have you not tried before? What have you always wanted to do, but have put off? Ask naive questions.

Like unusual places, if you do not ask *out-of-the-ordinary* questions, how do you expect to get to new ground?

- *Get fast*. There are many strategic benefits from speedy innovation: from leading insight, to learning faster, to returning investment quicker, to charging a premium, to reducing costs, so on and so on. But above all (and this is where your accounts will flip), speed increases *luck*... Again, if you're in more places over time, you get more goes.

- *Feed on positive feedback*. Fatboy Slim launches a pop recording called '*Funk. Soul. Brother. Check it out Now...*' (you may know the one). It is played over a few pirate radio stations and listened to by the dance underground. It gathers a small following on the club dance floors across the US. So a few network radio DJs get to hear and play *Funk* over the air at low-peak listening times; a bevy of the 100,000 listeners get to hear *Funk*, and 3000 listeners go out to buy *Funk*. The next week it hits number 62 in the pop dance charts. Because *Funk* slots in the top 100, it is put on the regular DJ play list, so 2.5 million listeners hear *Funk*. Two per cent of the listeners go out and buy *Funk*, that is 50,000 sales of *Funk* in one week. Now it reaches number five in the pop charts, and is played peak time over all the private, national network and international network radio stations. *Funk* goes to number one in 18 countries, peaking at a 100,000 sales a day for three weeks. Thanks to positive amplifying feedback, Fatboy makes it big time. Feedback is one of nature's most powerful governors (see Chapter 26). It forces order out of chaos, it inclines chance towards the central ground. And the Fatboy story is true. The guy lives in my home town, Brighton. A few years ago, he was an unknown. This weekend he is performing in front of 40,000 people. Besides clever marketing and positioning, Fatboy Slim has become a multimillionaire, due to the power of positive amplifying feedback.

- *Do not follow fashion*. Set trends. Whether a management fad or a booming product concept, the fastest way to go out of business, and the quickest way to negate luck, is to follow suit. This is a simple law of competition. If you are happy with mediocrity, if you are happy with being a *me-too*, then copy. But it will not get you very far. The only sustainable competitive advantage is to be sustainably different, but relevant. If you are distinct and germane, it is likely your innovation will catch the customer's eye.

- *Constantly gather information and knowledge*. Only by incessantly collecting new ideas and ways to specific projects, just-in-time, can you thrive on those unexpected changes on those multiple fronts. And forget education of the schooled type, learning via instruction is on its last legs. Hyperlearning via the internet on equally ubiquitous hand-held devices is coming at everyone at rocket speed.

- *Live on the fringe from time to time.* Watts Wacker, founder of First Matter, and Jim Taylor, Iomega's executive VP, say that only by sitting on the edges of life can you see clearly how life really is. To gain these enlightening perspectives, these six-figure-a-day consultants engage in activities that Mr Average would find quite discomforting – pan handling (begging), putting on disguises and mingling with street gangs, and so on – and by all accounts it works.
- *Build not only on home runs*, build on near misses, as they may come through in the end. Most near successes flunk for two reasons: poor timing or underdevelopment. In fact, it often takes decades for a radical innovation to go from inception to total market adoption. And far too many give up just before the turning point. So, stick with it, and you may luck out.

We cannot all win all of the time. The law of averages says that someone has to lose, and lose badly. But then again, not everyone has access to this little list of tips for strategic serendipity. Use them, and the odds of successful outcomes, will, *probably*, increase.

It is All in the Mix

Strategic hyperthinking capacitates hyperinnovation in these complexifying times. Multidimensional logic breaks beyond the borders of normal context, preparing the mind for an immense rush of ideas. Contradigms provide a faculty that fractures the paradigm, shedding light on what we are often blind to. Uncommon sense accommodates a mindset beyond the usual context, penetrating boundaries, offering new associations between ideas. Counterintuition liberates from the anxieties that sit with novelty and surprise, accounting the unexpected as a commodity to be cherished. In turn, strategic serendipity exploits the increasing aggregate of possibilities occurring as the result of increasing number of agents and their interconnections. Play each thinking mode atop each other, and you'll have patch work of multidimensional thinking strategies that enable hyperinnovation.

CHAPTER 3

Multidimensional Learning

Predictions about inventions – their successes, their proliferation, even their emergence – that dominate our lives today, have frequently proven to be wrong, and often quite amusing. Take the computer. In the late 1940s it was subject to the most comprehensive market research studies of the day. The conclusion was that cumulative market demand by the year 2001 would reach a mere 1000. The computer would never make for a sizeable market, and so, at that time, it was shelved... In 1880, with high expectations, the mayor of Washington DC speculated that every city in the world would have at least one telephone by end of twentieth century... The car at the turn of 1901 was predicted to reach 1 million units by 2001. Why? Because that is how many chauffeurs would be in employment. Not a bad guess for chauffeurs, but altogether wrong in actual conclusion.

Predicting the future with any accuracy, even 100 years ago, when times were relatively simple, was tenuous to say the least. Yet today, when events are perpetually novel, surprising, ambiguous, and all the rest, time after time, we fail to learn from this history.

In 1984 AT&T calculated that by 1998 the total demand for mobile phones would hit around 900,000 units. In fact, by year end 2000, over half a billion people owned a hand-held phone. In Bill Gates's, book *The Road Ahead*, published in 1995, a book about the future of information technology and its impact on society, he did not even mention the internet's world wide web (and he the most technologically endowed on the planet). In 1998, Boeing stubbornly declared that there was no sizeable market for commercial superliner (double-decker) jetplanes. By 2002 Airbus had received over 50 options on orders for the A-380 supercarrier, a $235 million-a-pop product.

All advance, even for the best and brightest, in the final analysis, is non-deterministic. The future simply unfolds differently than we can possibly anticipate… But *why*?… This is a simple question, that has been asked since man first began to ponder. The good news is that we now have answers to this question, thanks to emergence of the complexity science. In fact, we not only gain insights for the *why*, but also, on *how* we can gain *leverage* on such unreliable change.

Three Principal Drivers of Change

At the most fundamental level, there are three principal drivers that account for such blind, capricious change: *the acceleration of change, the nonlinearity of change* and *the context of change*.

The gap between the recent past and the immediate future has never been so gaping, because the future now arrives at a rate and a magnitude like never before. By my estimate, the pace of technological innovation is accelerating arithmetically, and the number of meaningful new possibilities is expanding geometrically. Which says something about our most immediate future. Research into both pure and application-specific science, ranging from the most complex, such as genetic engineering, to the most exotic, such as nuclear fusion reactors, has reached a stage where no government or independent institute can measure it fiscally, or in terms of volume and yield. Not because of the enormous amount of capital invested, but as a consequence of its diverse and spontaneous nature. And since we cannot measure it, we do not know what will emerge.

In 1800, the state of the art was the stationary steam engine, the size of a house. It was only 90 years ago when Orville and Wilbur Wright's primitive wooden plane made its short, but mammoth, breakthrough glide. In the Middle Ages, both these contraptions would have been perceived as witchcraft. A mere 25 years ago the entire US strategic early warning system was based on the Q7 mainframe computer; it took an area the size of a football pitch to house it. Today we can store 10,000 times the computational power in an area the size of a postage stamp. And think of this: the first draft of the infamous human genome mapping project was completed on 26 June 2000. When first planned, the entire genetic map of human biology was set to be completed around 2020. The project came in 20 years before time.

To underline all of this, the great Buckminster Fuller once estimated that about 5000 years ago a notable invention occurred every few hundred years or so. By AD 0 there was one every 50 or so years. By AD 1000 the time had shrunk to 30 years. With the advent of the industrial revolution it was down to a significant invention every six months; and 100 years later, down to only three months. By the middle of the twentieth century the time had shortened further, and a major breakthroughs occurred at the rate of one per month. And today, the rate of innovation is just too vast, and too fast, to measure with any meaningful accuracy.

Change is quickening, and its slipstream is the first reason *why* we cannot predict even the most immediate future. The sheer speed and magnitude of change going on, drown out any possibility of getting a grip on what comes next, and what comes after what comes next.

The tempo of technological innovation depends also on the interconnection of ideas. In fact, this may be the root feed for the acceleration of change. As we have explored, ideas interconnect in nonlinear, acausal ways, giving up both novel and unexpected innovations. Science and technology in one field can bring about tremendous, sudden changes in other sciences or technology. What will we discover in molecular biology or synthetic chemistry, or discover in high-energy physics in the next 10 or 20 years? What will be the interconnected and enabling effects of biotechnology or nanotechnology over the next 25 or so years? Professor John Marie Lehn of the University of Strasbourg says that one area that is limitless is chemistry. It is not like physics, which behaves within certain laws and is there to be discovered, chemistry is a creative process and only limited by the imagination. And when one considers the volume and speed of scientific and technological innovation going on today, the vast and increasing interconnection between minds and our ideas, it is not so unrealistic to speculate changes in the very way we live, to exceed anything we can now imagine. The fact is, change is not only accelerating, it is also multidimensional. For every innovation, there is an unexpected string of related and unrelated events and outcomes impossible to predict until they arrive. The transistor enabled the microprocessor and software code, with this came leaps in productivity, empowering more creative work, giving more opportunities, expanding possibilities. Microcomputing brought with it new forms of communications and media, which further improved productivity, with new possibilities in leisure and entertainment, home automation and domestic appliances. None of this remarkable enterprise could have been assumed logically from the primeval conditions around the humble transistor. The nonlinearity of change sees that sooner, rather than later, events will diverge from all rational projections, and often in counterintuitive ways. So when we naturally ask what changes nanotechnology will evoke, or what artificial intelligence will bequeath, the inquiry is met with a cold retort: we cannot know in all its detail what will happen until events actually occur. As only history is frozen in time, so it is only history that is certain.

At the extremities of rocketing nonlinear change, sits a third order to why we cannot anticipate outcomes in detail: the *context of change*. The actual future contexture in which our invention(s) is to interact and diffuse – has itself not been invented. The millions of initial conditions, and the zillions of resultant fluid variables that make up a future context have not even begun to stir. Therefore, all future predictions are taken out of context, and hence meaningless, even stupid. Who knows what unusual, freaky, idiosyncratic factors will emerge in the markets our inventions are set to create? A great many of the details of any future context arise from unforeseen combinations of ideas and events we have no concept of. Consequently, we cannot second-guess a *future context*, no matter how plausible. In short: future context is a commodity that in the end does not lend itself to a simple rational explanation. In fact, take any cataclysmic market failure, any invention that wholly bombed, and the forensic analysis of rational cause and effect breaks down. Common sense may tell that our brain-child flunked because it was fundamentally useless, or inferior in design. But many of the great commercial flops (for example Apple's Cube, Concorde, Delorean) were dream machines of unparalleled brilliance in concept and engineering. But acceptance by the public at large, simply was not forthcoming (at least in the hordes necessary to pass the critical point for a market winner) because the proposed market intent (slick design, supersonic transit, advanced materials transport) missed the real-world context of consumer moods, opinions, perceived risk, hearsay, apathy, and so on.

The message is, all long-term projections of future context, at best, are mere hunch work, since the future is not always as we think it or like it to be. When Boeing speculate no sizeable market for mammoth double-decker airliners, they are being quite reasonable. The advent of expansion in provincial city airports the world over means big demand for smaller, faster, point-to-point routes and aircraft. This is common sense to Boeing. And any reasonable enterprise would stick to its guns here. But we do not live in a reasonable world. Novel events, that we have little or no control over, pan out and accumulate in unexpected directions at the drop of a hat. Who knows what the future context for commercial air travel will be in 10 or 20 years? The glib answer is that nobody knows.

In unison, the acceleration of change, the nonlinearity of change and the context of change drown out any possibility of projecting the future with any accuracy. In fact, the more accurate and detailed our prediction actually is, the more we are merely describing a current reality.

Single Dimensional Learning is Not the Answer

Detailed *deterministic* planning is the favoured orientation to strategy development. As I walk through the corridors of corporations and medium-sized businesses the world over, I witness legions of senior managers engaged in a strategic dialogue that smacks of – yes – 'A' leads to 'B' leads to 'C' logic. Engaged in a process that often takes months, if not years, to quantify some tangible, but imagined future context. This orientation and its pervasiveness, are due, in part, to their straight *common-sense* appeal. Yet, as we have seen above, if we continue to believe that *causality* is predictable, and therefore can be enough understood, we are laying a short path to commercial demise.

The universal platform for deterministic planning is the much beloved *five-year business plan*. An institutional activity that sets strategic and operational objectives that define the course of the business over the next five years. Under this scheme, a business plan is modified in towering leaps. In a technical expressions, this kind of plotting is known as *single* or *lower dimensional learning*: the application of linear, step-by-step logic, where strategic goals and their actions are modified from year to year. In other words, if an actual outcome veers away from its intended objective – say a new product not hitting a sales target – corrective action may be taken to bring it closer to the original goal during next year's planning cycle. This occurs when an enterprise applies the same rules over and over to seek improvement in targets, continually honing the strategy towards greater efficiency. This in turn builds simple orderly learning, with simple orderly results. Consequently, this traditional strategic mode is a top-down, centrally controlled exercise, with learning at a steady orderly pace.

It might be seen that this kind of strategic blueprinting system is the equivalent of the nuclear bomb. Powerful if the environment is static, but leaves little chance of learning in complex, dynamic markets. Single dimensional learning will effect wheel spinning, hesitation and unrealistic premise, only to find that by the time corrective action has been taken, new issues have sprung from nowhere. For simple deterministic learning can indeed lead to predictable outcomes, but outcomes that may not be in synch with market realities. Furthermore, this kind of learning brings with it a false sense of security, it feels very safe indeed. It feels safe because in most cases goals and actual outputs are similar. Similar because goals and outputs are a simple and collapsed perspective of a more than complex reality.

And no wonder the goofy projections, like the computer, the telephone, the car and so on, were, and continue to be, so unrealistic and out of synch with today. The projections did not take account of the speed, nonlinearity and the context of real-world change. In essence, lower dimensional learning will guarantee simple and unrealistic forecasts, out of touch with live events.

So what to do?... If we cannot predicate or control the future within any meaningful tolerance even in the short term, even with every piece of up-to-date information, and even with superbrained analysts at our disposal, then how can we make any reliable strategic plans? How can we plan for uncertainties, when the issues themselves are driven by creativity, chance, counterintuition and uncommon sense? How can we innovate with any clarity under this scheme?

The answer is double-sided: On the one side, hyperinnovation is not built on the assumption that we can forecast or control what will happen in detail, rather it emphasises rapid response and learning as the world unfolds in real time. On the flip side, once we have gained this intelligence, we can use it as *feedback* to influence the future. What comes out of the system in *real time*, we can put back in the system in *real time* to direct in ways that benefit (A=B; B=A). After all, what comes next is not inevitable, it is not written in some sacred stone. We can learn in real time, then use this knowledge to steer innovation across wild and erratic terrain. In fact, this is a scheme of learning and imagination found in the utmost complex and creative of fields of all: the *natural world.*

Lessons from Nature: Hyperlearning

It is well understood by zoologists that in the ecology of species, innovation and learning are somewhat interrelated. In the zoological realm, linear and disconnected combinations are dumb and dying; nonlinear networks are smart and thriving. In the zoological world, interconnected systems learn as fields of evolving populations interacting upon each other; each adapting to the tune of their neighbourhood; the system at large learning, evolving and growing in value faster than the sum of its elements. As we will see, not only is there strength in large interconnected numbers, but *intelligence*: system-wide intelligence that learns and adapts in ultra-creative and value-multiplied ways.

At the carefree age of 10 years, while on vacation in Spain, I stumbled upon a nest of giant black ants. Instantly, thousands of them appeared from nowhere, and begun their attack. I jumped up quick as a flash, but the ants had already begun their assault. My bare legs were covered in a swarming, stinging black sheet. The pain was excruciating, the experience I can tell you, terrifying. But as luck would have it, the mishap took place next to a brook. Abruptly, and without a single thought, I jumped like a polecat into its middle, then with one great splash the ants discharged, trailing off downstream. My bacon was saved. Since that day, and with the experience for ever etched in my mind, I have had this ambivalent interest in ants and their lives. As I studied, I found that ants are quite extraordinary creatures, and that ants have rapid learning and *n*-innovation in complex environments all worked out.

A colony of ants consists of around a million workers, and a few hundred queen ants. The prime job of the worker ant is to keep the nest, and tend and feed each queen – but little more. Each ant is quite dumb, very tiny, and almost blind. But in spite of this, what ants actually achieve is all too remarkable. Our little friends can:

- Make and navigate a leaf-boat on a stream.
- Build a bridge across a chasm.
- Rapidly find the shortest path across a rugged landscape.
- Construct mountain-high cities, with spiral staircases, nurseries, storage rooms and living quarters.
- Keep the entire city at a steady temperature of plus or minus one degree, while the outside environment cycles around 40 degrees.
- Find the choicest food in pitch black, predator-ridden terrain.
- Carry eight times its body weight over the equivalent of 25 miles.
- Beat off a lethal predator at least a million times its mass (me).
- And adapt to an ever-changing, competitively ruthless environment.

Awesome, truly amazing and dumbfounding… But how do these little ant-brained creatures design, build and maintain such wonders?

Ultimately, we cannot understand the actual blueprints that make ant artefacts, like a nest, or ant activities like building a bridge, but what we can grasp is basic *ant system mechanics*. Quite obviously, there is no detailed list of instructions logged inside any ant's head that says 'Look for a fulcrum point for bridge leverage', or for that matter 'build a bridge'. Moreover, there is no single ant that has ever lived, that has grasped the concept of boat, bridge, shortest path, city, temperature, quality, mass, change or yours truly.

When zoologists study these creatures, they find that although individual ants are totally mindless, reflex-driven creatures, a large colony can produce ultracomplex properties and products, way beyond the sum of the composing club members. When a million blind, mindless ants are wired up as a vast interconnected network, they become a field of evolving populations, capable of coming up with brilliant solutions to complex problems that tax even us humans. Again, the complexity, the intelligence, is [not] in any singular ant (agent), but in the ensemble. In fact, we find that the amazing ant products above, are exclusively determined by a dozen or so simple chemical (pheromone) messages (rules). A particular pheromone might say 'follow', another 'stop', another 'back', and another 'grab'. But no more detail than this. But now multiply this handful of simple messages by a million ants, then scale up to the potential of interconnections across a thousand-thousand crumb-like insects ($\frac{1}{2} * \Sigma\alpha^2$), and you get massive real-time parallel computing, faster and more powerful than any computer we humans have yet devised. From such huge collateral crunching, you derive nonlinear cascades, amplifying in counter-intuitive structures far beyond any tangible human comprehension. Messy, overlapped webs and redundant connections giving by-products – bridges, boats, combat teams and so on – far in excess of the elemental bits. From a high number of agents, with even higher numbers of interconnections, are built the most profound emergent structures, amazing products that do not exist in the constituent parts.

Hyperinnovations as Learning Superorganisims

Like ant colonies, hyperinnovations are swarming multi-headed beasts, behaving as a great compound eye on the market. Each individual technical/functional feature is quite mute and blind. But when put into an interconnected system of ideas, and set to work in unison, the *n*-innovation wakes up, feeding crumbs of information into the whole. Just as colonies of ants can deal and thrive in complex, uncertain, rapidly changing environments, *n*-innovations can mimic nature by making churning populations of ideas behave as remote sensors, all experimenting and processing market information at once.

Since a multitude of ideas work in parallel, the population as a whole visits many regions of the market (diverse customer demands) concurrently. Hyperinnovation is the secret by which ants and corporations are guaranteed not only to find any value in the market, but premium worth. And how does an *n*-innovation make sure it locates this highest value? By experimenting and testing bits of the wider market landscape at once. How do you gain leverage on a thousand contradicting variables that eventually make up a future market context? By sampling a thousand comparisons simultaneously. How do you develop an *n*-innovation that can thrive in such harsh non-deterministic conditions? By trying out a multitude of slightly varied ideas concurrently.

Hyperinnovation turbodrives market learning (wholly deserving its name). The highest performing (highest value) ideas in the market landscape begin to interconnect with other star ideas. And since high performance increases the rate of experiments in that zone, it forces attention on the most promising bits of the marketplace. Equally, it diverts experiments away from unpromising, low-benefit zones. Thus hyperinnovation sweeps a huge lattice over the market landscape while reducing the number of experiments needed to find the highest value. Multidimensionalism is one of the ways around the inherent uncertainty of innovation. It is the ultimate counterintuitive supposition: that the smartest business plans, repeated in linear sequence year on year, lead to greater depths of nonsense and market irrelevance. While a thousand tiny experiments performed in parallel lead to peak value in unfathomably complex and unpredictable markets. An enterprise driving a multidimensional learning strategy may only be able to see as far as its own nose, but proceeding in this fashion can still bring that business to a fruitful journey's end.

Multidimensional Learning in Markets

Capital One's accomplishment is a parable of network learning in diverse, discontinuous markets. Multidimensional learning has lavished Capital with an explosive growth rate, while incumbent financial service providers tread water. Founded in 1990, an original spin-off from a Virginian bank, Capital has soared to $20 billion in managed assets, with 28 per cent return on equity, and now ranked among the top 10 credit card issuers in the world. In a complexifying world, personal circumstances shift at a rate of knots. Hence belated financial prescriptions are not only impracticable and dumb, they are totally and utterly senseless. In contrast, Capital profile bespoke trust plans: as each customer's state of affairs change, the trust plans modify too. When I visited Capital's European headquarters in Nottingham, UK, I saw a hive of parallel experiments at work. By testing a thousand slightly varied experiments on a daily basis, Capital's population of *5000* interrelated credit products moves across an extensive market landscape concurrently. Driven by a powerful Oracle database, each experiment acts as a market sensor feeding information into the whole, analysing demographics, pricing, interest rates and lifetime net present value of individual customers. This way Capital spots the highest value custom. This is ant logic at its best. A massive parallel computation of experiments giving up 99 failures out of 100. Some results are promising, a handful of real wins, but every so often Capital strike a golden revenue stream. Through an array of interconnected ideas, one or a few of the tests latch on to a higher value peak (repeat sales, more new custom), and from this 'win' a signal (message) is sent back into the network, for more sensors and tries in that zone. More successes generate more feedback, so starting a self-reinforcing learning loop. Capital's strategic focus is: (a) the rate at which financial innovations can be brought to market, (b) acute one-to-one market testing, (c) financial mass-customisation. Capital, thus, is a true hyperinnovator, thriving on the paradox of heterogeneous, erratic markets.

Hyperlearning is a powerfully objective tool in a bustling market of alternatives. By rotating a panoply of experiments, it is possible to accelerate learning of what diverse, often confused customers favour most. In *The 500-Year Delta*, Jim Taylor and Watts Wacker describe the endowment:

> Snapple iced tea, as bottled-tea lovers know, has an almost endless variety of flavours – seventy-two last count. Lay each variation end-to-end, and they would stretch almost from the great tea fields of the Himalayan foothills to the top of Mount Everest itself. This panoply of tastes, Snapple executives long thought, was their product's greatest strength. In fact, it was Snapple's greatest strength only if the company managed its customer's choice for them. Why? Because in a time-crunched world, no one has the raw minutes to sort through seventy-two flavours. Lunch would be over by the time you made a selection; the supermarket would be closing, the vital organs dehydrated and shutting down. How could Snapple get around the problem? How could they offer an immense variety of choices without turning a multitude of choices into a chaos of choices? We made this suggestion: Come up with a simple shelf-set of eight choices? Four would always be the same so that Snapple would offer customers the pleasure of familiarity. Four would be changed every week so that Snapple could continuously refresh and renew its product line and so that customers could work their way out on a limb – mango-raspberry flavoured or peach-papaya flavoured? – if they so choose.

Ant logic again! By putting thousands of these eight-set choice shelves out in the market, Snapple get to carry out tens of thousands of experiments each day. They can assimilate the rotation of choice, building up a profile of what is selling, what is not, what is most popular, what is growing, and so on.

The most inventive media corporation I have come across, leverage on a multidimensional learning strategy too. Sony, back in the 1980s, were content with an arbitrary launch of a platform product and to cautiously follow with around half a dozen derivatives based on the original platform. Today Sony are more likely to hit around 100 or so new platform models, followed with a divergent stream of designs. That is over a thousand new and improved products each year, or one every nine hours! The lesson here is that the more choice, the more turns, increases the opportunity for market feedback, which in turn lifts innovations further and faster towards fitter designs. This kind of hyperlearning allows an organisation to turn on, or turn off, what the market likes or otherwise. If customers adore the red woollen jumper with the bobbles on the shoulder, then more can be injected. If the reaction leaves the red woollen jumper on the shelf, then it can be quickly pulled off and replaced with another choice.

Virgin Atlantic hyperlearn at the intersection of fun, entertainment, dreams, pleasure, lust and jet thrust. They experiment with new inflight services at a rate unmatched in their industry, innovating hundreds of tiny comfort dimensions for the leisure and business passenger, to make their flight more entertaining and relaxing. They come in the form of very simple features such adding a special radio channel, a manicure service, even the odd magic show. When they made the decision to put in the sleeper cabin service for business customers, they introduced a whole range of pre-and-inflight features in less than *10* days. Now that is hyper-innovation inflight.

Another trick in nature for accelerating learning and growth, is *death*! By killing off older species, nature makes way for newer, more robust and intelligent genera. Vertebrates outgun their lower invertebrate cousins. Mammals outwitted and eventually superseded the terrifying dragons. And we humans outdo all (so far). It is the same with technological innovation. Technology – whether a language, a technique or tangible consumer products – is as much part of, and subject to natural selection of the *Darwinian* kind, as biological life! *Life* must adapt to competitive variations or perish. As in nature, in commerce, weak innovations die, the strong proliferate. What is weak (failure), and what is strong (success) is determined only by the ecology (marketplace). The strong innovations dominate, as the weak are swept aside. Callous-sounding stuff, but it works by all accounts.

Jonhson & Johnson's 120 years of innovation and growth comes down to abiding by the principle of natural selection in markets: culling the weak and building on the strong. J&J are wholly prepared to pull the plug on the utmost capital-intensive business divisions, if the market does not bite. J&J stopped selling an ibuprofen pain reliever, called Medipren, in which it invested millions over six years. But like several other J&J businesses – heart valves, kidney dialysis equipment and magnetic resonance image machines – Medipren simply flopped. J&J made no apologies, viewing innovation as a game of learning. Willingness to pull the plug on unpromising projects makes it a difficult company to second-guess. J&J, like all true innovators, never know whether a project is going to strike gold from the outset, but have set the business up to quickly learn and adapt to market demands. Over a third of J&J's revenues come from products launched in the last 3 years. Of the 21 units identified as the principal domestic operations, a third have been sold or shut down. Of the major businesses that make up J&J, more than half were less than 10 years old, in a business that is 120 years of age. As aggressive as J&J are at creating new businesses, it is even quicker to enter new markets. I find it hard to say which is more laudable: J&J's success in inventing new products and services, or the willingness to cut loose failures? Perhaps it is both. But in the end, it is J&J's acceptance of the fact that it is the competitive context that determines the winners and losers. J&J apply leverage using nature's culling and nursing practice, switching on the winners and dropping the duds, killing off what the customer did not respond to, only to focus on what the customer selected.

The Strategic Principles of Market Hyperlearning

Strategic hyperlearning's goal is to identify superior value, by performing a cascade of simultaneous tests across the aggregate market landscape. What follows is a summary of principles that guide such a multidimensional market learning strategy:

- One giant leap of the planned kind heads to impetuous failure, as data gained are neither immediate nor apparent. Market intelligence is lost in the prolonged gap between planning and outcome. Consequently, it is essential to examine market data as and when they transpire. This enables swift redress for the next learning cycle. It also motivates for action as the fruits of labour are direct and meaningful.
- Follow the path of greatest value. Pitch a lattice of tests over the market totality, to parallel crunch the numbers. As the population visits miscellaneous regions of the market simultaneously, the law of averages

locates premium value without human intelligence. Remember, nature's dumb search techniques are smarter then human pioneering. As the messages come in for the choicest custom, throw more experiments into that zone, this thickens the stew of amplifying feedback signals for yet more value. In pure computation terms, the capacity to find value in any market goes up as the square of the sum of the population of tests. This is not only a law of nature, it is a law in business.

- Provide as many tests to the market as possible to compound outcomes, even duplication across the landscape is virtuous. Quick-fire tests cannot be optimised or supercoordinated by assembling a perfectly balanced system. There are far too many fluid variables to control completely. A potent strategy of experimentation – as in nature – is a soup of messy, parallel webs, at times overlapping, sometimes displaying redundancy, mostly diverging, but collectively giving up market facts far in excess of the elemental tests.

- The magic that breathes intelligence into a bed of indifferent entities is in the *interconnections*. Each test is almost sightless. A group of examinations see a little further. Yet wire each test up as an enterprise-wide hyperexperiment, and the activity springs forth like some bloodthirsty animal in pursuit of live bait. To enable the interconnection of market tests, provide your people with hand-held gadgets and gizmos for outfield communications, and intelligent web-based tools to collect such field data in real time. Construct this on smart agent-based (ants again) software technologies (for example Intelligenesis's webmind product) to enable teams to meta-tag and collate data in easy-to-navigate hyperindexes; to build heuristic profiling of customer demands based on common themes; and to automatically and intelligently route customer information to those most interested. There is much to do here. Chapter 14, Hypermachines, details a functional model for such data/idea interconnection technologies.

- Rules, few in number and simple in form. Complex systems reach high levels of dynamic learning and innovation when the system is subject to a few simple rules. Elaborate order is not inevitably buried in the rules; complex order emerges from active compounds. Make sure the applied rules promote network learning with real prototypes, in the real markets, with real customers.

- Design a market test kit (à la Snapple) to continuously sample the market for real-time customer trends and demands. Then measure the rate of experiments: (a) per associate, (b) per customer, (c) across the aggregate market. Next, gather feedback to build up a profile of where the value is in terms of what is selling, what is not, what is most popular, what is growing.

- Listen to the signal-to-noise ratio, it is an important yardstick in effective market deduction. Ultrachoice, rapid technological fusion, and all the rest, leads to yet one more sandbag on the road to market learning: confused markets, to the point where customers can simply turn off. The marketing experts term: *noise*, and considering the first chapter, there is one awful din. The other part of the equation: *signal*, the impact of information coming in from the market. For effective market learning, the signal (high value information) must be greater than the noise (market entropy). The secret to intensifying the signal-to-noise ratio is to identify the most uncertain tests in the market. This is because the least probable test result yields the most valuable information, therefore the highest value experiments are those that have the lowest probability of outcome, yet are proven feasible. Consequently, the value of market information is inversely proportional to the probability of its event.
- Experiment differently than the competition. To maintain differentiation from the competition there is a vital need to enrich with radical test campaigns. What relevant, but rebel-like experiments can be created? Do something outlandish. Drop a million ping-pong balls from a helicopter over a football game, with a description of your new product stamped on it. Ask the customer to log on to a website designed to capture insightful knowledge of the customer. Those that reply have a higher interest factor. Tell the press you are going to do it, media coverage will reinforce the testing. Most important: tests must grab attention of the right people; specific targeted customers (lead users, advanced buyers, early majority, and so on). There are many tactics that can be applied here, games, quizzes, contests, whatever is relevant to the customer.
- Outexperiment the competition. Test where your competitors do not. Test in places where your competitors are lacking or weak. Measure the rate of experimentation vis-à-vis the competition.
- Mistakes are okay. Life in general, and innovation in particular, the quicker you make your first 1000 mistakes, the more learned you are going to be. Innovation (and life) is a high-risk business, so get over the phobia of mistakes, it comes with the job. Failure is part of the culture and nature of innovation too. In a world where more stuff happens, more failure simply happens. Praise failure, or people will stop taking

risks. If people stop taking risks they will not effectively test the market, and innovation of the relevant kind will evaporate into the ether. Does management actively praise a failed set of experiments? It will happen, remember this is also a probabilities game. An effective way to evoke learning in the face of error, is to set targets. This heads up the test in question, if a team misses the mark. The bottom line here is to learn from failure faster than the competition (much more on this later).

- Design the task of market learning and innovation into everyone's role. Capital One's job specifications obligate each associate to, (a) suggest innovative product ideas, (b) carry out experiments in the market and (c) champion their innovation projects from pre-concept through to commercialisation.

Each experiment interconnected to the network, offers the opportunity to learn what the market is selecting for, and where the highest value rests. Each test allows fine tuning to what the customer says is important, while at the same time lots of experiments inch up and transform the *n*-innovation in total, within a very short time, expanding the innovation in multidimensions.

'But,' you may ask, 'How can I experiment with a pioneering wind turbine, or integrated office furniture systems, or a new platform car with a development budget of $-billions?'

Inherently large, high investment, resource-intensive innovations do not stop multidimensional learning. Narrow, strip the product or service down to its fundamental features. Its simplest number of subsystems. Work on them quickly. Get a working prototype to market fast. Only then can you evaluate with real customers, learn and feedback for the next cycle. If it bites, rapidly deploy a team to carry out more trials within months, less time if possible. Learn from these new tests in the market. If the swarm of tests bite again, connect more to the tune of the feedback, so on and so on.

Accelerating Learning

We live in a time where the latest laptop computer is out of date as soon as it leaves the box it came in. Where new software code can be downloaded via the internet to any point in the world within seconds. Where if it ain't broke, we chuck it anyway. The ephemeral is everywhere, technological advance marches on without compromise. This creates one more headache in a complexifying world. To remain competitive, enterprises have to move along faster than at any other time. Thus, not only is network learning per se central to successful innovation, but the *speed* of learning plays a major role.

A key to *accelerating learning* in the market, is to build up so-called *iterative capital*, the ability to carry out prototype experiments at a rate of knots, at least cost... 'The new economies of innovation is transforming global business', says Michael Schrage, codirector of MIT's media lab. 'The marginal costs of prototyping products, simulating services, and modelling business systems, are rapidly shrivelling into insignificance. It's becoming ever cheaper and easier for ambitious organisations to explore new ideas faster. The inevitable result? Hyperinnovation.' Schrage asserts that an extended capacity to iterate within the innovation process enables companies to experiment with more versions of ideas in less time.

Iterative capital, a surplus of prototype process capacity – like an excess of financial or intellectual capital – gives many advantages. By cleverly deploying virtual reality simulation tools (see Chapter 14), and rapid prototyping technology (below), the cost of *design–test–learn* cycles in the lab and in the market, shrinks. Think of a new checkout service at an airport, or an in-car entertainment system, even a simple spotlight? The attractiveness, relevance and performance of the new concept depend on feedback from both tests in the market and lab, and potency of the feedback hangs on the number of concept iterations over time. The great news is, in the digital era, the cost of such repetition is falling towards the free, and turns out to be a smarter initiative than any of the contrived schemes yet seen.

Concord Lighting is a world-class manufacturer of high specification commercial lighting products, and gives an excellent example of what iterative capital can accomplish. Yet, not so long ago, Concord had a major bottleneck in their new product development process. The design of reflector/lens systems (the elaborate parts that actually focus the light beam) often took months to perfect. Several products I know, run to years before all the optical problems were ironed out. Then, Concord came across a computer-aided reflector design system, called Cadlite. The design engineers were sceptical at first, as Cadlite promised to reduce the reflector design process to a matter of weeks. Yet by the second week of use, the first reflector was specified. The surprise, they thought, was how much more flexible the system was, enabling hundreds of design iterations in a fraction of the time and cost. In fact, one reflector took a single afternoon to develop, cycling dozens upon dozens of options. The benefits were threefold. The reflector design process went from several months down to one afternoon, technical performance went up leaps and bounds, and the capacity to try out multiple options in one hit (iterative capital) went up by at least five orders of magnitude.

Prototype experiments are also essential to risk management in any innovation process, because *learning* is the single most effective way to de-risk – anything. Iterative capital enhances and helps accelerate learning in the market, again through increasing the number of tests over time, at least cost. Again like the ants above, you may only see a little way ahead, but the capacity to iterate in rapid cycles gets you the choicest food (superior design specifications) faster, even if you do not exactly know where that food is in first place. It is a simple strategy, that is set to dramatically enhance both market and technical learning. Here are 14 guiding principles to build up iterative capital:

- *Generous capital investment*. Innovation is several orders of magnitude more difficult and time-consuming than any other activity in business – fact. Prototyping is the single most significant activity within innovation, in terms of the value-adding information it gives up – fact. Prototyping de-risks in high uncertainty and accelerates learning – fact. Whether you are in traditional manufacturing of big machines, or leading-edge development of genetic pharmaceuticals, or radically innovative financial services, your capital investment programme had better be *the* most generous when it come to iterative capital. Of course, it is not just how much, but how funds are spent that has impact. But without a significant budget in the first place, you will not afford the kit that gives the order-of-magnitude jump in prototyping productivity necessary for hyperinnovation.
- *Collocate learning facilities*. Facilities that manifest fast results and accelerated learning, mean having prototyping facilities collocated dead centre of the project working environment – that is designing, prototyping, integrating, experimenting, testing, concluding and feedback. Very few do this. The amount of businesses I visit, whether service or manufacturing, that lack any such facility, is still much too high. Even so, many that do, still have these facilities dispersed around the organisation. This cannot deliver what is necessary for even a reasonable amount of innovation, let alone hyperinnovation. A collocated facility gives the opportunity to carry out downstream prototyping, upstream. That is, service infrastructure or component assembly machinery being mocked up at the same time as initial product experiments. This may turn out to be a vary large, chaotic area. The scene is quite different from the typical office environment (see Chapter 13 for such a working example).

- *Build in redundancy*. Multiple parallel tools and processes eliminate prototyping bottlenecks (do not get caught up in the *one big machine trap*). I know of a major manufacturer of gas turbines, that invested heavily in a *mega* integrated piece of test kit, to replace the older test kit which was made up of about half a dozen smaller, discrete systems. As the integrated mega-kit was commissioned, they decided to chuck out the 'scruffy' older kit. After all, the new mega-kit would do all the jobs at once – they thought. In reality, the mega-kit caused a major bottleneck, as the downtime in set-up and set-down took much longer. Furthermore, even when one particular test was needed, the mega-system was the only kit available to do the test. Straightaway, queues of work-in-progress mounted up, which caused major delays in the development process. So lots of smaller kit is the goal here. Build in redundancy to enable simultaneous prototyping, it is the law of complex networks again. And as for the ever-growing and vast offering of rapid prototyping, instant production technology, and services themselves (for example stereolithography, 3D powder printing, laser deposition, fused deposition modelling, vacuum casting, metal spray moulds, and so on), there is little point in discussing the finer points here, as the technology is developing faster than this book could do justice to. Therefore I suggest that you subscribe to the journals, click the websites (for example www.rapidnews.com), attend the exhibitions, and hold talks with the service and technology providers. Personally, I am astonished what can be achieved today, with so little time and expenditure.

- *Accelerate learning before output*. The primary objective for any prototype experiment is to effect high levels of learning about how an invention (physical equipment or people-based services) *behaves* in its working environment before launch (output), both into production operations and the marketplace. In too many cases this kind of learning is achieved *after* a new product/service is launched. For large-scale projects (for example aerospace, automotive, internet banking and so on) this causes an acute learning disability, and reason number one why we see quite poor design performance in many big-scale projects. Follow the guidelines here, and rates of learning before launch (output) will accelerate.

- *Test criteria*. Quantitative performance targets must be identified, and the tests to qualify those targets must be defined. This includes such measures as component *technical* characteristics performance, process *characteristics* performance, and end-process *controls* performance (see the structured matrix in Chapter 24 to capture such test criteria).

Equally, operational and field performance and test criteria now come from an increasing number of international technical and safety qualification standards. These give a *baseline* for performance, that is, they set the minimum performance requirement. In some situations it is important to exceed these standards to achieve competitive performance advantage.

- *Accelerated strife*. So-called *strife* (stress-life) experiments push the design to its limits prematurely. After all, the true nature of any experiment is to move what you are trying to learn to its breaking point. If not, *learning* before production and market launch will be wholly disabled. This is achieved by gradually raising the loads and changing the environmental strains to the point where the prototype or final product, passively or catastrophically fails. This gives insight into areas for improvement and potential early failure in the field. For example, a superstore checkout counter service can be stressed by overloading with groups of customers impatiently waiting in a long line. Through observation, it is possible to detect bottlenecks and weaknesses in the service process, thus enabling design of significant improvements and unique innovations. Jusco supermarkets in Japan do this. They have completely redesigned the checkout process for high-speed service, no high technology, but uncommon sense. They have quadrupled the speed of checkout throughput, simply by removing bottlenecks and re-engineering the service process lay-out. Iterative prototype experiments were key to this. Further still, durable products, such as the Sony Playstation II, go through traumatic strife experiments and tests covering any failure mode from zapping with static electricity, dropping on to concrete from 3 metres, baking at high temperatures for months on end, and on and on. Through rapid prototype experiments Sony are continually finding new ways to make their product's performance more robust and reliable under extreme environment stresses and strains.
- *Lots of false starts are a good sign of innovation*. In all of the innovative enterprises I know, you can wade knee-deep in the projects and experiments that just did not make it off the ground. But in the same breath, these companies do not hang around, these innovators are prolific. The knee-deep false starts, happened over months, not years.
- *Exit early*. Paradoxically, a key to de-risking a project, is to fail earliest. The earlier you fail, the faster you de-risk and/or learn. As James Dyson says, 'If it works, and especially if it works first time, you learn nothing!' Here, the management maxim of right first time is out, and

accelerated learning is in. So, treat all prototype failures as learning experiments. The late Soichiro Honda, co-founder of the Honda Motor Co, often said: 'My success comes from 99 per cent failure and introspection.' He lived by the belief that a failed experiment can tell you what direction to go next, or how a design could be improved. So think about why a project failed? Ask others why they think it bombed. Ask who the project affects (the customer) why it flopped. Ask successful people why the wheels fell off. Equally, ignore commentary that sounds like 'Why bother,' or 'It can't be done,' and especially disregard 'You can't possibly do that.' Negatives do not help here. Prototypes, first and last, and all in-between, are there to learn from, to toy with, to take to their limits, to see how they behave under duress. And now, after all, we know why our kids break their toys so readily, they are not merely being destructive, they are simply learning, playing, toying in the extreme. As Chapter 2 shows, we can learn a lot from children.

- *Test the highest value and most sensitive experiments first.* To achieve an early exit strategy, *focus on the highest value and most sensitive experiments* earliest. The greater the success rate experienced with the most valuable and sensitive experiments, the more reliable and valuable an innovation is likely to be. A high value experiment is one that is unlikely to be successful, yet is successful. That is, if a complex and highly novel piece of technology or process is made to work reliably, you are likely to gain a competitive advantage and increase the premium for that technology. By contrast, a sensitive experiment is one that is either uncertain in terms of outcome (the basis of true innovation), or one that dramatically affects downstream activities. Without attention to the highest value and most sensitive experiments earliest, a prototype can move down a less than satisfactory path. Tom Peters and Nancy Austin tell an amusing, yet pithy example of the significance of sensitive experiments, in their book *A Passion for Excellence*: 'Aircraft engines have to contend with the possible ingestion of flocks of birds. So one of the important things you do to test an aircraft engine is to go out at some point to your local chicken farm, buy several gross of chickens, put them into the barrel of a huge (several feet in diameter) 'chicken gun' and fire them at the engine. It's the ultimate pragmatic test. Now consider this: Rolls-Royce spend several years and about a quarter of a million dollars on a new graphite based engine, then it fails the chicken test. *Reworking* cost them a big share of the markets.' Furthermore, if the more sensitive problems are left until later, many of the more certain outcome experiments will simply be a vain and wasted effort. The key here is to search for the most uncertain problems or concepts. Ask 'what can we quickly do right now, without fuss, that will prove or unprove the direction we think we should go?'

- *Prototype both product and process simultaneously*. If you do not, you will be limited in process innovation. Remember, product and process co-evolve (A=B; B=A), so it is best that the process design work begins at the basic product prototyping stages. For example, in manufacturing, production ramp-up; and in service, full throughput capacity (the time it takes to reach full volume capacity) is a critical issue for *breakeven time* (the time it takes to recover capital investment). Hence, production and service process proofing must start way before development ends. From this standpoint, we have to adopt a mindset that product–manufacture–delivery, or service-process infrastructure development, are one whole. No one piece of the product/service can be conceptualised, developed and commercialised in isolation. All things here need to be considered in the light of other things. Motorola insist that production process development is collocated with product development. Motorola's Message Pager division broke time-to-market records for introducing a new range of pagers. Each experiment considered both product and process as an integrated (A=B;B=A) system. By the time product development had been completed, all the major production process problems had been ironed out. Each stage fed from each other. Unorthodox design and process innovations were realised, impossible under the old regime. Ramp-up to full-scale production happened for the first time without fuss. This is simple stuff, but few do it.
- *Usercentric*. Centre the prototyping activity around the customers and providers who will purchase, use, abuse, transport, make, serve, maintain, and recycle the contraption. The reason, as I will expand on in Part V, is that what is considered high value in the market, is not determined internally. Unfortunately, too many firms ignore the customer when experimenting with prototypes. At the end of the day, it is the customer that is both the judge and jury. The message here: get the prototype into the market, today. Knock something up. Get some customers in. Try it where it will be ultimately be judged. Tom Peters, again, forcefully tells companies to get the 'thing' (service or otherwise) among real customers asap. Within 10 days for a light machine, within 60 days for a new car, it does not have to look pretty, comments are what you want and lots of 'em, and do it again and again until it ends up in the market on a full-time basis. Apply the customer demands analysis methodologies in Chapter 20. Learn and feed back into the prototype.

- *Phased passes.* Iron out the bugs flawlessly, whether software code, electronic circuits, mechanical fits, human factors or service sub-processes. Only until you are quite satisfied you have squeezed out all the information possible about the first pass prototype is it then astute to move on to the next level. Again, to do this, you need to get prototypes tested, played with, abused, and so on, out there in the real-world market. Microsoft had, for example, 40,000 copies of its Windows 95 product in beta-test, with real customers. Now think of the dollar return here. Say 20 test hours each customer, times $100 dollars an hour (customer personal time), times 40,000 copies? One billion dollars of bug testing for free!
- *Do not change the proven ideas.* Once you have objective test data that says that an idea is durable and reliable, do not change any of its parameters. This is about fixing trustworthy information into the prototype.
- *Inch upward.* Interconnect new layers of ideas over the results of simple prototypes. Build on what you know will work flawlessly. Make the new layers of ideas work as flawlessly as the simple.

Follow these simple guidelines over the longer term, and you will build up equity in iterative capital. As the equity ascends, the cost of prototyping falls, in turn raising the capacity to experiment and test more options, thus learning at a faster gait. An enterprise can significantly expand its range and diversity of a product portfolio, as learning is ultra-accelerated through iterations. As with the logic above (strategic serendipity, concurrent experiments in the market, and so on), the more attempts amplify feedback from the market and the lab, and so boost learning and adaptation in real time.

Amplifying Learning

There is a fundamental law of innovation that can be leveraged to further amplify learning in complex markets. When at least *3 per cent* of the total (population) market has accepted an innovation, it will not go away. When the number rises above *15 per cent* of the population, it takes off like a rocket. Evidently, finding and learning from the first 3 per cent is critical to the survival of an innovation; learning from the first 15 per cent is crucial to the confirmation and sustainability of an innovation. But who are the leading 3 per cent and sustaining 15 per cent in the first place?

To begin to do this, it's possible to pinpoint each *class* of customer by their *orientation to innovation*. It is clear that for different reasons some people, indeed entire businesses, are simply more open to new ideas than others. Some just hate the idea of innovation. And the reasons for the likes or dislikes are identifiable, successively giving up information on who is most likely to adopt a new product or service platform. It tells where a firm should focus its learning at various stages through an innovation cycle, and then later during commercialisation stages, where to focus marketing. Here is a simple breakdown of the five major customer classes classified by their orientation to innovation:

- *Innovative customers (5–10% of population)*. Educated, well connected, technology appreciative. Often risk takers, science believers, ambitious, and less dogmatic. Innovative customers are people with a mission in life, or businesses that live on the leading edge of science and technology. They are not only open to innovation, they are predisposed to it. They include the so-called *passionate specialist*, always on the look-out for the unique or the exclusive. The techno-geeks, who like to lose themselves in the wonders of new technology. Sometimes they are fashion or life-style experimenters, having an unquenchable desire to stand out. This class is hard to attract, and even harder to keep. However, if they switch on to your innovation, they can be used to gain revenues during early learning and proto-commercial stages. They often enjoy finding squeaks and bugs, sometimes the fixes too. Silicon Valley, for example, is chock-full of innovative customers.
- *Advanced customers (10–20% of population)*. Opinion/thought leaders, respected, proactive decision makers, they watch for new ideas and technology. They are individuals or organisations that have real demands and new needs that conventional products or services are failing or limited in meeting. They are relatively small in numbers, but because of their credibility, they have significant impact on the proliferation of innovation. They are also reliable for rapid word of mouth, due to their technological endowment (e-mail, faxes, mobile communicators, communities of interest, and so on), and so have great power over confirmation or rejection of an innovation. To find this class of customer, individuals are likely be reading highbrow literature and/or media that tells them how to get ahead in life. They often belong to institutional bodies or clubs. The businesses usually reside in technologically intensive, highly competitive, and/or fast-cycle markets.

- *Early majority (20–30% of population).* Analytical, have their wits about them, and try to avoid risk. Slightly older, they can sense a good thing or potential winner, but they can also smell a stinker a mile away. They are also hard to attract, but once convinced – often after much convincing – they are loyal. They are also good for word of mouth and the deeper confirmation and eventual establishment of an innovation. Experiment and learn from these customers. Sales target these customers once it can be shown that advanced customers have gained real benefits. To achieve effective learning here, target high-profile early majority types with (a) real tangible needs, and (b) the power to make/influence the purchase; without these two criteria driving the learning effort, it will not work. Significant effort is needed here, as the numbers that make up this class can either make or break learning and eventual total market adoption. Early majority classes are often professionals, or managers, or high-grade trades people with higher disposable incomes. They read a lot of non-fiction literature and often watch a lot of factual television. And if you have done your customer analysis homework here (see Chapter 20), they'll also come and find *you.*
- *Late majority and gradual adopters (30–50% of population).* Limited disposable income, traditional, sometimes suspicious of the new. Peer pressure to stay the same and fit in the group. They are often less ambitious and more fatalistic. This class of customer sometimes reject the whole notion of the new. Gradual adopters, they often have specific or latent needs, so learning through direct marketing is a reliable way to reach these people. They are often provincial, homing in on media such as local radio, and local and tabloid newspapers. Small start-up firms, on tight budgets, come into this class. Local exhibitions are good inroads here.

By performing experiments with the applicable customer class during appropriate stages of a given innovation cycle (see Chapter 15 for four key stages), it is possible to significantly amplify market learning. The starting block is the *innovative buyer.* They represent a mere 5 per cent of a market, but this class is often willing to give up time to interact with early prototypes. They are also good for focus groups (see Chapter 20) to help define early concept designs. They will not in themselves tip the market, but will give invaluable indications of what the emerging demands are going to be. The next stage is to learn from *advanced customers*, again they only represent a small percentage of the total market population, but will give up much more detailed information about explicit demands.

Once you have refined a prototype, it is important to move on to mass market learning, the so-called *early majority*. These represent a percentage of the population that will make your innovation both profitable and sustainable. They will tell you where to improve your inventions, give indications to where it could be augmented, and tell you about the most effective marketing channels. By the time market learning has reached the *late majority* and *gradual adopters*, it is a done deal, you have already innovated.

And a final word here. Anything sufficiently new, whether a bright new piece of knowledge, even a brilliant and essential breakthrough in technology, will be doubted and readily rejected, even laughed at, at first. Then, slowly, the idea progressively creeps in through innovative thinkers and lead users. Next, it moves up through wholesale adoption via the early majority. Lastly, it becomes a commodity and is eclipsed by yet another innovation. So, each customer class has distinct attitudes towards and demands of, innovation. As the saying goes, you can lead a customer to a market, but you cannot always make them drink. On the other hand, if you identify and learn from the right class of customer, at the right time, you'll seriously improve your chances of obtaining that vital first 3 per cent, and sustaining 15 per cent of the total customer population.

Multidimensional Learning

No business, no matter how smart or technologically endowed, can predict the future in all its detail. Yet, by combining and applying lessons from nature's network learning, and by accelerating learning by building equity in iterative capital, and by focusing learning from the right class of customer, it is quite possible to find the highest value, even though the market and/or technological landscape ahead may not have been defined or thought of yet.

But it does not stop here. The learning strategies above are just where hyperinnovation begins to take off. As we shall explore in the next chapter, not only can a firm offer a broader portfolio of product platforms, not only can a company effectively compete in a range of unrelated markets, not only can a business win in totally disparate industries – but! – can create an enterprise that interconnects an amazing diversity of ideas, technology and customer demands in single product and/or service concepts. In short: multidimensional learning ignites a sea change in business dynamics: the strategy of *focus* is now transforming into *multidimensional enterprise*.

CHAPTER 4

Multidimensional Enterprise

Study the lateral frontiers between dense oak forest and open wild flower prairie, and you will discover that no single species dominates the slender terrain. The narrow band between two distinct ecologies fosters the most prolific, often counterintuitive arms race between competing forms of life. The strategies and tactics found in such trenches are unimaginably creative, outinnovating any close cousin found deeper in the ecologies beyond. For example, ants live in thorny bushes where no ant-eaters can prey, yet ants eat the thorny bush as their staple diet and burrow deep inside the bush's body for ant habitat. By supplying an abundance of sap and juicy leaves, the thorny bush encourages the ants to live within its torso to keep out other bush-eating predators like caterpillars and small rodents. Together, they thrive.

This is a marvel of complexity in all living fields, not just in zoological ecologies, but in human-made spaces as well. Whether science, politics, the arts, or here, business and technology, at the fringe between dissimilar domains, the magnitude and diversity of innovation is unbelievably prolific. As the first principle of hyperinnovation tells us, when an increasing number of disparate technologies and markets combine, the number of new possibilities for innovation goes up exponentially. And when this happens, you begin to get highly novel product offerings, like Sony providing financial services such as credit cards, with discount incentives on their electronic products, music, games and film CDs. You get surprising ventures between distinct enterprises, such as Monsanto pharmaceutical operations working with a carpet manufacturer that weaves nylon fibres, who together produce a new inert vascular skin graft for heart surgery (carpets and medicine!). You get the likes of Microsoft moving into consumer electronics, with its X-BOX concept. As a long-held software publisher, this may look like a bold move, but the multidimensional interconnection of ideas, in synch with a heap of capital (intellectual, financial and iterative), enables Microsoft to confidently criss-cross market borders to create new value where none existed before.

So What Business Are You in Now?

Question: what is the difference between an acorn and a DVD? The answer is as profound as it is alarming. As genetics and computing merge into the biotech industry, the packaging (that is, the husk of the acorn, and the plastic of the DVD) become less significant. But the source code (that is, the DNA of the acorn, and software of the DVD) becomes all-important. Deep inside the acorn lives a genetic code, software that defines the acorn's final product, a great oak. Likewise, on the DVD lives another kind of code, the software that defines the make-up of its ultimate product, a Hollywood blockbuster movie… Now think of this: it is now possible to put up on computer screen the complete genetic code of an oak tree. The computer armed with some clever genetic sequencing algorithm can recode the genetic software of the oak tree. So if you can do that, you can put up the genetic code of any living thing. Put up the DNA code of a spider and put up the DNA code of a goat, and blend in a way so that the goat manufactures spider silk for industrial application. Thrilling or chilling, it has already happened! Nexia Biotechnology, who live on the borders between genetics, agriculture, industrial manufacturing and computing, have produced a herd of goats that produce molecules in their milk that mimic the long molecular chains the spider produces in its silk. The product is called 'BioSteel' and has far-reaching applications, from aerospace to entertainment to medicine, new orders of strength built into abundantly available materials, *without* the need for large-scale, chemical manufacturing plants.

Intriguing. But it is not the end-products or processes per se I want to highlight, but more the new kinds of industries they shape. Interconnected concepts in general, and emerging technology in particular, cause gross shifts among the boundary definitions of long-held businesses. And when that happens, most of the old ways of doing business, much of the experience built up over the past, become superseded by new ways and means. As above, biotechnology is drawing in agriculture, high-end computing, cosmetics and retail into one multidimensional business. All of a sudden, cosmetic companies need to become computer wizards, farmers need to understand genetic engineering, retailers need to think about biological manufacturing and infrastructure. And this kind of dramatic collision and redefinition of business boundaries is happening in every conceivable business today. Clearly, the famous Peter Drucker question 'What business are you in?', has never been so pertinent. Microsoft are asking Drucker's question more and more, so are Sony and Monsanto above, and many others alike.

Ford ask this question, and have found that they are no longer in the traditional automotive business. No, they are partnering with the likes of Motorola to build a new generation of *infotainment* vehicles, radically shifting the locus of Ford 's business model. But it does not stop here. As Ford further stretch their product concepts, they begin to work with even more extraordinary organisations. Biotech outfits, theme ride designers, sports equipment makers, who and whatever can further transform the definition of Ford's product. So Ford's short-term future may be embellished with infotainment, but its long-term prospect may be in ever more unique and radical business arenas. Who knows? But one thing is for sure, Ford's inevitable higher value creation will not merely be in the hard lumps of engine performance or eye-candy body design, but in the networking of software, entertainment, communications, biotechnology, nanotechnology and artificial intelligence. Each, a disruptive technology in its own right, and when brought together as a multidimensional enterprise, the results will be of unimagined scale, complexity and value creation. So considering all of this, what business are you now in? What mix of businesses *should* you be in to increase and sustain your enterprise's future value?

Creating Higher Value at the Intersection of Ideas

In an era of the multidimensional, the highest kind of value creation is a consequence of the intersections an enterprise can make between novel, sometimes conflicting, but all too often disparate, ideas, technologies and customer demand. To begin to actualise such higher value, we can look to four multidimensional strategies, namely: crossing boundaries to create new industry definitions, multipositioning, value-multiplication, and price positioning via positive feedback.

Crossing boundaries to create new industry definitions. Multidimensional innovation gives higher value not by dominating a single business niche, nor an entire industry; but by progressively interconnecting different concepts across technological and industry boundaries. This kind of boundary crossing either changes the competitive ground rules within

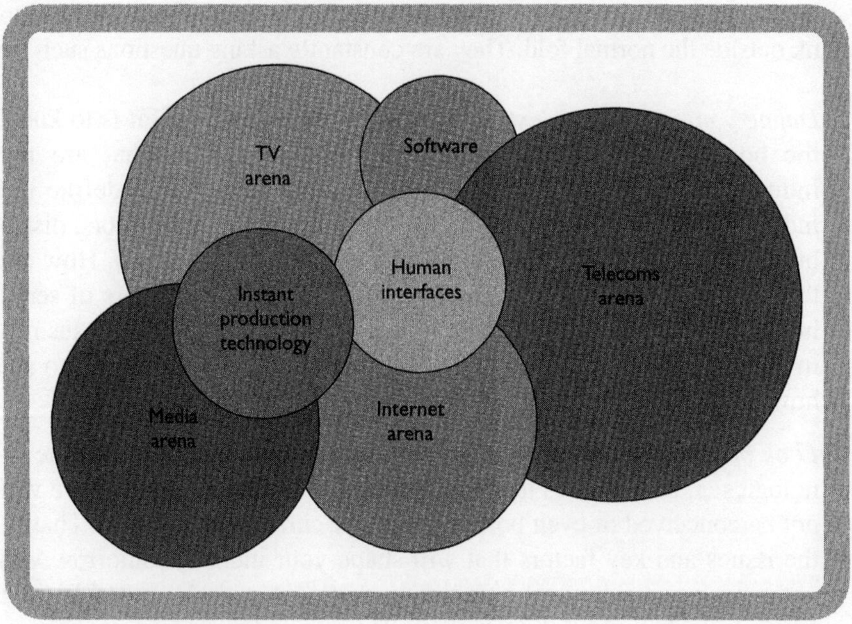

Figure 4.1 Hyperinnovation in the broad band communications arena

incumbent markets, or gives fresh seed concepts that create entirely new industry definitions.

NTL, as one example, ardently challenge long-held *linear* business stereotypes with radically new interconnected concepts. They are developing a total communications business, *merging* once disparate technological tracks across separate niches. NTL's COO, Stephen Carter, told me: 'We are building a webcentric gateway to the broadband communications and media arenas... offering high-speed access to an interactive [department store] of online content and bundled services... '. And so the boundaries between software, media, television, internet, telecoms, human interfaces and instant production technology intensively *blend* to create a brand new value proposition (as Figure 4.1). For NTL and others alike, new higher value lies at the intersection of adjacent domains, as the next new market space, the next new product platform, and thus the next new value wave comes from the ability to expand what a market, product or basic value proposition is meant to be. Here, the greater the number and diversity of connected agents (ideas, knowledge, customers, technologies), the greater the potential for more interconnections, the richer the potential value creation.

NTL, like Ford and Sony above, know that to sustain value they have to think outside the normal fold. They are constantly asking questions such as:

- *Define your existing industry boundaries.* The starting point is to know the borders of your own backyard. Ask yourself, 'what are my industry's city limits? What are the key ingredients that define my industry?' Think about the customer, the technology, competitors, distribution channels, the product and service concepts, and so on. How are they defined? Are they old linear abstractions, based on years of serial innovation? Most are. The point is that when you appreciate industries in terms of their functional and process outlines, you will begin to see how constrained your industry domains really are.
- *Look beyond the boundaries of your industry.* Many of the ideas, technologies and enterprises that will mould your industry in the future will not be conceived or even born within your current line of sight. That is, the issues and key factors that will shape your industry tomorrow will not only be outside your own organisation, or even just outside your present markets, but come from quite unusual origins outside your industry.
- *Innovatively interconnect with adjacent industry domains.* What new technologies near and far can you interconnect to your current industry outline, that would begin to create a new industry definition? What unarticulated and unsatisfied customer demand could you fulfil by expanding your business concepts with ideas from outside the current fold? What emerging ideas in other industries could you interconnect to reinvent your industry? Reference NTL's broadband communications and media gateway, emerging from the telecoms, software, internet, media human interfaces and instant production technologies. This is ultimately a game synergy of ideas, where the *new whole* is greater than the sum of the individual old elements.

Multipositioning. A characteristic of any sufficiently advanced hyperinnovation, is that it is chameleon-like in nature. That is, its identity, and especially its market positioning, can change dramatically, depending on where and at what time you look. Take Microsoft's X-BOX concept. Is it a PC or a games console? A DVD or a telephone? An internet URL or hi-fi? It depends on when you make the call, because the X-BOX concept can be dynamically repositioned as market demands and preferences shift. If the games market is up, then of course it is a games unit. If the video-on-demand arena becomes bullish, then it is a video-on-demand centre, and so on. Again, as new technologies emerge, expect the X-BOX to criss-cross boundaries at an ever faster pace, and reposition in markets as far flung as home automation, teleworking, immersive virtual reality, and eventually all kinds of domestic life support systems.

This kind of dynamic positioning within fluctuating and rapidly evolving markets not only changes the whole perception of a given innovation, it can also occupy *multipositions* across many different minds and demands simultaneously. It is that swarming multiheaded beast I mentioned in Chapter 3, where streams of ideas are turned off, and turned on, to the tune of the customer.

Take the Superbowl. Is it a sporting event? Is it a business venture? Or is it a multimedia event? Again, it depends on who is looking and at what time. The Superbowl is a multipositioned product, where new higher value is created by dynamic positioning in the minds of many different people – coaches, pundits, players, merchandisers, TV programmers, fans and enthusiasts and so on – at different times. Clearly, multipositioned products and services can mean many different strokes to many different folks at many different times. And as markets themselves complexify, this kind of multipositioning strategy is set to proliferate. Some issues here include:

- *Multiple customer demands*. Ask: who are my potential customers? What are their emerging and unarticulated demands and preferences? What ideas (technologies, concepts, and so on) can be integrated to answer these questions? See Chapter 20 for method here.
- *Multidimensional branding*. Names like Borders or Netscape reflect the multidimensionality of the product or service proposition. Here a brand can change the whole perception of the innovation, occupying many different positions across many different minds, appealing to multidimensional demands.
- *Whole branding*. Here brands can be viewed holistically from the product itself to letter heads and stationery, to uniforms and livery, to buildings and company cars, even the personality, background and ambitions of the people employed. You'll not have to look too hard to find companies that do this. Virgin Atlantic's corporate colours of red depict a daredevil, fun-loving, energetic organisation. They employ A-type personalities. Virgin crew would probably not fit so well into the people profile of British Airways, who employ more conservative types. The difference in the recruiting policy reflects in the whole branding effort.

Value multiplication. This strategy boosts the value a given innovation provides. An illustration of the power of value multiplication can be found in the so-called *i-MODE* concept. The brainchild of NTT's Do Co Mo. On the surface, it looks like yet another common or garden hand-held media-phone. But, in fact, the nucleus unit interlinks with many other kinds of units and systems. In your pocket is a palm-size satellite uplink gadget, hosting a 350 mm focal length video screen giving the illusion of big projection definition; it is your magic window on the world. The device acts as a hyperhub, sucking in any form of digimedia. It then acts as video-voice-data injection system, interconnecting to any domestic and work appliance, and all of your personal tools and toys: digicameras, digipens, digigames, digimaps, digimusic, even your digitoothbrush for direct links to your dentist… i-MODE's logic?… First, recall that established domains in networks tend to disintegrate suddenly, then get replaced with fresh nodes and patterns of interconnection. By offering an ever-expanding, developing *portfolio* of interconnecting units, it is possible continuously to supersede the older network domains they make up. Consequently, this enables the i-MODE concept to remain perpetually novel, and perpetual novelty, again, equals a perpetual higher value proposition. Second, in the simplest terms, i-MODE knows that for every customer who joins the network and/or purchases a new i-MODE unit, not only does the customer buy a hard electronic lump – say a digiscreen – the number of ways that customer can communicate or play games or send video streams or whatever, goes up exponentially. In other words (assuming that each customer makes one transaction a day), hyperlinking 10 customers via the i-MODE concept does not mean 10 linear transactions between peers, but 45. One million customers would mean 500,000,000,000 possible transactions. Hence, the i-MODE value proposition is not only sustainable, it is multiplied.

And the one that proves that value multiplication is possible through even the most basic product, is that of AMP – 'a world force in interconnection'. AMP, who deal with virtually everyone in the cut-throat electronics market, have managed to turn *commodity* electrical connectors and cables into a business with revenues in excess of $15 billion. There's not one car that arrives on US shores from Japan, that doesn't have an AMP interconnector assembly linking its systems. AMP CEO, Jerry Sanders, calls his strategy 'moving up the food web… ' He believes that his customers want components that do multiple jobs simultaneously, to cut-out time consuming assembly. And the potential here for AMP is phenomenal, as the first principle of hyperinnovation ($\frac{1}{2} * \Sigma\alpha^2$) reminds us: AMP have 6,000,000 connectors in their catalogue, and that means no less than a dramatic 18,000,000,000,000 potential value propositions. So…

- *Think connectability*. Create units (idea technology, customer demands, and so on) that can be interconnected in some way. Another law of the network says that as the number of agents with a network goes up, so the value of that network multiples.
- *Think interfaces*. Are your interfaces connectable? Are the protocols, size, standards, universal (for example internet protocol, size 6, 110 volts, English)? Innovations that promote interface standards multiply the chance of wholesale adoption.
- *Think scalability*. The pace at which value multiplies is governed by the speed and limits to which a system can be scaled up. Again standards are key here.

Price positioning via positive feedback. There is yet another side to the *n*-equation here. How can manufacturers and service providers afford to keep the cost of core technology and processes down, when functionality dramatically expands? If more and different ideas are being interconnected, surely the cost of any given end-product or service is going to skyrocket?... Yet the evidence points in an altogether different direction (as those vast warehouses chock-full of cheaper goods and services give testimony). Think of the latest digital televisions. More and different technology, and thus functionality, is packaged in much less volume of space, yet the end-price point of any given digital TV continues to fall. How? It is mainly down to the law of positive feedback found in complex networks. Current designs and production tools build better designs and production tools, and these improved tools build smaller, cheaper, more efficient technology. In the same vein, past knowledge gives way to new scientific knowledge, and this deeper knowledge eventually leads to even better, more creative design tools, which in turn lead to ever more efficient design work. As cheaper, better, smarter, quicker production systems emerge, marginal costs will continue to fall. Everything, even the most arcane, sophisticated, complex technology of the day, will eventually simplify towards a commodity. Hence, the latest digital TVs, microprocessors, fast food services, indeed all artefacts and soft processes, now fall in cost faster.

This kind of positive feedback within innovation can be used to position prices so that higher value propositions can be offered at a keener price point. Clearly, in an ultra-competitive context, pricing to (a) maintain a competitive position, and (b) attract new customers to make a purchase, are the most difficult challenges of all. The keys here are:

- *Innovation productivity.* Continuously seek better and more innovative ways to increase the productivity of novel design work. The more effective an outfit is in its innovation activities, the greater the positive feedback becomes, and the more price positioning can be used as a competitive weapon.
- *Find innovation leverage points.* What are the most significant features and functions the customer demands? Ask: what specific details can I enhance to further increase the value of the innovation? The tools in Part V will help achieve this.

Accelerating Interconnections

Clearly, the faster an enterprise detects and interconnects new ideas across conceptual boundaries, (a) the more costs will fall, (b) the higher the potential value proposition grows, and (c) the more sustainable the value proposition becomes. The most virtuous circle of all. So, what is needed now are ways, tangible ways to facilitate such an accelerated *n*-innovation. Here are three key means to begin with, hyperconcepting, fusion, and spider webs:

Hyperconcepting. At the heart of multidimensional innovation sits the hyperconcept, a product or service concept that cuts and stretches across market and technological confines. For example, in biotechnology today, it is not so much a case of swallowing a pill to grow a thick head of hair, biotech products now multidimensionally connect with lifestyle commodities, such as beer, ice cream, chocolate, even breakfast cereal and Swiss cheese. In turn, smart technology moves towards *n*-conception. Jogging shoes with microprocessors and fuzzy code uplink your split to a home database. Now combine biotechnology with smart technology, and fundamentally new *n*-concepts emerge. An *internet toothbrush* that reads actual mouth acidity, bacteria and plaque density on teeth, then formulates and discharges a precise chemical compound for tooth maintenance. The internet toothbrush then uplinks information to your dentist… and so on.

Okay, so how do we begin to break the perimeters between disparate concept domains and generate such hyperconcepts? One powerful means here is the *n-metaphor.* Start by searching for, and interconnecting, unlike circumstances, antitheses, even unrelated objects, that if drawn into different domains of technology/markets/customers would impart a breakthrough (hyperthinking in Chapter 2 assists here). Look for contrasting parables, stories, fables, yarns, that if brought into a new and remote context would lead to new insights and original inspirations.

Take the ensemble of *fish, reeds, algae, insects*, and imagine them as *information units* in a lake, *the actual computing bits in a pond*? Now apply this to the context of home automation and furniture design? Gary Natsume is a product designer who applies such an *n*-metaphor to his work. His 'data pond' concept was inspired from such a contrary metaphor. Coffee table in size, looking much like a modern fish tank turned on its side, digital fish represent flooding information swimming in an electronic reservoir. To access information you need the 'data cell' which can captivate but not send information. To transmit information you need a bevy of what Gary calls in his very own words 'hypercomponents', each having a particular utility: digital camera, infrared transmission, satellite uplink. The data cell along with a selection of hypercomponents is wrapped in an electronic matrix skin. The end product is what he calls a 'hyperpersonal assistant' that is different every time it is assembled ($^1/_2 * \Sigma\alpha^2$ again).

The power of the *n*-metaphor in innovation proves invaluable. So some further examples: *user-friendly* software has become a household term, yet back in 1982 the term was almost unheard of. Of course, Apple put paid to that. So what is next, new and *n*-dimensional? What about *user intimacy*?... What about energy supply, what metaphor would inspire the future of domestic energy service? What about *energyplex*?... What of the future of retail sports equipment? The future here is smart Bluetooth and internet technology integrated into traditional equipment such as footballs or tennis rackets. What about the *smartfeet*, or the *sharp racket*?... What of inflight cabin services? First-class or upper-class concepts are well worn nowadays, what metaphor could spark the future of inflight services? *ultra-glamour class*? *Hollywood class*? *Hyperclass*? What *n*-metaphors can you think of to break and cross normal business context boundaries?

Fusion. Innovation thought leaders Watts Wacker and Jim Taylor describe the process of *fusion* as a way to further accelerate the search for interconnections across customer demands. They talk of the fusion of culture, from *foods* (for example South-east Asian and French cooking techniques), to *gender* (for example men taking up traditional women's roles), to global values (for example, a Chinaman now aspiring to the very same goods as an American or Brazilian). But they have a word of caution too: *fission*, the process whereby two or more concepts actually tend to repel each other. A good example of fission is when Hostess decided to experiment with *Twinkie-Lite*, a snack that contained the notion of weight-watching with the notion of a product that was supposed to be a heavy weighted sugar food. Twinkie-Lite flopped because watching the waistline and a sugar-boosting meal just do not sit together in the mind of the muncher (whether practical or otherwise). On the other hand *lite beer*, which has been a resounding success, is a great example of fusion. In the mind of the beer drinker the product works, 'a social lubricant, while not gaining any weight'... Here's a couple of fusion vs fission examples, that test the logic: superquick-dry paint (practical) vs superquick-dry cement (impractical); on-line shopping for innovative gadgets (easy life) vs on-line shopping for fashionable shoes (uncomfortable life)... fusion thinking, turns out to be a simple, but effective way to accelerate the interconnections of ideas.

Spider webs. Perhaps the archetype of counterintuitive logic, having a central idea, such as a meaning or anticipated customer demand, or some other kind of anchor that shapes the network. Spider webworks couple chains of ideas mimicking nature's silk fly trap. Spider webs of ideas can be used to link knowns, in unusual ways.

For example, what if a surge in demand for ultra-efficient home heating systems occurred? Conventional domestic central heating is less than efficient, it heats up large open spaces that often need not be heated. Could an original, ultra-efficient heating system, that heats up relevant areas of a room, be created? Start by writing the keywords that describe the customer

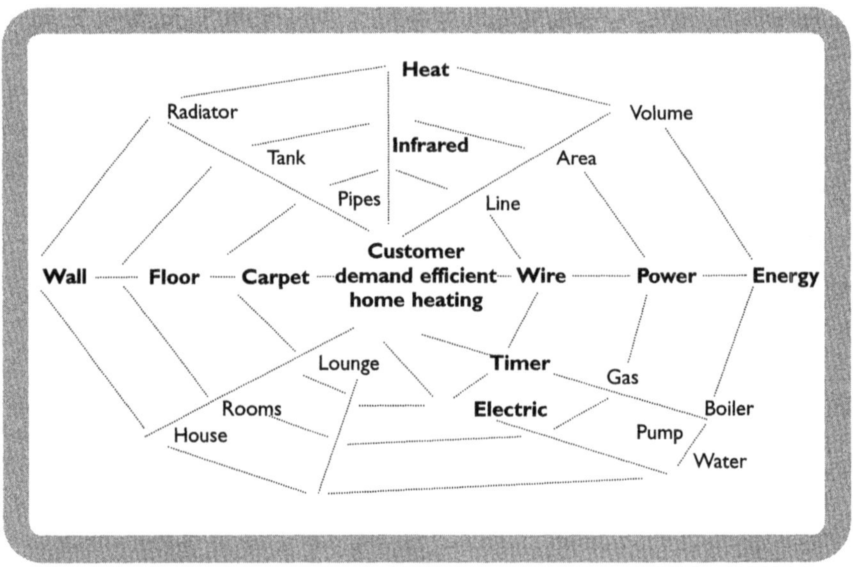

Figure 4.2 Spider web: hyperlinking key words for electrically heated carpets

demand. Then around that demand scribble the keywords that describe a conventional home central heating system. Then draw lines towards the customer demands from each keyword. Now write associated words inside the web's strands (see Figure 4.2). Keep on going until you have a dozen or so keywords inside the spider web. Now *hyperlink* the words, and see what springs to mind. By linking the keywords inside the spider web and ordering them in meaningful ways relative to the spider's (customer's) demands, a concept for *electrically heated carpeting* leapt from the web. Perhaps a range of automatically adjusting electrically heated carpets that heat up the room temperature to a comfortable 22°C. The naturally large surface area makes them incredibly energy efficient.

Multicompetency

Another powerful strategy for criss-crossing the borders of business concepts, is the *multidimensional competency* perspective. And in a market where fun is a serious business, Disney personify the traits of *multicompetency*. Intensively catering for a total panorama of demands, fantasy and entertainment being the panorama; theme parks, movie making, media, merchandising, even now leisure ships and whole new towns interconnecting in various dimensions. To imagineer that holistic experience of one whole, Disney build multifaceted strengths and abilities, including: ride and theme technologies, theatre management, intensive guest care and showtime efficiency.

We can see that moving beyond any linear market perspective, towards the creation of multidimensional markets, does not necessarily mean moving away from current knowledge bases, skills, experience; even technologies, processes or distribution channels. No, stepping into the multidimensional means a reconfiguration and/or alliance of these basic intellectual assets, to yield an original but germane system of innovation. Here are some key questions on multicompetence development:

- What emerging markets can we enter into with our existing know-how and turn into a multidimensional market?
- What and how can we combine existing competences and innovate in other dimensions?
- What transdimensional innovations lie beyond our existing market, that could exploit existing competencies?

- What multicompetency do we need to develop or acquire to realise the multidimensional opportunities we have identified?
- Who do we need to ally with/acquire to complement our current core strengths and abilities, to realise exciting multidimensional opportunities?
- What emerging technologies and customer demands have we recognised that can conjoin with existing products or services that would begin to multiplex their design?
- What longer-term latent demands and technologies can we develop and bring together in extradimensional ways?
- How can we envision fundamentally new and exciting transdimensional markets based on these simple questions?

Virgin constantly ask these types of question, developing their businesses through this kind of multicompetence orientation. For example, what has running an airline to do with running a cinema multiplex? Virgin have won a string of awards for best inflight service. Virgin's upper-class inflight service competes with the big global players, and to win custom, they have reinvented the back end of the passenger airliner towards a total entertainment experience. In the correlation of inflight ideas, Virgin have developed multicompetency in on-the-ground entertainment. So when MGM cinemas came on to the market, it was an insightful move for Virgin to buy it up. Virgin are now actively shifting the notion of the multiplex cinema away from the stereotypes of old, towards a total upper-class entertainment encounter.

Multidimensional Enterprise

The main message is that by entering the margins between distinct industry sectors, by exploiting new technologies that redefine market boundaries, and by seeking new definitions of business context, both perennial corporations and small start-ups are assured revolutionary combinations among technologies and infrastructure that give extraordinarily new and extremely high-value business platforms. And because of this, multidimensional enterprise is set to become the defining success factor in creating and sustaining the industries of the future.

CHAPTER 5

Collaborative Commerce

Collaborative commerce is a further and deeper strategy for multidimensional-enterprise, and turns out to be the most adaptive scheme yet seen: hyperlinking ultradiverse pools of often remote, *conflicting*, sometimes *strange* businesses as one whole. In the extreme, networks of rival, once cut-throat head-to-head enterprises are learning to work together; sharing not only manufacturing and/or service centre resources, but core R&D, key talent, secret recipes, even high-flying executives.

NBI Capital, as one example, is a collaboration between DeNational Investeringbank ABP, PGGM's structured finance expertise, Parnib, Alpinvest and Van Den Boom Groep, creating a multicompetency not found within any of those single businesses. NBI Capital maintain: 'The new economy demands new connections between companies and suppliers, partners and customers – creating cross-organisational synergies of skills, talents and resources, that were either previously overlooked, or simply unimagined…' From this approach, NBI Capital offer comprehensive, coherent innovations from a single source. For NBI, this is not about being all things to all people, but being a diversity of interrelated things to the relevant customer.

Another example is that of AOL Time Warner, and is perhaps the largest collaborative enterprise on the planet. And do you know what? They hardly make a thing you can touch. They create conglomerates of fantasy, intangibles and infotainment. Through the symbioses of digital publishing, movie production, multimedia, popular music, virtual reality, cable and satellite TV content – a trillion dollar market burgeons. By networking with technology researchers such as MIT, Microsoft, and AT&T with content providers such as Disney, Viacom and Newscorp; AOL Time Warner are growing into a heterogeneous corporation that flows to the multidimensional interconnection of ideas.

On a smaller, yet still potent scale, Trimension, Sussex, UK, is the world's first virtual reality systems integrator; an *n*-enterprise of 120 people, with revenues in excess of $50 million. Trimension design so-called reality rooms, virtual domes, and total immersion environments, giving full-blown stereoscopic 3D imagery for application in science, design, architecture and entertainment. By co-innovating with other systems enablers and content providers – such as Barco (the world's most powerful projectors), Silicon Graphics (the world's most powerful visualisation computers), Stereographics (interactive 3D-image eye-glasses) and Seos Displays (world leader in visual displays for simulation) – Trimension integrate the most advanced virtual reality systems yet seen, including the Hayden Project at the American Museum of Natural History, the world's first digital planetarium.

Consequently, we can see that these kinds of extradimensional enterprise are not so much the result of giantism, but a roll-out of the number and kinds of collaborative networks created. *Collaborative alliances will be affluent, not the isolated corporation of yesteryear...* So, let us take a look at some of the opportunities and benefits that lie within deep *collaborative commerce*:

- *Multidimensional reach with lowered risk.* Clearly technological and market breadth of many systems innovations today stretches beyond the capacity of the lonesome enterprise. In fact some systems innovations are so complex that even companies such as Microsoft are collaborating with hundreds of smaller companies to develop technologies and markets outside their normal scope. After all, starting from scratch in any project is an expensive waste of time and effort, if others have already invented parts of the wheel. For the lone inventor, even medium-sized organisation, developing advanced technology is all too often out of reach. Reasons ranging from technical proficiency, financial capacity, resource, and of course time, can deny business aspirations. A partnership between two or more organisations can open up opportunities for products or services that would otherwise have been out of reach, while lowering both risk and capital investment.

- *Walking light.* The need to interconnect, sign up and collaborate with other, often competing organisations, is becoming a salient way to move fast and build capabilities. In fact, this disposition is becoming a favoured way to walk light and thus simultaneously reduce overheads, while allowing more time to devote to value multiplication. Nintendo have built a business on this strategy, employing less than 900 people directly. Nintendo's core competency is based around game software design/development, product design, electromechanical packaging design, high impact marketing, product life-cycle management, strategic networking and supply partner development. Almost everything else is handled through a network of collaborative partners. A truly pan-enterprise of 900 people, handling $16 billion turnover, now that is walking light.

- *Value multiplication.* Enterprises as teams, as swarms, as bees! Pooling your resources along with theirs, for the same ends, is exactly the same as your internal objective: synergy, where total value is greater than the constituent parts. Bringing different insights, experiences and knowledge from a collection of organisations with the same interests is a salient way to multiply value. Core technologies, and the associated specialist skills spread far and wide, can come together for specific projects, interconnecting competency to achieve a multiplied end, a multiplied value. Here, the 3G mediaphone market is a panorama of technology, design and multiprocessing demand. The necessary 3G core-technology is in R&D now, and when the broadband telesats go up, hyperinnovation – big time!
- *Spreading the cost.* The cost and risk of commercialising any innovation may be prohibitive for the lone ranger. IBM have formed literally hundreds of alliances in attempts to contain costs. Ranging from small software developments and marketing agreements to large-scale joint development programmes with their most avid rivals. Names such as Toshiba, Siemens, even Apple and others, are an integral part of IBM's strategy. The result is highly interconnected technology and end-product getting to market with lower direct costs and overhead.

In Search of Criticality (Goldilocks Alliance)

In complexity science there is a process known as *criticality*. Essentially, when the number of agents and the interconnections between them is rich enough – not too hot, not too cold – combinational explosions take place, unleashing major and continuous innovation within that network. This kind of *criticality* generates richer, ever more profound, yet coherent innovation than is ever possible with independent agents. By far the most amazing aspect of networks approaching criticality is that the largest proportion of invention is a result of *serendipity* (as above, more stuff happens in a complex world). The recombination of new and existing agents that result in cogent and meaningful innovation is driven by intense and open *chance*!

In the business world, initiating and heating up a collaborative network towards this kind of criticality is not so removed and impractical as it may seem. First, the business world is becoming ever more network like; and second, hyperinnovation thrives on networks moving towards criticality. The key is to get the network activities going, and follow the handful of guidelines set out below.

- Initiate constant experiments – attempt, trial, strive, test with new economy ideas (say a Dot.com with IP Mediaphones), and radical ideas (say Disney with NASA for the ultimate in theme-park rides). Without this kind of perpetual creativity and generous volume of trials, co-innovation criticality will never tip.
- Seek common business interests; whether creation of a panoramic product (say Lockheed-Martin with Honda for hands-off ride-by-wire motorbikes), research and/or development of *n*-technology (say DuPont with Glaxo-Wellcome to develop nanomedicine), and/or market penetration (say Toys 'R Us with McDonald's).
- Look for unique/creative competency spread between different enterprises that could achieve synergy if held concurrently – it is business as swarms! Bond a virtual reality technology integrator (say Trimension), a training provider (say Learning Tree), a computer games designer (say Game Freak), and a furniture maker (say Steelcase Co), and you create VR entertainment and learning systems for the home. A potential mega-market, that is yet to be tapped.
- What direct multidimensional opportunities, and exploratory possibilities, have been identified that lie beyond existing strengths and abilities? What enabling technological or process characteristics have to be brought together to achieve these multidimensional ends (say internet electronic retail of digibooks, with say Macmillan with Casio)?

Competition through Contradigms (Oil and Water Alliance)

Criticality is not the only recruit. The *counterintuitive* pursuit of alliances that at first seem *conflicting*, often springs a surprise. As we saw in Chapter 2, special kinds of conflict can be the harbinger of creativity. Even in the face of initial cultural collision, the resultant technological paradox gives rise to surprising outcomes. Specifically, diametrically opposed institutions and firms that work in unison can offer an option on a bright future that was not there before. Again, the opportunity is not in the individual business units, but a synergy across the whole.

Look for opposites, conflicts, contradictions, that if brought together in a creative way, cracks open a contradigm. What greater conflict than oil and water? But now add an emulsifier and you hold something greater than the original disharmony!... So?... This metaphor equally, yet paradoxically, carries into the world of hard-nosed innovation. Think of Amoco Oil and Greenpeace. Conflict – big time – right? Now concoct an emulsifier, say a global vision called 'Beyond Petroleum', and you spring a contradigm that *contradicts contradiction* itself (paradox indeed). But this is no dream! As I write, members of Greenpeace now work within the so-called 'Beyond Petroleum (BP) Alliance', with British Petroleum, Amoco and Castrol. The result: *competitive advantage through contradigms*!

Strange Alliance

This may not be so much the product of strategic alliances (critical, contradigm or otherwise), but the *strange, weird, alien, total wild* relationship. It's one sure way of securing business diversity, thus richer emergent patterns within hyperinnovation.

To wit: San Francisco International Airport plants relations with the Royal Botanical Gardens at Kew, the Moscow State Circus, Trimension Virtual Immersion, Disney, the Three Tenors – and from this variety of disparate vocations, spring concepts for a 24–7–365 entertainment/relaxation centre for delayed, quite bored, often stressed-out passengers. The stranger the better: Manchester United, the most successful soccer club in the world, in and off the pitch; their brand is now associated with high performance. Now extend the 'Man-U' brand into Formula 1 racing, who team up with TAG/McLaren, who tie up with MIT's artificial intelligence labs, now developing swarm system assembly lines; that is, production lines manned by rodent-sized robots working as a swarm. Bring in DuPont to develop bioengineered substrates, grown like sticks of celery to exact geometric specifications for use in such ultra-specification car-frame fabrication. And Manchester United win a Brazilian Grand Prix with a racecraft like no other?... These kinds of critical, conflicting, altogether strange collaborative networks give requisite measures of novelty, surprise, and as yet untapped value multiplied. This is perhaps the ultimate boon of such collaborative commerce.

Strategic Guidelines for Collaborative Commerce

It is clear that searching, initiating and developing these kinds of collaborative businesses models (strange or otherwise) can have a level of mortality, especially at the initiation stage. Again, cultural, organisational, conflicting strategies, clash of methods and practices can all contribute to this. Other reasons are down to human nature; examples such as paranoia (the competition will find out), political (power seekers that keep information back), the not invented here syndrome, the so-called NIH factor (having other people do *your* work, or giving *you* ideas, is a sign of weakness) and the age-old buyer's belief of purchase at the lowest tender. However, if seen and managed under the right conditions, the results can be quite fruitful. Here lie 10 key points that assist in the development of collaborative commerce:

- *Strategic top team.* Set up a small strategic top team, made up of relevant senior people from across the organisation(s), give them ownership of seeking, initiating, developing, monitoring and ending strategic alliances. The very act of collaborative networking must have problem owners. Then set them to work using what follows as a guide.
- *Win–win teams.* Collaborative corporate webs can only triumph if the whole succeeds, thus an alliance means less head-to-head competition, towards a positive-sum game. Move the emphasis away from I win, you lose; to a win–win for all disposition. Team building is essential here (see whole-team building Chapter 12).
- *Significant.* If undertaken, an alliance is viewed as important and therefore must obtain adequate resources, management attention and sponsorship. The importance is amplified if put into the context of overarching long-term goals.
- *Long-term goals.* There must be an agreement for long-term investment which tends to help equalise benefits over time. The development of long-term goals supports this (see Chapter 6), giving direction for longer-term investment agreements, thus holding credibility over the long haul. What limits longer-term investment is lack of longer-term thinking and goals!
- *Positive politics.* Diverging opinions will no doubt occur, but do not brush them under the mat. Disregard for difference of opinion will jeopardise even the possibility of fruitful outcomes. There is a need to convene regular forums, seen as credible by all stakeholders, addressing

the dilemmas and trade-offs inherent in intercompany projects. But it is also an opportunity to enhance the synergism and benefits for the meeting of the clans. Treatment of general concerns is not just a public relations exercise, but a strategic initiative that is hell-bent on making this orientation work. By seeking out the views at all levels – the arcane scientist and the pragmatic business fronts – we see that people are effective in thinking in different ways and at different times, giving unforeseen consequences. Thus, this is not just about the connectivity per se, it is about the alignment for success of individuals as well. (Again, teambuilding in Chapter 12 will assist here.)

- *Independent framework.* The partnership must be independent which will help balance power. Many alliances are given independent management structures, facilities and liability/incorporation. This is often necessary to allow fit-for-purpose culture and organisation. So the partnership must be institutionalised, that is, a framework of supporting mechanisms should be instigated from legal requirements to social ties, to shared aims all of which make trust possible.
- *Integration.* At the top there is a definite role for a top team of executives to act as initiator, middleman and alliance coach. To smooth the edges, to set objectives, to focus the alliance on end-results, and to set the pace. However, a key to effective collaboration between divisions and stand-alone enterprises is to interconnect them at the operational level, so appropriate points of contact and communication are fed laterally. Without horizontal communications at the team level, the alliance will progress at glacial pace. There is a need for some hierarchy of control, but it must be heterarchical – with information flowing from the top down as well as from the bottom up, and laterally too. These kinds of heterarchical alliances facilitate the most acute n-networks, allowing a diverse range of issues to be addressed. Which is exactly what is needed for hyperinnovation.
- *Collaborative technologies.* People may work face to face, but equally, and more often these days, teams are spread across vast distances. Collaborative technology needs to be in place to facilitate virtual teams inside the firms, and across co-innovation alliances. This we will expand upon in detail in Chapter 14.
- *Informed.* All organisations should be informed about the strategies and direction of each other organisation, relevant to the particular strategy and project at hand. Formal communication channels and briefings – top

down, bottom up and obliquely across the alliance – need to be set up, and carried out on a regular basis.

- *End game/next game*. Without an end game, or a next game declaration, an alliance can often lose sight of its aims and objectives, and in the extreme result in unnecessary political repercussions. In simple terms, state the criteria for the end of an alliance, or a position(s) when it is time to move on to new projects.

Innovative Collaborative Supply Webs

The *collaborative supply chain* is a spicy topic today. Open any industrial journal or visit any trade exhibition, and collaboration along the supply chain will dominate the ambient language. Indeed, collaborative commerce has a significant role to play, as new product and service platforms become more complex.

Only, there is concern here. The mindset and language that surround the collaborative supply-chain effort all too often destroy the very objective of collaboration in the first place. The mindset is lean and mean, the language is cost containment and right-first-time. The anxiety here, is that this orientation is crude *negative feedback*, where a system tapers itself closer and closer towards equilibrium (see Chapter 26 for technical explanation of feedback). To understand the consequence of this, think of the kind of seashell that spirals into itself. Many a creature with this kind of shell has become extinct, because as the shell scrolls into itself, the creature has little or no room to adapt and evolve. It is the very same for much of industry, particularly manufacturing. The manufacturing sector in the EC and US is leaning and costing itself out of business, as the overwhelming evidence shows. Manufacturing now accounts for a minor percentage of most major economies today, due in part to the dogmatic application of negative feedback.

So what is the alternative position? The key here is the right balance of *negative* and *positive* feedback. That is, a balance between the pursuit of optimisation (negative) and innovation (positive). As Chapter 1 shows, if a supply partner is not spending at least 25 per cent of its time on creative and innovative issues, then that collaborative network is not going to be sustainable. Costs are important, for sure efficient on-line business processes are sacrosanct, but these ambitions will not give endurable competitive advantage. Remember, absolute perfection (if ever it existed) is an objective for a world of permanence and stability, but in a world of interconnections the pace of change accelerates. So if a firm stubbornly sharpens and grinds towards perfection, by the time that company reaches any level of utopia, the competitive context would have moved on. In this world, innovation and learning becomes the positive, not excellence and efficiency.

Edward de Bono has maintained for at least two decades now, that being the *best* and most *proficient* is not enough or even sustainable. There will always be someone who is bigger, faster, cheaper or whatever (didn't we learn that in the school yard?). So the only sustainable competitive advantage within any supply chain is to be consistently different. The problem is that this orientation is a major move not only in direct action, but consciousness itself. If collaborative commerce within the supply chain is to be sustainable over the longer term, then learning and innovation, and other positive feeds, must dominate the corporate mindset and agenda.

Because of the gross shifts in market definition and positioning (for example IBM becoming a biotech company, Microsoft entering consumer electronics, Sony extending into financial services), tired old mindsets just cannot keep up with such breathtaking transformations. So the goal must be to create new mindsets and language that can hold pace with such displacement. To obtain such a breakthrough in thinking, we can look for and apply axiom antithesis (re: Chapter 2). Here are some examples:

Axiom:	*Antithesis*:
Supply chains	Supply webs
Lean manufacturing	Hypermanufacturing
Right first time	Learn every time
Cost containment	Value multiplication
Improved production	Breakthrough production
Zero defect	Extraordinary supply

Take the axiom *zero defect*. Who could dispute that this goal has no value? Of course, it does have worth, and must be strived for. Only, it is no longer enough, for reasons above (negative feedback). However, extraordinary supply, a supply process that exceeds expectations, gives positive feedback. Extraordinary supply goes beyond the shallow confines of specification, by performing beyond the anticipated. And when processes are performing beyond expectation, you can bet that attention is being spent on innovation, not optimisation, and therefore they tend to be sustainable over the longer term.

Again, axiom antithesis breaks the dogma of lean, keen and mean supply chains, giving distinct perspectives from which to grasp new context and goals. In fact, the list of antitheses above, opens up completely new possibilities and horizons for the materials management. Concepts that are not only inventive, but truly endurable.

Hyperinnovation Strategy

Multidimensional interconnections hold no bounds. From the paradox it delivers, to the counterintuitive initiatives it derives, to the learning strategies it provides, and the multidimensional enterprises that emerge, hyperinnovation is the new genre of business. The strategies are brand new, the end-products obtained are unique, as shift in business outline moves like never before. Whether the inspirations come from nature, or the uncanny logic of the network, hyperinnovation strategy is already unleashing a new kind of order, of unimagined creativity and value, of incredible leaps in complexity and innovation... Like it or not, hyperinnovation is coming your way.

PART II

Hyperinnovation Culture

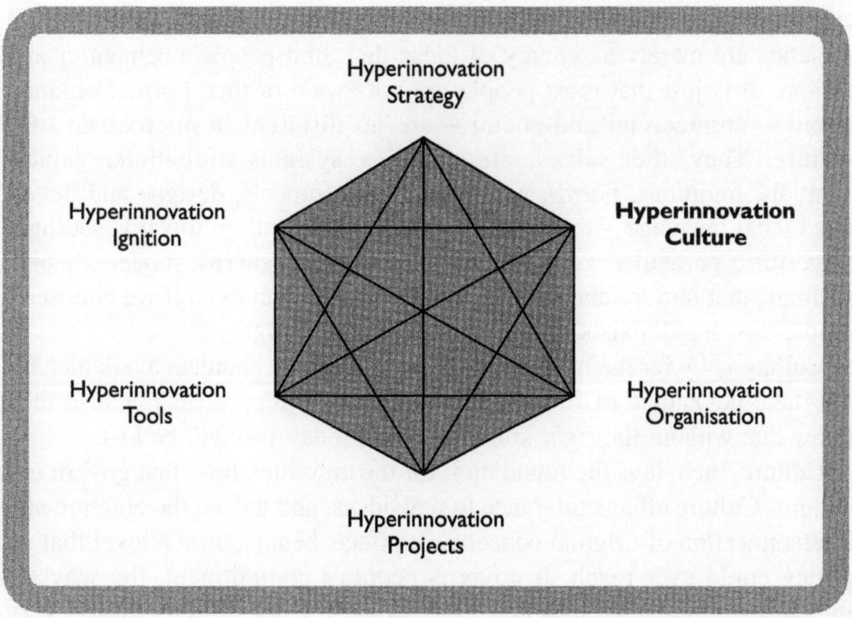

> Man is not born human. It is only slowly and laboriously, in fruitful contact, cooperation, and conflict with fellows, that he attains the distinctive qualities of human nature.
>
> R. E. Park, Anthropologist, 1915

Multidimensional innovation depends not only on strategy – as crucial as it is – nor does it boil down to organisation, methodology or performance measurement. It goes much deeper than that; and into the very hearts and minds of the people working within your organisation. Human behaviour and emotion play a lead role in hyperinnovation. Mould behaviour, and tap and direct emotions in the right direction, and whoosh: an endless stream of *n*-innovation. This is exactly what the *hyperinnovation culture* is all about; building a work climate that motivates people to search through and interconnect ideas at untold pace.

Towards a Hyperinnovation Culture

As one well-seasoned manager put it: 'Culture! Culture! We haven't got a culture. What rubbish!' But he, and many others, are quite mistaken. All societies are merely a synergy of ideas that mint people's behaviour and actions. It is just that most people are not aware of this. Formal organisations – commercial and social – are no different, a microcosm of a culture. They, themselves, are complex systems of beliefs, values, symbols, traditions, norms, politics, status, protocols, designs and developed local language – the stuff of culture. Which all go towards setting a stage for a particular way. You know: thoughts, patterns, models, habits, feelings, that nurture and guide people's actions. But even if we choose to ignore this, it still exists, whether by default or design.

Culture is by far the most powerful leadership mechanism available. Yet few take advantage of it. The most innovative jump at it. Because they know that without the *right* kind of culture, today you will be lost.

Culture, then, lays the foundation for the unwritten laws that govern our actions. Culture affects tolerance to new ideas, and indeed the creation and interconnection of original concepts. It affects behaviour at a level that no policy could ever reach. It governs people's commitment, the way we interact, communicate and make decisions. It even impacts on the very *way* and *what* we think. And for these reasons and more, culture is equally, if not more, important than the other parts outlined in this book.

To hyperinnovate, it is clear that we need the kind of culture that stimulates and supports the multidimensional interconnection of ideas. Four key cultural building blocks go towards this:

Chapter 6 – High Concept Futuring: New *stuff* happens unpredictably ever faster; so we cannot know in any detail what that future will hold. Yet, even with such levels of ambiguity, the future can also be a matter of choice and design. On the larger, global picture scale, we can premeditate the future. In fact, a strong view of the future has never been so important, precisely because the world changes so rapidly and so unpredictably. Consequently, all enterprises need to outline an innovative high concept picture of the future to give long-term bearing. Here, a method for the design of such *high concept futures* is outlined.

Chapter 7 – Values that Connect: Values inform our behaviour and the actions we take beyond any fragile plan, or strict set of operating rules. Hence, the need for a set of core values that animate people towards hyperinnovation.

Chapter 8 – Multidimensional Leaders: Leaders' behaviour profoundly shapes cultural values, and the way in which people think and behave. Therefore, to develop a culture of *n*-innovation, leaders must explicitly express the kinds of values and behaviours that shape such a culture in their daily actions and deeds. To effect this, leaders must adopt the art and discipline of *multidimensional leadership*. This chapter examines the key issues that actualise such a leadership disposition.

Chapter 9 – Nurture Multidimensional People: Hyperinnovation culture, likewise, emerges from people that gravitate towards a diversity of ideas and discipline. The personal development of these special people must be considered too, because *how* and *what* these people *know* and *think* impacts on how they organise ideas. All of this is underpinned by specific motivational forces and factors that can ignite such a kaleidoscopic culture of innovation.

CHAPTER 6

High Concept Futuring

The future is not a single destination, it is an endless space of growing, living, connection possibilities. In direct terms, an enterprise is not held to one preordained destiny, its fate is not fixed in the stars, but open to an unlimited choice about the future. All enterprises can stimulate an imagination to invent many kinds of future, and then develop the capabilities to build those futures. Chance, of course, plays its hand, as the space of innovation possibilities holds a complex juncture of twists and turns. Despite chance, there is much we can do to steer along towards an innovative future: *high concept futuring*, in particular, can help give this bearing.

The Need for Innovative High Concept Visions of the Future

We are all enthused when we hear of some bright prediction about the future. Whether a new technology or a new way of life, we all hope for a better world, a more interesting and fulfilling place to live. But *prediction*, as we began to explore in the first part, is the wrong practice to take up in the first place, because no matter how much information a firm gathers, no matter how smart or empathic that enterprise is, the longer it projects out, the more that prediction will deviate from eventual actuality... So what to do?... A big picture outlook for your enterprise some years hence is not wholly about prediction, it is about design work, a mass of design work. It is about vivid, insightful imagination, then working to make that imagined future become a reality... Only, there is more here. There is much more to vision design than first meets the eye. In fact, there are three basic mandates that drive a strong sense of the future.

First, we all search for some level of meaning in our lives, our significance in this world. Bruno Bettleheim, the eminent behaviourist, goes so far as to declare, 'If we hope not just to live from moment-to-moment, but in true consciousness of our existence, then our greatest need and most difficult achievement is to find meaning in our lives.' In fact, it is a well-debated topic among scholars of human culture, that if *purpose* is absent, even one of mythical proportion, a society will lose its desire to advance and develop. Essentially, a purpose, imagined or otherwise, is the principal spur for human endeavour and innovation, beyond merely surviving day to day. But even beyond the academic point, it is easy to pick out those with a strong sense of purpose. Whether it be a career, or a love for family, or a wise system of belief, even an arcane or practical aspiration, people that hold a sense of mission are often the most fulfilled and productive people of all. But the evidence suggests (homelessness, displacement, crime, alcohol dependency, and so on) that a complex and paradoxical world makes finding or creating a meaning in our lives more difficult. Yet in spite of all this, one dependable way to develop a sense of purpose, whether for an individual or the largest corporation, can be found in an innovative and exciting vision of the future. A high concept picture of the future can give a sense of collective purpose across the organisation, and when you get that perception of resolve, that sense of deeper meaning, you get the Holy Grail of management: *commitment*. In my experience, the most effective way to secure long-term commitment from your people, is to think in the longer term, and the best vehicle for that is to design an all-encompassing high concept picture of the future.

Second, even though we cannot know the future, people, all people in all walks of life, need a sense of certitude. As Bertrand Russell once wrote, 'What people want is not knowledge, but certainty.' In the extreme, without some level of certainty people tend to stress out, our sense of perspective goes haywire, our reasoning overloads with anxieties; and in answer to such distress we incline to lower our expectations and life goals, and when we do that we begin to turn off and become indifferent – the most dangerous of all positions. It is the very same for the enterprise. Without a vision of the future, I would argue that an enterprise has no point of reference, no sense of confidence about tomorrow (imagined or otherwise), in turn losing perspective, and its people left anxiously wondering about tomorrow. Several companies I have worked with had little sense of vision, little idea of what the future could hold. Many of these companies competed in the fastest growing markets of all, such as telecommunications and application software. You might only imagine the kinds of distress these enterprises experienced. So, there is a distinct mandate to design a high concept picture of the future, to give a strong sense of certainty.

Third, a high concept future is a strategic architectural issue for managing complexity in a holistic way. It gives a locus to market learning. As market information flows inward, a future picture imprints meaning, acting as a filter for what is strategically significant. It also enables a firm to ask pertinent questions (see below) about the future, within new, often breakthrough context. Further still, with a high concept vision in mind, decision making becomes concrete, goals tangible and concordant. In contrast, a firm without a sense of bearing, is a firm that swings from tree to tree in any direction. Again, there is a need for the design of high concept futures to give bearing.

In sum, imagining and designing a high concept future is an express human need, as well as a strategic architectural need. It gives a sense of collective purpose, a feeling of certitude, and gives direction signs for which way the enterprise is heading. In fact, the most innovative enterprises I know, that are winning in the same adverse conditions as their competitors, that set new market precedents, that create new business platforms where others see no opportunities, time after time, design a wholly innovative and motivating picture of the future.

Key Components of High Concept Futuring

High concept futuring is both a tool and a way of thinking – a multi-dimensional thinking tool for conceptualising the future. It further creates a legitimate space and time in which to consider the future. Essentially, high concept futuring captures a predetermined design about the future, in turn establishing a broad direction and sense of collective purpose, without restraining actions to black and white dictum. At the fundamental level, high concept futuring is about prototyping the future, it is about building models for testing and breaking, openly playing and toying with possibilities on the big commercial scale. For the purposes here, there are 12 key components that build a high concept vision that is both technically potent, and commercially relevant, in the context of *n*-innovation:

- A vision is *not* a prediction or premonition. The corporate planning offices and high scholarly seats, that see visioning as some kind of scenario planning scheme, still live on. In fact, some of the most eminent business strategists in practice today have not recognised, or at least not yet acknowledged, that a vision is *not* about strategic soothsaying.

- A vision is descriptive, not prescriptive. It is the strategic what, not the detailed how. In other words, it is a big picture of the future, a large sketch outline of what a firm or industry wants to become. An example here is NEC's vision of the unification of computers and communications, the so-called C&C. Back in the early 1970s this was truly revolutionary thinking. Each industry, and the technologies and markets within, were miles apart mindset wise. Yet the very act of envisioning C&C gave new insights into possibilities that just were not perceived before. None of the breakthroughs we now take for granted, such as internet works, mobile phones, and so on, originally came from detailed planning, just big concept futuring.
- It has future tense... obviously? I see many vision statements that seem to look to the future, yet actually simply maintain the present. Hyper-innovation, in particular, is not a maintenance game, or even a catch-up and play game, it is fundamentally about inventing the future. So a vision must explicitly pre-empt the future. Look at the difference: 'To be the *best value* retail bookseller in the city', against 'To *create* a book retail service that customers want'. At first glance, each statement may seem very much alike. But the first statement is merely a maintenance declaration; *best value* can be obtained from initiatives such as cost containment or best quality service, but these initiatives are simply not sustainable over the longer term (re: the dynamic competitive context). The second statement, in contrast, has an explicit future tense, to *create*.
- A vision is purposeful, it outlines the *why* we are here, the value a firm provides to its industry or creation of a new industry. It defines a coherent strategic market intent, in a creative way. Think of General Magic's vision for personal communications: 'We have a dream of improving the lives of many millions of people by means of small, intimate life support systems that people carry with them everywhere. These systems will help people to organise their lives, to communicate with other people, and to access information of all kinds. They will be simple to use, and come in a wide range of models to fit every budget, need and taste. They will change the way people communicate.' Purposeful and future tense orientated. Succinctly, it offers up an innovative proposition – General Magic want to make reality that benefits the customer and creates future market value.
- It embeds an overarching commercial philosophy or theory for doing business. Think of this: 'We shall build good ships here. At a profit – if we can. At a loss – if we must. But always good ships.' This was the

vision statement of Collis Huntingdon, founder of the Newport News Shipbuilding and Dry Dock Company, in 1886. Today his vision still thrives. Now owned by Tenneco, you can actually read the vision statement on the side of a 16 tonne monument to Huntingdon. One hundred and fifteen years later. The philosophy/theory must be doing something right.

- It has integrity. To build sustainable futures, the vision must have explicit integrity. Ethics impacts on every level in business, from direct stakeholders (employees, customers, shareholders, suppliers, managers), to local communities, up to and including the spectrum of politics, environmental issues, economic and social policies. Take Johnson & Johnson's vision statement: 'We believe our first responsibility is to doctors, nurses, and patients, to mothers and all others who use our products and services.' Well, it has served them well in sustaining J&J. One story in particular makes the point. When a lunatic put cyanide in a batch of Tylenol capsules, which then killed five people, J&J did not merely withdraw the batch in which the suspected poison pills were sighted, J&J pulled the entire stock across the United States, backed up with network TV news bulletin every half-hour. At the end of the day, it was not really J&J's problem, as the products were tampered with at the retail store level. What gave them moral guidance was, of course, their commitment to their vision. And the impact the decision had on the perceived integrity of J&J, only reinforced customer loyalty. The level of trust between the consumer and J&J was fortified, and J&J's stock market value, in turn, rallied.

- It proposes collaboration. A great vision leads to a great advantage, but an advantage that is not competitive in the traditional sense of *I win, you lose* (a zero-sum game), but emphasises *win–win* for the whole network (re: Chapter 4). However, it does emphasis offensive progress, in pursuit of advancement in a wider competitive context. The world marches on after all.

- It will be unique and different from the direct competition's vision. For a vision to be competitive in the wider context, it will have to identify potential opportunities that the competition have not yet perceived. Here, the context of high concept futuring for any given organisation needs to be specific in many dimensions, from the very meaning, through to the definition of focus.

- It contains what is right to create value and grow. Take Toyota's vision back in the 1990s: 'To build automobiles people everywhere will love'.

What do you think of that statement? Was it rhetoric maybe? Some I recall spat at such propaganda. But was it? Look at the result. Have they achieved a consistent value creation and growth? Do people love Toyota cars, in Germany, Australia, Pakistan, Brazil, Egypt today? I have met lots of people who work for Toyota. Quiz them about their job, and what will they say? 'To build automobiles people everywhere will love', just about sums it up, and by all accounts it works, as Toyota have outperformed all of the big auto-players over the longer term.

- It identifies the essential and tangible issues that bring the future into reality. Vague or aphoristic statements like 'we want to be the number one in X market', or 'best quality, least cost', or 'service excellence' or even 'world class' will not only lead to bland, vague behaviour, but a business to suit. In fact, these statements are blind dogma. By contrast, the high concept vision should be a powerful pragmatic communication that inspires and inflames the imagination. OKI Electric, for example, have a dream of bringing anyone together anywhere, instantly. And when they say *anywhere* and *instant*, they mean *anywhere* and *instant*. Think about the word *instant*? What does *instant* mean to you? To me it means quicker than a snap – instant! Impossible today? Yes. But this very statement projects a path to a particular future. It literally attracts the organisation in a vividly defined direction. It sets the road map. The technology may not exist today, but that is a point. The vision sets the agenda, it stirs the creative juices, and gives an overall direction no document could ever outline.
- A vision must be simple to understand. It contains no technical jargon or management phrases. It can be plainly understood by the man/woman on the ground. A good example here is Hewlett Packard's vision: 'Make people's lives easier and more fun at home and at work through information technology'. Simple, but effective.

Boiling down and interrelating these 12 key abstractions into a technically potent and commercially relevant vision of the future is a rigorous, often time-consuming task. The method outlined below will assist here.

Voracious Ambition: The Dream/Reality Ratio

One major factor to effective high concept futuring is that it must be *ambitious*. Not only in terms of pushing the edge, but going way beyond what is thought probable today. Remember, it is the seemingly unreasonable individual, the chimerical enterprise, the audacious institution that see what others do not, and create what is thought not probable. After all, without this orientation, ground-breaking innovation would never arise. It is a case of asking for the improbable, the far-reaching, the scary, the beyond the limits. It is about counterintuitive logic and walking positively on *terra incognita.*

So, are you personally ambitious? Is your innovation strategy ambitious? What would you call ambitious? I know a large group of wealthy individuals, who have an ambition of constructing their headquarters in a geostatic satellite by the year 2020! Is that ambitious? Most people's immediate reaction is that they must be 'nuts' or 'that's garbage'. But these people believe that setting skyrocket ambitions is the key to achieving the impossible and waging war on achieving their ambitions is the certain route to unlevelled growth; whether personal, or economic... So, is your organisation setting mega ambitions?

Take Fujitsu's high concept vision: 'What man can dream, technology can achieve.' Here, Fujitsu are forging ahead in technological R&D, that, without this kind of fantastic-like ambition, would never emerge. The key is to imagine voraciously ambitious high concepts of the future, big ideas that stretch way beyond what is probable today. And while on the subject of dreams, what is your organisation's *dream/reality ratio* (D/RR)? Gary Hamel, the London Business School Visiting Professor, declares that 'the gap between reality and imagination has never been so small'. So, is your D/RR something like 'that'll never work divided by feet on the ground' kind of scale? Or 'incremental innovation over what we really know well' ratio? Or is it of the Fujitsu kind: 'What man can dream, technology can achieve', ratio? *The message: do not try to predict the future – wildly imagine it, then make it happen.*

Long-term/Short-term Paradox

A central question that invariably raises its head when developing any future vision: *How far into the future should we look in the face of uncertainty*? If all future context is ambiguous, and the space of future possibilities is so vast, how on earth are we to plot with any reliability, move in directions with any real meaning? One answer is the *long-term/short-term* paradox: even though it is improbable to predict actual outcomes in the distant future, longer-term visions set an overall bearing, but at the same time, small-scale projects facilitate rapid learning and feedback... In a

Harvard Business Review article 'Technological Fusion and The New R&D', Professor Fumio Kaodama, wrote:

> Instead of planning R&D investments out 1 or 2 years, companies should think out 10 to 20 years, to how R&D effort can satisfy today's latent demand even when the technology does not exist or is just emerging. Thinking long term was critical in the evolution of the home-use video recorder market. The product concept can be traced back to 1955, when TOSHIBA's Noritake Sawazaki invented the helical scanning system for video recording and play back. Sawazaki's innovation enabled professional broadcasters to use narrow tape and smaller systems. But just as important, it set TOSHIBA and other equipment manufacturers thinking about the potential for home use. By shrinking the machine and developing ways to mass produce it, they could develop a viable home unit. Over time, with great effort and expense, they solved both problems.

Long-term thinking set global patterns and flexible migration paths, and eventual market innovation. On the other hand, without short-term results-focused experiments and projects, it is not possible to learn what the market is selecting for. And Toshiba know this well. Long-term research is injected with doses of reality. In the ultracompetitive laptop computer markets, new technologies come and go at rate untold. Consequently, learning and feedback from the market become pivotal. To gain the kind of swift insight needed to stay at the edge of research and innovation, Toshiba launch more new laptop computers per unit time than any of their competitors, interconnecting new ideas to keep ahead, learning at a rate matched by few others. Hence, Toshiba live the long-term/short-term paradox: their typical product life-cycle is less than 12 months, but these ephemeral cycles work within an extended 10–20 year high concept vision.

Extradimensional Questions

The next step to high concept futuring is to ask questions, great questions. Anthony Robbins, the leading consultant on the psychology of human excellence and achievement, is adamant that the most successful commercial and social organisations are the ones run by leaders that ask *better questions than their rivals*… I have honed them down to four.

Searching questions. A good starting point is to ask searching questions: 'What multidimensional businesses should we be in? What dimensions make up our business already, and how can we expand upon them and interconnect further?' The answers to these kinds of question are quite often taken for granted. Furthermore, in an interconnected world, change accelerates, context obliterates, and new technologies emerge that transform the competitive landscape. Recall Microsoft in Chapter 4. What business are they in today? What business is Ford into today? So, ask questions that probe, dig deep into the nature and future of your business in new context. And if you are in matchsticks, *do not* ask 'what business are we in' and say 'matchsticks'. Calling a spade a spade does not help here; look deeper. The Japanese are masters of this. To the Japanese, poor quality does not only mean a defective product, or even customer dissatisfaction, but a 'great loss to society'. So, think now 'What is my business now, what are our strengths, our best capabilities? What transdimensional innovations can we bring to our business tomorrow, in 5, 10 and 20 years?' 'What are the most important discontinuities that will impact on our future markets?' The point is that enterprises must think in terms of creating the future. 'What are the key influences on the future businesses we decide to develop?' 'Who are now our most demanding customers?' and 'What are their demands?' 'Who will be our most demanding customers with emerging or latent expectations?' 'What extradimensional demands can we anticipate?' 'How can we be different?' If an enterprise cannot answer this question, then it is not going to be that innovative. So, 'what differentiation can we achieve by creating a transdimensional market?' 'What differences should we compete on?'

Positive questions: Questions that uplift. 'What would be good for the customer, the student, the patient?' – 'What could reignite the market ecology?' 'What could be developed that would help, improve, amaze society?' 'What extradimensional concepts would blow the customer's mind?'

Projection Questions: 'What can we do to project the future of our business?' The answer is to imagine the future, then make it happen. The only accurate way to project the future is to invent it! So, based on the answers from the two previous questions (searching and positive) what can you imagine about the future? What amazing questions can you now ask yourself about what your business and its markets (traditional and multidimensional) are going to be? 'What could ignite a hypermarket and excite multidimensional customer expectations in the distant future?' 'What would fundamentally shift and multiply value?' 'What could we do to transform the whole notion of the market focus, towards market panoramics?'

Fantasising questions: It is time to push further, to the fantastic, the profound, the amazing, the magical – to fantasise. Ask what spectacular business concepts, whole new markets, could exist in the long-term future. Do not hold back, even if the ideas that come into your head seem impossible in today's world. Ask: 'What transdimensional wisdom would a time traveller from the year 2025 bring?' 'Could we write a short science fiction story to give new extradimensional foresight?' What about your dream/reality ratio? Is it feet on the ground, or is it near improbable-like thinking? Do not let limited ambition or conditioning get in the way.

Build and Share Your Vision

Until now you have consciously asked your inner self, constructing internal mental pictures of the future, based on your own knowledge, imagination and wisdom. But this is only the beginning, the platform. It is important to build on your own ideas and ask your customers, partners, academics, consultants – (direct/indirect) at their site, at your site, at the point where they use your product/service, at exhibitions, conferences, and so on – what they imagine about the future of your market ecology/new market ecology/use or interaction with your product/service. Expose them to the multidimensional strategies in Part I, and ask them for extradimensional market concepts. Talk to the best technologists, both the sceptic and the radical schools. Go to the most innovative universities or research organisations. Ask them audacious searching, positive, projecting and fantasising questions. What/how would your customers/society gain/benefit from a multidimensional innovation that is so spectacular that it would pop the top off the current market ecology and/or create an entirely new and exciting panoramic industry, yet in today's technological/market/regulatory constraints is wholly impossible?

Futuring Workshop

Now, set up a weekend retreat, far away from the mindset of the company. Invite key people (executives, technologists, marketing, doctors, lecturers, operations people); just as important, invite people outside your current mindset (strategic partners, consultants, new graduates and apprentices). Set an agenda based around these vital future-building questions:

- What will/should/could/possibly be the extradimensional future of an industry that does not exist yet, in say 5, 10 and 20 years' time?
- What are the overriding internal, external and seemingly (now) remote influences that will diverge that industry over the next 5, 10, 20 years, technologically, economically, politically, socially and organisationally?
- Who will/could be the highest value customers in 5, 10 and 20 years time?
- How could we define the industry in terms of hypermarkets, n-products, and extradimensional service structures? What hyperinnovative distribution and marketing channels could be introduced?
- Ask challenging searching, positive, projecting and fantasising questions (above).
- Give a significant reward for the group and individuals that smashed the mould, battered convention, pursued the unorthodox.

Put significant energy and importance on this. Make 'em sweat. This is the future of your organisation, your growth, your job and all that goes with it. Document the conclusions and reiterate this process after some digestion period.

And remember, visions are made for breaking and raising the standard. Visions need to be dynamic and grow, they must be continuously on the move and in development. In contrast, the closer a firm moves towards a static vision some time in the future, the further that firm falls behind the competitive context, because by the time a firm eventually arrives at that ideal destination some 10 or 20 years hence, the world would have moved on… *The message: the more adept a firm becomes at designing the future, and the faster it is at making that imagined future transpire, the faster it can move on to the next level of speculation, in turn, the better it becomes at disabling even the most contemporary competitive context.* As a consequence, the futuring workshop must become a frequent event.

Construct Key Wording through a Powerful Metaphor

At the end of the futuring workshop construct a powerful metaphor that typifies the conclusions. Metaphors can act as creative springboards, engaging higher levels of reasoning that extract new insight, often breaking through to new context. I recall Tom Peters, using a powerful metaphor to describe the processes of modern and often radical management practice: *Business as carnival.* The picture it formed was quite extraordinary. In my mind's eye I could see bright multicoloured lights, fireworks rocketing off and exploding in a dazzling array of patterns, funfair rides with people pitched to the point of screaming ecstasy. Of course, Tom's point is that organisations need to be exciting and highly interactive places. Certainly a powerful metaphor... So, from the above futuring workshop, describe in metaphorical ways the amazing interconnected vision you have in your mind's eye.

Expanded Meanings

Interpretation of any given word is informed by an individual's knowledge and experience, so it is vital to expand the meaning of each word that makes up the metaphor. For instance, what does the word 'fast' mean to you? I asked a random group of people what they thought. The range of answers: 'hunger to incorrect time, to speed, to fixed position, to dishonesty, to heaven knows?' Recall OKI Electric's high concept vision 'to bring anyone together no matter where they are in the world instantly'. Focus on the key word 'instant'. I have asked this before, but what does the word 'instant' mean to you? What other words does it bring up in your mind? Now do this exercise with your metaphor, and the answers to your fantasising, projecting, positive, searching questions.

Depicting the High Concept Future

So, in sum. Wording is most important. Clearly depicting the future in a way that is clear to the man on the ground, but also excites every member of the organisation. The future tense must stand out, giving some last thoughts here. The *challenge* of givens, axioms, traditions that have for so long been the norm, must be emphasised too... So, from the above expanded *meanings*, write down your high concept future vision in the box provided on the next page.

High Concept Futuring: The Way to the Future

It is about metaphorical signposts across the company, high concept futuring points the way to the future. It is not a panacea, and it is not about setting everything with certainty. That is just not possible. What it is, is about learning; learning in multidimensions, a great theme of this book after all. It takes time, effort and practice like the rest of the topics in this part. But once a firm begins to build and see that big picture in the future, so it begins to see the light. A light that that will guide that firm to innovative and multidimensional ends.

Your High Concept Future

CHAPTER 7

Values That Connect

What we value, our deep-held beliefs, constantly and intensely inform our actions. How we rise to new life challenges, how we communicate, our relationships with others, and most important of all, what we pick out and focus on in the world around us, acutely depend on the values and beliefs we hold. Our values are nurtured within the family, through schooling, in contact with peers and community; and now in a rapidly complexifying and interconnecting world of ideas. What is practised most, the customs we cherish, the protocols we experience, the knowledge we take on board, all go to make up a system of belief. 'Give me a child until the age of seven and I'll give you the man', remarked the inimitable George Bernard Shaw. When you consider the ideas that a child takes on board up towards this age, they will affect the way that the eventual adult thinks and behaves for the rest of his/her life.

Enterprises, themselves, often hold deeply ingrained values, etched by their leaders' habits, beliefs, priorities and expectations, and by the experiences, challenges, knowledge and ultimate outlook of people across the organisation. Company culture can turn out to be a hotchpotch of negative and conflicting values, some downright treacherous. Other enterprises and institutions, however, seem to have a magical, an untouchable winning, often quite delightful way about them. Sometimes the product of an enlightened leader; sometimes simply good fortune; but more and more the result of conscious design.

Traits and Behaviour Patterns

What moves people – ordinary people – to make connections, to forge relationships? What lifts them to a point of excitement and urgency? What gives them a sense of pride, builds mutuality, trust and openness among their thoughts? What gives them a lust for the new and the creative? What inspires them to collaborate and work in cross-organisational teams to surpass their goals, to experiment and play with ideas, to see what no one has seen before, to achieve what no one has done before?

On the other hand, what switches people off? What isolates people? What makes them disparaging of their fellow workers? What makes people manipulative and calculating? What breeds paranoia and segregation?

Take a look at the difference in traits and behaviour patterns between Company A and Company X. Where would you prefer to work? Which company is likely to thrive in a world of interconnection? Which company is likely to build relationships with partners, with employees, with competitors, with unusual, novel, diverse ideas? Who is likely to hyperinnovate?

Company A	*Company X*
Dogmatic	Intelligent
Bureaucratic	Effective
Autocratic	Creative
Fatalistic	Visionary
Political	Candid
Fearful	Confident
Suppressed	Exciting
Takes Space	Gives Space
Boring	Playful
Suspicious	Trusting
Conventional	Have ideas
Sombre	Friendly
Abusive	Respectful
Deceitful	Have integrity
Indifferent	Caring
Harsh	Forgiving
Disconnected	Mutual

The list goes on... But do any of these traits and behaviour patterns originate from a predisposed personality? Is there nothing we can do? Culture just is? People are simply out for themselves?... Or can we build a positive value set that stimulates a Company X culture?

Some Living Values that Interconnect

As in society, as for business, what is rewarded is generally practised. If you want to induce a certain behaviour, reward it, praise it, hold it with high regard.

Take Mars, the foods people. They have a clear set of values guiding daily business operations: *freedom, quality, mutuality, efficiency* and *responsibility*. These values are not mere ideology, you can feel and observe the Mars way the moment you walk into any of their business units worldwide. The Mars values signal for a kind of behaviour that integrates people, that motivates people to collaborate, to break down the barriers, to share and expand world views, to interconnect with ideas, peers and partners. And it evidently works, as the Mars culture has kept 6 of their products in the top 10, in a market of 6000 alternative products! By rewarding for specific behaviour, these values have come to be ingrained in the Mars culture. Mostly the rewards are a small 'thank you,' but Mars go all the way and reflect what they value within their remuneration system.

Ideo Product Design, the top industrial design excellence award-winning consultancy, have a highly effective value set when it comes to stimulating hyperinnovation. They call it FLOSS: *Fail* sometimes, be *Left*-handed (right-brained), get *Out* there, be *Sloppy*, be *Stupid*! It is these kinds of playful value that motivate Ideo to interconnect ideas in original and unusual ways. Try doing that with set of top-down rules.

The Centre for Business Innovation (CBI) at CAP Gemini Ernst & Young, have a lucid set of values that interconnect: *Explore the New, Recombine, Ship Quality, Make a Difference*, and *Enjoy the Experience*. CBI's values are designed to create a culture of hyperinnovation, creating new services and businesses, providing new value for their clients, communicating to a broad audience around the world. They collaborate with a diverse network of lead thinkers, synthesising what they learn to catalyse change in the business world. CBI's vision of an increasingly interconnected economy drives their research and consulting agenda. They say:

> There's no doubt that connections and ways of connecting have proliferated wildly among firms, people, computers, and more. In a highly interconnected world, things don't simply happen faster. Different things happen. Industries behave in non-classical ways. Firms take on different structures. Different types of assets drive competitiveness. All this calls for new theories of management and new tools for management.

Hyperinnovation is fast becoming CBI's bread and butter work, already applying breakthrough thinking and tools in the connected economy.

Throw Out the Rule Book

Without a premeditated and engendered value set you will probably end up with a mixed bag, conflicting and dividing people in general, and wholly limiting in practice. Historically, organisations have tried, without much success, to control people's actions through a complex set of rules and procedure, but the value set is and always has been a much more powerful method of control than any rule book. Mostly, the policies and procedures developed by a committee of managers often have little or no controlling power. It is not so uncommon to find people spending inordinate amounts of time fighting or finding, by stealth or otherwise, ways around the rule book, to actually achieve intended real results. The reason is, deep-rooted values. Putting a superficial rule in front of any group will bring out the militant, to some degree. My point: if approached in the right way, leaders can use these basic instincts as a behavioural tool. A tool surpassing any other method of directing.

So here, rules limit rather than service: rules, policies, reporting lines seem to fade into the background when there is a rich feeling of what the organisation as a whole is aiming for, and means most. If people feel at a bone-deep level, know what it is all about and where the business is going, then a *rule* becomes irrelevant.

Yet another reason for limiting rules and procedures to a set of key values, is that it fosters creativity. Procedures and standards mean exactly that: standard – nothing new.

One requisite for innovation, of even the mundane, is to burn the procedure book. Most executives get the logic, but do not come close to doing anything about it. Creativity means toying, tinkering, experimenting with ideas. Moreover, so does getting the XYZ product/service to market faster. Procedures get in the way. I asked a designer at an ISO : 9000 approved company, whether the procedure assisted or clarified her job. She replied:

> Everyday I have a unique situation blow up from nowhere. These procedures presume that I live in a static world not accounting for the odd exception to the rule. But in my job (innovation) the procedure becomes the exception to the rule… as every day is different.

Unique events are the rule in this interconnected world, and because of this, I am unsure of the value of binding up an innovation project with internally focused quality standards. As my observations of *ISO-certified* companies show typically that they do not and cannot adhere to any standard as more and more novel, surprising, discontinuous situations blow up. One company that I would like to name, has a 200-page, 20,000-word procedure just for its purchasing department. One of its competitors that is chipping away at the margin has a two-line statement:

> To procure reliable materials at best life-cycle cost against a jointly agreed specification and schedule.

Sixteen words vs 20,000... no contest! I asked a senior buyer at the 20,000-word company to describe his role in a nutshell. He said something along the lines of above. So I asked him why he needed a 20,000-word procedure to do his job. He said he does not, and did not adhere to it. I then asked his boss to justify the procedure. 'If all of our buyers were to leave us we would lose all of our built up knowledge, so we decided to document it.' A rational answer to a reasonable question. But right off the point. If the procedures were there in case of an emergency, I can see the point to it. But working by them to the letter, that's a different matter. The 16-word company employs just two buyers to procure around £50 million worth of inventory a year. It takes the 20,000-word company an army of eight buyers and secretary to manage a budget of £60 million per annum. That's a difference of 1:25 million to 1:7.5 million.

Action over Procedure, Results over Rules

For an enterprise to survive, let alone grow within the context of continuous interconnection, there is a basic need to move fast. Speed is the result of action. The stuff that stops action are the very rules, procedures and functional structures that we put into place that are supposed to give action. We have grown dependent on this way of working, and in turn end up with bureaucracies that turn people off and limit their potential. If your people are to meet shorter deadlines or a new venture is to take off, then the people working on these projects must be given the scope to develop their own culture and ways of working. Forcing them to adopt a homogeneous system does not give the stimulus and the scope needed to achieve any of the goals I have been talking about here.

In her classic management book, *When Giants Learn to Dance*, Rosabeth Moss Kanter probes in much more detail for the need for more than one way of managing:

> The era in which corporations could operate by the pretence of a single management system is over. Playing in the global (commercial) Olympics, corporations cannot succeed by valuing uniform treatment over flexibility, adherence to procedures over fast action, rules over results. Instead, they must recognise that the ability to invest in new opportunities means letting internal enterprises go their own way.

The bottom line for Rosabeth here is that different things take different strokes, and trying to force homogeneity among operations can lead to nothing less than a calamity. Teams need to develop their own way of working. It is basic human nature to have some freedom of expression and self-control. Demanding that people work in a homogeneous and fixed way suppresses creativity. Letting groups of people develop their own processes and methods is a core trait of the most innovative organisations I have observed. Honda in particular. Honda call this: *simultaneous competition among different approaches.*

Above all, I think the critical contribution of a set of guiding key values is the very freedom they give to people to develop their own and best way of working. If, say, exceeding customer expectations is an aim, a mandatory list of procedures and given working methods will restrict, rather than assist. What is right in one situation, probably is not going to be in another. On the other hand, an open and positive set of key-values gives people the opportunity to develop their initiative, their orientation to risk taking, and today's necessity to be in a continual state of hyperinnovation.

Precipitant and Higher Values Development

There are values I call *precipitant values.* Values that must first be set in place to bring about what I call *higher values.* In basic terms, precipitant values are the kind that cause other values to occur. Higher values are the kind that actually give rise to a behaviour, such as *team collaboration.* In other words, there are specific values a firm must have in place first, to gain any hope of achieving higher values and resultant behaviour. For example, to gain the higher value of *trust*, a firm must have the precipitant value of *integrity* in place and functioning first. Trust is without doubt a key to team collaboration. But until a firm has the value of integrity in place, the value of trust will be limited. Integrity, is then, a precipitant value. Trust, a higher value. Figure 7.1 shows how a chain of causality leads from precipitant values to higher values to desired emergent behaviours.

The method for defining *precipitant* and *higher values* is straightforward. It starts by defining a desired behaviour; say *risk taking*. Risk taking is a behaviour essential to innovation. The next step is to define the higher value(s) that will animate risk taking. In this case, the higher value of *support in failure*. If your people are left out in the cold, or heaven forbid, punished for failure, risk taking will dwindle, and innovation with it.

The next stage is to define the precipitant value(s) that animate a support in failure. In this case, the precipitant value of a *learning disposition* (see Figure 7.1). Only until failure is valued as a learning process, will support in failure occur, and in turn, sustain risk taking.

The key is to keep asking and asking *what are the deeper precipitant values that must be in place first, to create higher values which in turn motivate the behaviours that give rise to hyperinnovation*?

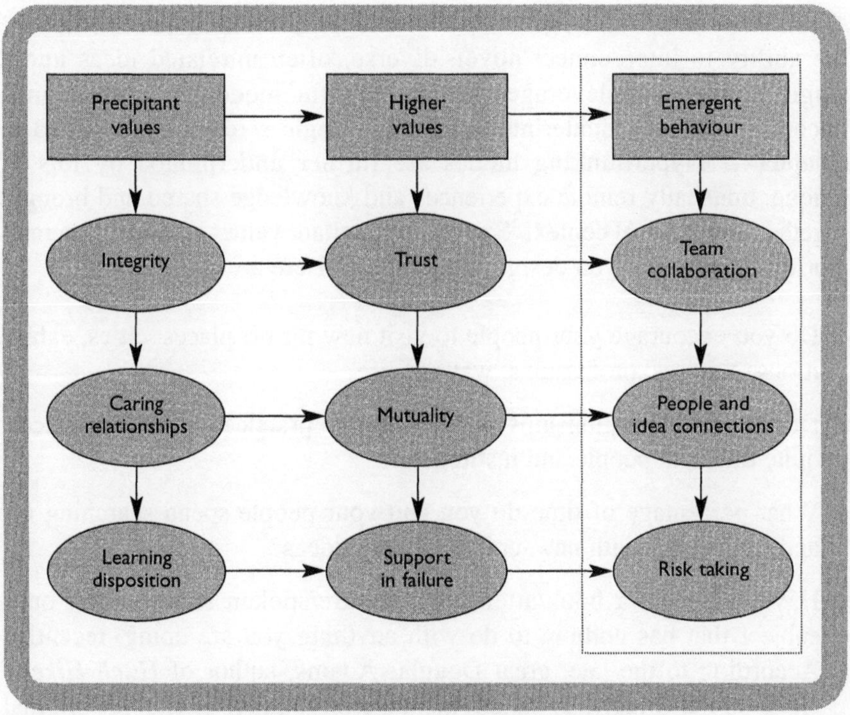

Figure 7.1 Precipitant and higher values, and the web of causality to emergent behaviours

Notice, further, how each precipitant value in Figure 7.1 is mutually reinforcing. *Integrity* reinforces *caring relationships*, which in turn reinforces a *learning disposition*. Clearly, if a chain of causality is carefully thought out, it is possible to build a value set that fortifies each desired value and ultimate behaviour as a whole. This only intensifies the potency of this approach.

Cultural Immersion and Hyperinnovation Values

One of the most effective ways to shape people's values, is to immerse them in activities, exercises and environments, that explicitly exhibit the values you want to make happen. Therefore, if we are to encourage people to think, collaborate and innovate in interconnected dimensions, they must engage in deeds that support such ends. Here is a set of activities that gives rise to hyperinnovation: multidimensional thinking, accelerating the interconnection of ideas, and exceeding customer demands:

Multidimensional thinking: Multidimensional thinking is precipitated by the ability to interconnect novel, diverse, often unrelated ideas under single concepts. It leverages on the thought modes of contradigms, uncommon sense, counterintuition and strategic serendipity, outlined in Chapter 2. Hyperthinking modes are further underpinned by lots of unique, unusually remote experiences and knowledge shared and brought together under novel context. So what precipitant values embedded in real-world activities can you design and activate? Here are some ideas:

- Do you encourage your people to visit new far-off places, cities, exhibitions, cultures, professions, ways of life?
- Do they build relationships with innovative practices, strange alliances, quite different people and institutions?
- What percentage of time do you and your people spend searching for and connecting with new, crazy, uncanny ideas?
- Have you read a book/attended a lecture/spoken to an expert on a subject that has nothing to do with anything you are doing, recently? According to the late, great Douglas Adams, author of *Hitch Hiker's Guide to the Galaxy*, so-called 'mental crop rotation' is vital for original inspiration on a long-term basis. So, have you worked in a different role for a day/week/month/year/decade? Have your people?

- Do you encourage your people to take sabbaticals? Accenture Consulting, have what they call 'flexi-leave', 6–12 months, with up to 80 per cent of salary. It gives their associates a sense of self-control, a chance to expand their minds, to build a wider world perspective.
- Have you promoted someone for pushing the edge, even though they fell short?
- Have you hired multidimensional people?
- Do you play games, have toys in and around your work environment, flood your time with creativity-enhancing activities and devices?

Multidimensional thinking is a product of the seemingly (at first) crazy, weird, arcane, even strange venture. So what exercises and proto-games are you executing, to inject multidimensional thinking into the blood of your working culture?

Toyota hold *playful* competitions every year to exercise the imagination. One of them is the *Idea Olympics*, an exhibition of car designs ranging from the ridiculous to the downright wild. The object is not to conceive feasible concepts, but to expand world-views, and enter into and interconnect novel design concepts. I saw a design for a double-decker car. An anti-bump car. A car that you swim in and a car you never need to reverse. A car with legs and a motorbike with triangulated wheels with off-set axial shafts. Untamed stuff, but does exactly what it aims to achieve: *new insights*.

Toshiba hold an exhibition called *Art and Innovation*. It is often designed to criss-cross the boundaries of sometimes dull technology with the abstract and pure nature of art. Students, designers and artists are invited to take Toshiba products, core technologies, even discrete electromechanical componentry, and produce new art forms. This leads to insights impossible using traditional specification-driven approaches. When I made a visit to their London exhibition, I was bowled over by the quite unique, beyond the fringe concepts these techno-artists had created. But once again, that is the point. So what events, trials, environments, challenges can you think up to develop mindsets and values that stimulate multidimensional thinking?

Accelerating the interconnection of ideas: A key to rapid idea interconnection is break down the barriers among people and the knowledge they hold, to encourage people to build relationships in and outside the firm, to enable teams to weave diverse concepts and unique technology together. So what *integrity* (precipitant) and *trust* (higher value) enhancing events, challenges, proto-games can you think up to build a culture that gives relationship building and connections among a diverse range of people and what is on the mind?

When Honda say fast to market, they mean it. They can bring a new car platform from clay model to the showroom in under 24 months, in one case, the Today micro-mini car, it took Honda only 12 months. Honda V.P. Shoichire Irimajiri says that swift innovation cycles are part of the culture by intent and underlined with action. Each design engineer is circulated through the Formula one engine design team, where they learn instinctively to work within a subsecond time culture. This is part of the so-called 'Spirit of Honda', a business philosophy that brings out the best and most original in people. Honda unequivocally believe that unusual, sometimes high-pressure events and exercises outside the fold can grow the diverse and swift mindsets essential to create the automobile products of the future.

St Lukes, the award-winning advertising agency, continue to easily outpitch their much larger rivals. St Lukes accomplish this through a credo of *honesty*, *trust*, and *friendship*; unusual in a power-driven industry of this kind. This is accomplished – in part – by constant forum and dialogue on business ethics and codes, about creative chaos and the higher concept needs of clients. People at St Lukes often work in several simultaneous teams, so contact with a larger diversity of people is guaranteed. Again, work outside the fold, such as community projects, is encouraged to nurture relationship-building values. St Lukes' aim is to constantly reinvent itself as it grows, integrating the best of the past, with lessons anew. All of this breaks down barriers between people, building a capacity to accelerate the interconnection of ideas.

Exceeding unexpressed customer demands: Customer demands and expectations are not only on the up, they are multiplexing and complexifying. Demands for the new and diverse contained in single product offerings are now the expected. To inject the philosophy of *demandplex* into the heart of a culture, teams need to spend generous amounts of time visiting local and far-off multidimensional places (airports, theme parks, disk worlds, mazes, whatever is relevant) with the customer. They must analyse *n*-dimensional innovations (complex synthetic pharmaceuticals, *all-in-one* services, internetworks, inflight entertainment systems, whatever is relevant) with the customer too. Study customer reactions and demands in multidimensional situ, learn from this, and build the results into hyper-innovations. So what precipitant and higher value exercises, events and proto-games are you executing to exceed customer demandplex?

Marriott Hotel executives spend generous amounts of time soliciting customer opinions, holding literally hundreds of focus groups with lead customers, sifting through thousands upon thousands of comment cards and letters every year. Tough, when day-to-day operations often bark louder. Yet from this orientation, Marriott have found a mass shift in custom. Customer expectations, again, are not only on the up, they now expect service suites that cross cultural boundaries. In the past, the Anglo-American business executive was a key benchmark. Rapidly emerging is the generation-Y, multicultural, worldwide traveller, and his/her demands are diverse and complex. Marriott executives now spend even more time travelling to far-off places to absorb different cultural contexts and customs, consequently multidimensional service innovation is trailblazing Marriott's culture development.

Philips Electronics have gone so far as to build a complete environment for the customer to experience and play with new product concepts. It looks a little like the kind of environment you would see in an episode of *Star Trek*. A large glass-fronted, two-storey house called 'the home of the future'. Within the surroundings, Philip's innovation teams observe customers using prototype concepts in 'live' settings. One concept is a toothbrush, designed for a child, that starts a two minute cartoon in the mirror while they are brushing their teeth. This interaction with authentic, irritable, dizzy, run-around kids, has given Philip's people unorthodox insights into the development before the product has even been launched (recall Chapter 3, learning before output). But the environment is not just for customers. No – Philips have gone the extra mile, as 'the home of the future' is also a laboratory for engineers and marketers to do real development work. This is exactly the kind of emissive environment that speaks a thousand values.

Values that Connect: The Glue of Culture

Values are the substance that glues the fabric of hyperinnovation culture, the conceptual adjustments and emotional adhesives that bring it all together. To be clear, if the values are not aligned for hyperinnovation, if company values do not bring people and their ideas together as a whole, then innovation of even the ordinary is unlikely to transpire. So, an organisation needs to spend serious and generous amounts of time building and developing *values that connect*.

CHAPTER 8

Multidimensional Leaders

Leadership is not management. We know the role of management?...it is about planning and setting goals... it is about breaking those plans and goals into manageable pieces to hand down the line of command... it is about appraising, measuring and informing... and it is about enabling people to carry out tasks in a timely, productive, cost-effective manner... This is management at its very best: *tight and uniform control* (equilibrium and optimisation); and precisely why management is simply not enough for innovation... What we need more than ever before is *leadership*.

So what is leadership?... There are many kinds. What works in one situation, is limited, even disruptive in another. The braveheart leader of a cause, is the common model. Leaders from the front, and gung-ho types of leadership are seen on occasion and necessary under given circumstances. Some have specific processes to lead and take on the role of teacher and coach. Some people are perceived as gurus, they have acquired unique, enlightened knowledge that captures the imagination. Others encompass roles such as moral guide and mentor, setting principles and values. Some of the most successful leaders have had little official position and authority, yet through their beliefs, have managed to change people's thinking, and in the extreme, have changed the direction and fate of a nation. These are some of the characteristics of leadership. But here, I am aiming at something more specific: *multidimensional leadership*.

Leadership Behaviours and Actions

Anthropologists tell us that one of the most significant factors that shape human culture (in business or otherwise), is the visible behaviour and actions of the leader. His or her expectations, priorities, ambitions, beliefs, express knowledge, and daily habits and traits, impact directly on the way ordinary people working at the coal face think, feel, communicate and act.

Think of this. If you have one hell of tyrant at the top, who yells and humiliates, who threatens and intimidates, then you can only imagine what that company culture is going to reflect down the hierarchy. If there is a pinstripe bureaucrat and efficiency fiend at the top, who thinks that changing the office window blinds is a risk, then you can be clear that that company will not be doing anything that new, if at all… Are any alarm bells ringing?… What about the wise old owl, who knows all, tells all, takes all? What sort of culture will emerge? Probably an inch-deep one, because no one will have the space to learn, expand, and make their own mistakes and judgements. What about the highly creative type who dominates with his flamboyance and creative rhetoric? Probably a culture of procrastination… I could go on, as there are countless kinds of leadership personalities and traits. All of them distinct, but equally influential on the breed of culture that will develop.

The point is, that there is no universal algorithm of values and leadership personality or traits that fits all circumstance. No precise and right set of behaviour patterns that work effectively in every unique situation. There are certainly behaviours that categorically do not work in given situations, and there are behaviours that are just not acceptable. The best answer I can give is that each circumstance must be addressed as it comes along, and hyperinnovation is no different. As we shall see, it demands a unique set of values (above), and the multidimensional leadership traits (below).

The Life-cycle Stages of Leadership Development

We all grow throughout our lives. As the biological clock ticks, and as our experiences unfold, we all change and move on to new life challenges and priorities, we evolve new needs and wants, we even begin to see the world in different ways. And it is no different for the business leader. As leaders gain more experience and knowledge, their priorities and perspectives transform. They begin to develop new insights. They identify and engage with a wider context of strategic issues. And it is here, where we take up this very issue of leadership development and its impact on hyperinnovation.

Contrary to popular opinion, there are no instant leaders, at least not the kind of leader who is refined for a specific duty. In particular, multidimensional leadership is an experience set, mindset and skill set that should be continually stretched and nurtured. In fact, there are four potential life-cycle stages to the ultimate zenith of the multidimensional leader (see Figure 8.1).

First, the *functional* stage. Naturally, all managers, in all kinds of roles, begin with a rudimentary functional knowledge and outlook. That is, the technology, the methods, cost containment and internal objectives, like quality systems or cycle time, are pre-eminent in the mind of the manager. Essentially, people confined to this kind of thinking are *management technicians*. They work at the day-to-day level. Their skill set and world-view are focused on company maintenance. At this stage, managers are unable to perceive and work the kinds of issues now essential for higher-dimensional innovation. In fact, most people become stranded at this first stage, and reason number one why most careers in management begin to plateau early.

The second stage is the *transactional* orientation, where a leader recognises the significance of achieving wider external goals, such as customer satisfaction or total quality management systems. However, their experience and knowledge prior to this stage have been functionally focused, so leaders often apply previous-stage functional tactics to achieving external goals (paradigms again). And when they apply functional tactics to such external goals, there is every chance that actual outcomes will be unsuccessful. Again, management careers plateau for this very reason.

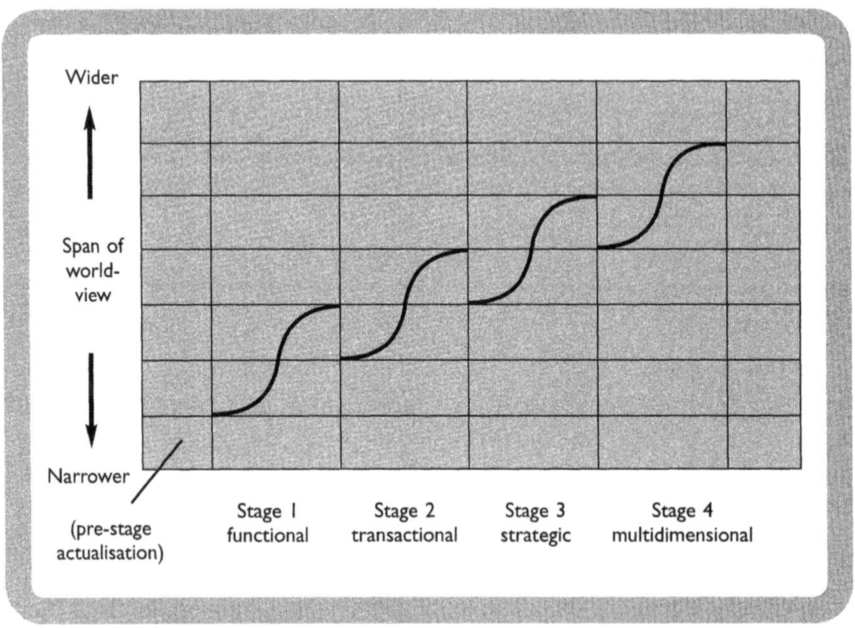

Figure 8.1 Life-cycle stages of leadership development

The third stage is a *strategic* focus, where a true *transformational* leader begins to burgeon. At this stage, the leader is competent at a portfolio of approaches and strategies to achieving external goals, and begins to develop the enterprise's strategic aims and value systems. At their height, they are exceptionally competent, and often recognised within their industry with high regard. They have learnt to manage conflict between the many different approaches to solving distinct problems. Their people-development skills are highly polished, having a perceptive capacity to shape, even rebuild, people's beliefs and outlook. The best here, hold a charismatic, sometimes mystical, charm about them. Most importantly, they begin to see and develop the bigger, high concept picture for a business. In a word, they are *future* oriented.

But it is the fourth stage, the *multidimensional* leader, that is all-important. This life-cycle stage is the most evolved form of hegemony, constituting highly developed sensibilities to the business world. Multidimensional leaders can conceive and integrate higher business philosophy, theory and practice. Their knowledge and experience are of broad expanse and highly developed. They are clear-sighted about the nature of complexity in the business world today, and all the paradox that comes with it. In particular, they recognise and regulate internal and external uncertainties and discontinuities that now sit with such complexity, and are attuned to the kind of counterintuitive and uncommon issues that spontaneously emerge. They can think and learn in multidimensions, and are holistic towards the building of a total business systems solution. Hence, the multidimensional leader is essential for the building of a culture that manifests hyperinnovation.

The Art and Discipline of the Multidimensional Leader

Multidimensional leadership is a science of noble arts and codes of discipline, and as in any science, there are laws, principles and hypotheses. The weakness in the science/leadership hypothesis, is that it is an anthropological science, one of the soft sciences. Although we can be observed to follow certain patterns, we humans are inherently unpredictable. Nevertheless, leadership that stimulates multidimensional innovation does have some definable protocol:

- *Iconoclast*. The first multidimensional leadership act must be a breaker and contradictor of tradition, seeker of counterintuitive reason and enlightenment, devisor of the novel. Clearly in a world of increasing amalgamation, we have little choice but to seek and bring in new ways. The ability to see beyond the norm, the quo, the quip, the turbulent, and even the seemingly rational. Yet have the wherewithal and perseverance to turn dreams and concepts into tangible, touchable global visions and values that the ordinary person can relate to. The task here is to act out rule breaking. Only then will your people take what you say seriously.

- *Connector*. Taking the lead in fashioning a culture that brings out the most inventive in people, and allows them to effectively achieve open combinations of ideas... So, how do you flood your company with plural values? Live it yourself, lead by example: be the interconnector of ideas, people, technology, organisation itself. The key here is to get out there. Spend time and effort greasing contact between people.
- *High concept visionary*. Without a high concept picture set sometime in the distant future, your organisation will lack an essential mechanism to steer great diversity, in often unfathomable complexity, towards some imagined future reality. Many high concept visions are a product of one person, they are not shared by the many. Until it is shared by the many, the vision will remain a figment of the leader's idiosyncratic perspective. The leader/s must sell and develop the higher concept(s) in the minds of the relevant people. The most important point is to make the vision tangible; wear the future in your daily actions. Ask people for their views and ideas on how the global visions can be achieved. The more the leader involves people in the global vision, the more it is shared. And yes, the visions will morph and change over time, that is the point; engagement with people means that their ideas will have impact, which will promote shared ownership of the vision.
- *High expectations*. Whether parents, teachers, president or crown, what our leaders anticipate and foresee, the lines they draw, directly and forcefully impinge upon people's behaviour and outlook. If our leaders' expectations are less than ordinary, then expect the less than ordinary outcome. If our leaders want to create where there is nothing, bring forth new venture and industry, then we can only anticipate that the best and different are yet to come.
- *Lifetime learning*. Learning drives innovation. Lifetime learning leads to fundamental innovation. If this is to be the case, intensive cross-enterprise learning (outlined in next chapter) must originate from the very top. The multidimensional leader quests for knowledge and motivates others to do the same. Building learning environments both physical and cultural, that assist individual and team knowledge building.

Seeking the most inventive thinkers and innovators in and around both relevant and irrelevant industries, exploring cultures far and wide. Pursuing disciplines and thought morphologies that break through to the unexpected, the deeply paradoxical concept.

- *Uncertainty guide.* When inventions start to grow in terms of the numbers and kinds of technologies, people often experience frightening, almost mind-bending change. When suddenly events and tasks do not string out in some linear causality, when innovations demand skills and knowledge that no one is proficient in or even aware of, when ideas come at them and interconnect faster than they can get to grips with, anxiety will swim all around. Thus in the dark of unpredictability, and in the dithering of ambiguity, there is a real need for leaders to see beyond the now and known. We need leaders that can steer the unfamiliar, the strange, the novel, that in themselves exist in shaky, nebulous environments.
- *Host.* Dialogue is fundamental to building relationships and learning, in turn innovation. If the company culture is one of fear, politics and suppression of ideas, then that company will be severely limited in linking both within and throughout alliance networks. Host is a leadership metaphor that tells of a role of encouraging people to openly explore ideas. To candidly, and sometimes doggedly, discuss what is on their mind, in a group, without the fear of threat – difficult?… Yes!… Yet if leaders are actively seen to encourage open dialogue, then frank collective inquiry will eventually emerge and lead to inventive insights. Think about this for a moment. Recall bumping into a colleague in the corridor or by the coffee machine, how often has this kind of happenstance conversation taken you in unexpected, yet positive directions? Now think of a team meeting that went exceptionally well, did it give the same unexpected and positive insights? This is a result of synergy. In contrast, isolated mindsets and knowledge are limited to fractional outcomes. Whereas two or more minds engaged in fruitful dialogue bring together a whole that is not present in any of the individual participants. If open dialogue can be effected on a continuous basis, across the entire enterprise, you will open up a doorway to novel concepts of unlevelled magnitude. It is about networking ideas once again. Intel's chairman, Andrew Grove, says, 'How do we know whether a change signals a strategic inflection point? The only way is through the process of clarification that comes from a broad and intensive debate.' Andrew is Intel's host. Opening up the team talk show on an ongoing basis is central for innovation.

- *Ritual setter.* Shared habits or rituals that point to a correlation between daily events and something much bigger, regular ceremonies that give deeper meaning. Rituals are powerful culture-building tools. Ceremonies that hold tangible symbols and passages, such as innovation tours, team building programmes, performance marathons and reward ceremonies. The point: inventive leaders must design rituals that foster the values of innovation.
- *Referee.* If you wish for your best, most creative, energetic people to leave your organisation, then book 'em every time they are out of step. Your most valuable people will be recalcitrant, even unruly from time to time, it comes with the personality package and is part and parcel of innovation too. Watts Wacker and Jim Taylor tell leaders to study the best NBA referees. If they send off every player for every bump or illegal step, the game would not flow. Learn to call the most important infringements, and the players will sense the scope of possibilities and turn on the creativity jam. I would go further. Even in the face of a full goose company felony, if you see genius in his eyes, promote him. If she cannot get out of bed in the morning, and steals the ball each time she rolls in, her official start time is around noon. Can't do it – then you don't get it!
- *Pace-setter.* In many types of competition, the role of the pace-setter is central, this is in fact a major act for any leader. Pace is set in the visual actions of the leader, the intensity with which s/he carries out rule breaking, hosting spontaneous debates, and dramatising all these. All the leaders of successful enterprises I have met exemplify this. You can capture in a New York nanosecond, the purposeful and positive pace just by walking into their den. No balance sheets, cash-flows or files containing acquisition data; but a room brimming with what the enterprise is about. Products and customer/competition information not filed in a cabinet, but stacked and displayed everywhere to touch. Pictures of company events, with people receiving awards for customer installation of products. Competitors' products torn apart and again displayed for all to see. Not a door into the office, but a gigantic hole with people flooding in and out. Many of the leaders I see do not have an office, they work in the same room as other executives and managers and rove where necessary minute to minute.

Again, all of these protocols are brought to life in the daily actions of the people at the very top. If it does not happen at the top, forget hyperinnovation, and omit all the benefits and advantages that it brings.

Developing a Culture of Multidimensional Leadership

Multidimensional leadership does not stop there. Because in an era when everyone in the company must hyperinnovate, in times when everyone must take on the responsibility for managing a transient career, and in an epoch where the world moves at rapid pace, the topmost initiative for the *n*-leader is to coach yet more leaders through each stage of life-cycle development (as Figure 8.1). Acting out the protocols above, will bring about the general behaviour patterns needed to bring about hyper-innovation. However, as we shall see below, there is a basic set of actualisation skills everyone, without exception, needs to build. Again, all this starts and stops at the top, the executives at the apex must actively nurture and develop a culture of leadership.

For people to take responsibility, and for the average person working on the front line to become engaged, they must have a tangible sense of influence and control over their destiny. And to gain that sense of control on destiny, people, all people, must gain basic leadership skills. Absence of support and development here can lead to wholesale failure. I have seen many a good candidate for project leader or product champion, left out in the cold through lack of training, support and/or coaching, and as a result falling way short of original intent and expectations. So, there are three things the leader atop must do here.

First, everyone must be seen as a potential leader. As the modern maxim goes, *leaders are not born, they are made*, and they can only be made in the first place if the team at the very top recognises this at every level within the organisation. In effect, it must be understood that people often have more to offer in the workplace than are given credit for… Test this if you like: simply ask your people what they do when they are not working for you, the boss?… You will find that the average person has some impressive pursuits or hobbies outside company time. You will find scout leaders, church leaders, community leaders, band leaders, charity leaders, club leaders, sports leaders. You will discover writers, magicians, thespians, pilots, dancers, fine artists, cybernicians, comedians, and so on. All of them committed, creative, loyal, progressive and purposeful. And if they can do all this outside work time, then what are they doing during the time they are working for you? Again, if the leader does not have high expectations for his people, then what games will be played at the front line? So the first act is to recognise that everyone has a leadership potential waiting to be developed.

Second, even though many people pursue great extracurricular adventure outside the workplace, not everyone is cut out or destined for executive office, or great ventures, or even greatness itself. Many people, of course, hold values or a personality that draw them away from such high position. The aim of leading large projects, or winning major contracts, or whatever, is just not in their blood. Yet, at the same time, we all, from time to time, have to put on the hat of leader, whether it is for guiding our children through life, or merely going out to buy a new car. In fact, if you think about it, we are all leaders in our own lives. We are the directors and producers of the ambitions and goals we set. Again, everyone has some level of leadership abilities and needs. So, the second act, then, is to help people build an awareness of their abilities and potential.

Third, and centrally here, innovation *is* about leadership after all, so it requires leadership skills and competence at all levels. Whether it be ownership of a project, or the design of new machine, or the negotiation and purchase of materials, it demands leadership proficiency. Like values development, the enterprise needs to nurture people with the appropriate skills and knowledge in leadership. So the third leadership act, here, is to support a learning programme that lifts people through each life-cycle stage of leadership.

Pre-Stage: Basic Actualisation Skills

Before we begin to address such a learning programme in the next chapter, there is a pre-stage to people and leadership development: the so-called *actualisation* stage in the life cycle (see Figure 8.1). A stage where people begin to orientate for leadership. I have honed down three basic pre-leadership skills that everyone needs to hold, to be effective in this inter-connected, fast-paced world. Skills that begin to *actualise* the traits of self-direction. They include: *self-awareness skills* (knowing what you want), *people skills* (influencing what you want), and *negotiation skills* (getting what you want):

- *Self-awareness skills*. Without knowing what you want in the first place, and then figuring out your strengths and weaknesses, you will be hard pushed to make it past the first-stage, *functional* life cycle (re: Figure 8.1). The inaugural step, here, is to find out what your *goals* are in life so far. List them. Next, ask yourself what you value most in life, what is most important to you? Ask yourself why you are drawn to those values. Actually write down a list of your top five values. If what you thought you wanted (your goals) does not align with what you aspire to (your values), that is a real issue. You need to rethink what you really want out of life. If you do not, you will be working against your true values, against what you think and feel is most important in life. Next, think of what your strengths and weakness are. List your top five weaknesses first… But a warning! This calls for a bit of soul searching. If you have not done this before, it can be a little painful. Be honest… Next, list your strengths, be realistic, what have you consistently been good at over your life thus far? Think long and hard. List your best achievements at each stage of your life. Now ask yourself whether your goals and values are aligned with your strengths and weaknesses. That is, do the things you aspire to at work (or life), sit well with what you are good or bad at? From this you should be able to pick out whether you are merely kidding yourself about your life aims. If your strengths and weaknesses are not aligned with what you're aiming for and value in life, then you have one hell of roadblock in directing your career ambitions or life in general. However, the good news is, if you've been honest here, you should be able to pick out areas for real improvement, or moreover, the values and goals you need to realign. You may even begin to see new possibilities. Everyone needs to think hard, and spend personal development time here. Only until you do all this, can you really begin to move on to the next stage, influencing where you want to go.

- *People skills*. The greatest power is not money, nor knowledge, nor imagination, but *influencing power*. Dealing with people is probably the toughest problem we all face. Even in the most technical roles, such as engineering, only about 20 per cent of success is due to technical abilities; yet 80 per cent of success comes down to people skills, to leading and influencing people. Here is a list of basic influencing skills that can give life-changing results. First, try to see the world from the other person's point of view. No one is really that interested in you (sorry!), but all interested in themselves. So think of what they want, think and feel about the world and the task at hand. Second, if you want to learn what people really want, you have to learn to listen. People often respond to people that listen. At a young age, I went to visit the head of manufacturing at the Jaguar car plant, at Cowley, UK. He said that he could give me an hour, no more. But I ended up staying all day. The reason?… I was on the edge of my seat with enthusiasm, I really wanted to hear what this man had to say (and boy did I learn a thing or two). The lesson: no one is more persuasive than a good listener (I even got in to see some undercover prototypes). Third, respect other people's ideas and views. There is no quicker way to turn people against you, than to trivialise or underappreciate their values and beliefs (even if you think what they say is eyewash). Tolerate, do not criticise or try to give an alternate opinion, even if his ideas wind you up; take a deep breath if she sounds like a bitching cow. If you criticise, or opinionate, turn off they will. Again, show some interest, try to see some good in their ideas, even if it is vanishingly small. Fourth, honest praise. People love to hear a compliment or a cheer, especially if it is well deserved. Do not, whatever you do, make flattering remarks when they are not justified, it only sends out a confused message. Lastly, smile… Now, all this sounds one-sided so far… Right?… Wrong! If you have followed these steps, you have got their undivided attention, and it is time to move on to the next stage, negotiation.

- *Negotiation skills*. These are basic leadership skills needed in all walks of life. There are three key stages to *basic* negotiation: *opening*, *mediation* and *closing*. Opening starts with defining what you want from the situation in quantitative terms, such as time or money or some other tangible deliverable. Then consider what the opponent wants in objective terms. Next, what are *both* parties' limitations, what can you both actually do? Next, what is the *minimum* plausible position you are willing to accept before you walk away from the table?… Mediation begins with asking for more than you expect, after sizing up in the opening stage. Next when an offer is made, flinch, do not accept it. Or if they say no to what you asked for or are willing to give, query what *they* are willing to give or take. If the opponent comes in below your minimum plausible position, tell them you are not in a position to make a decision below that point, that you will have to get back to the big boss. If they are unsure, that is good, as it means you are still in the ballpark. If they offer to split the difference, make the split go your way, ask for 80/20 in your favour. If they have gone this far, that means you are *well* in the game… Closing initiates with making the opponent feel comfortable about the situation (re: above people skills). If they ask for a concession, give it to them, but make it a small one and state it in terms of a tangible gain, such as money or time saved. By now, you have almost got what you want. So now ask for the deal, the moment they say yes, shake their hand, then follow with the agreement in writing in your own words with objective measurable goals (it is a binding contract). Now go out and practise. The shopping mall is a great place to practise negotiation. And that is it, the basics of negotiation.

These three pre-leadership skills must become as second nature in everyone from school leaver to schoolmaster to shop worker to chief executive. Without them there is little chance of moving through the four main stages of development, in turn nurturing a culture of leadership.

Hyperinnovation Leadership

All of this is both an art and a science. An alchemy and a practice. Becoming a multidimensional leader takes insight and application. Of course, some *are* born, we have all met them, but most are made, are developed and nurtured. Even the top cat must continuously grow along each life-cycle stage. So start today – now in fact. Act out and bring to life all the factors above. Begin to ignite a culture of hyperinnovation.

CHAPTER 9

Nurture Multidimensional People

Multidimensional culture also springs from people that gravitate towards a great number of new and diverse thoughts and ideas. These people are not too hard to find; you will, without any doubt, already work among such special types. In many cases it is just a case of collection, nurture and motivation.

Collect Multidimensional People

Teams that create what others do not see, then hit the market at bullet pace, gel a unique character – a mentality that enables interrelation among diverse knowledge, experience and ideas. To lay the foundation of this kind of collaborative psychology, we must continually collect people with *one or a mix* of the following traits:

- *Inquisitive people.* Curiosity is without doubt the most important personality trait, as all that is creative and ultimately innovative, is derived from curiosity. I was often told as a child that curiosity killed the cat, but lack of catlike curiosity most definitely kills innovation. Inquisitive people have a never-ending urge to acquire knowledge and learn new things, they have an infinite desire to pull things apart and analyse, an irresistible addiction to exploration. These types are never satisfied, they will always find new and better ways, because they are always searching, looking, wondering.
- *Optimistic people.* They see positive outcomes and ways through to fruitful ends. Optimists often infuse other people, and this is important. Positive thinking can lead to positive results, setting the virtuous circle of success breeding success. Most of all, optimists receive new ideas

with open arms, and because of this they open up and develop new ideas further.

- *Critical people*. The naysayer or cynic has no place in an innovation team. But cynics are not critical people, critical people are very different, and absolutely belong in an innovation team. Critical people stop to think and weigh the situation, they differentiate between reliable and unreliable information. Critical people do not (less) often jump to conclusions, conclusions that may lead down blind alleys or compound risk.
- *Persistent people*. Pitbulls that dig their teeth in and never let go. If the project is worth doing, they will see it through to the end, come criticism, hell or high water. All high achievers are persistent. No one is born with world-class skills, persistent people hone and polish their skills until they reach the apex, whether it is sport, acting, writing, designing, speaking, or here, innovation. Persistent people overcome uncertainty too, they find a way through to certainty via persistent learning and problem adaptation.
- *Integrative people*. Integrative people think holistically and in several dimensions, fusing ideas from unrelated subjects into idea arenas and cross-related pools, in turn building unique knowledge and creative concepts. This personality trait is key, as more and different problems become multifaceted we need hyperthinkers that can put together equally manifold solutions. Peter Cochrane, BT's former head of research, a man who had an annual budget of £100 million to spend on innovation, says:

  > The true polymath is probably not possible any more. But we do need a few people who are more holistic, who say 'how the heck does this all knit together? When I do this – what are the implications for tax, for health, and so on. How many people are going to be put out of work'... What we look for is a small number of people that can actually cast their eye across the wholeness. And that's a trick. They're not easy to find. When we find one they're a little bit like gold.

- *X-factor people*. That magical, unfathomable X-factor that produces the extraordinary. Look out for people that have done and do amazing, unexplainable things. After all, it is better to have an unfathomable individual producing the extraordinary, than a well-understood individual producing more of the same. So buy 'em, swipe 'em, hook 'em, but get 'em. They are centrally important to a systems innovation team. Do not forget that these people will need ultra-wide scope to do what they do.

They may trip, blip and blunder, but this comes with the territory, only the return is often multifold.

- *Diverse people.* She has backpacked the globe more than once. She has seen real poverty and riches juxtapose, she has panhandled, waited tables and mopped floors. She has partied and played very hard. She has studied very very hard too. She has ideas bleeding out of her ears. She has set-up businesses, they have flopped and she has tried again. She has run corporate or charity or homemade projects. She writes poetry and essays of inspiration. She may read Banks, Pratchett, and maybe the Pixel Juice of Noon, she may enjoy the ideas of Aristotle, Descartes, Marx and Popper, she may ponder the conflict of Hawking and Dyson, the marriage of Dawkins and Dennett, she may be in love with Dostoevsky, Shakespeare or Lawrence, and may devour the text of Prahalad, Porter and Peters. She may walk and talk confidently at all levels, about all subjects, about all things. She may speak more than one tongue, sing more than one song in life, and behave in a culture more than most could know. She may listen to the mix of the Wizard Cox, or the master Rachmaninov's Second. She loves her friends, her family, her significant other. She moves in circles most cannot, do not imagine exist. She is a true innovator in life, and would do even more amazing things in the right team… Do you have any of this in you? Do you see any of this in your peers? What kind of questions are you going ask the next interviewee? Check out their MBA? Or the colour of their shoes?

Notice thus far, no mention of skills, experience or knowledge? Most recruitment drives in the corporate world are now as a matter of fact based on competence and graduate selection; a complete contradiction of what I purport here. Because in a world of mix, the smartest qualified graduates do not always make the cleverest, productive and most creative people (smart does not equal results!). Furthermore, hyperlearning, JIT learning and rapid project cycles destroy conventional learning wisdom. A young man taken on last year has just completed his first electronics project and delivered it to the customer on time. He has had eight different part-time jobs since he left school, he first picked-up a CDI on electronic circuit design eight months ago, and only went on an ECAD course three months ago. He has a wonderfully inquisitive and critical mind, he is just 19 years old – this is the world of mix!

- *Adventurous people.* These types take calculated risks and can handle high levels of ambiguity and uncertainty. They are often ready to venture into the unknown, and sometimes offer leadership qualities when things are not so clear, or not going as expected. The traits to look for here are worldly, well travelled, well read, leathery, battle hardened, scarred storytellers, yet have their feet on the ground and have the track record to prove it.

- *Humorous people.* Whatever you do, collect and cherish people with a sense of humour. Humour is so important for so many reasons. Stress is busted with a joke or a story. Further, studies have shown that when people are humorous they are in passive mode, that is, they are open to other people's views and ideas. Psychologists tell us in fact that humour is the dead opposite of aggression, and that aggressive people rarely take on board other people's thoughts or needs. Just as important, humour is the sign of creativity. Spontaneous wit is the product of an acutely agile creative mind.
- *Playful people.* As I said in Chapter 2, play is centrally important for experimenting with new ways of thinking, and in turn innovation. People who love music, fashions, current affairs, hobbies, and so on, are people who are on the case. They have often set adventurous goals in life, they often take risks and see their ideas through to fruition. Playful people are generally people people, they interact and communicate well. People who work 6 days a week, 9 or 10 hours a day, are good for no one, even in the short term. They give out the wrong messages, and suffer stress burn-out in the longer run. A brain doing the same thing over and over is a dull brain through and through. A high performance brain is a mind engaged in diversity of activities and lifestyles. Some traits to look for are people who play quizzes, enjoy sports, hobbies, have an active social life, partake in charities, fun runs, even run clubs and events.

And how do you discover such people? Photocopy this list, then ask people to grade themselves out of 10 on each trait… Simple… Once you have detected and engaged such characters, it is time to move on to the next stage, the nurture of multidimensional people.

Learning Bank Account

Do you have a *major* learning disability?… Does your company?… Okay then, do you have a *minor* learning disability?… When I ask this question, people – bright people from all walks of life (CEOs, doctors, teachers, engineers, marketers), often react as though I have thrown an insult at them. But I assure you, it is a genuine and mindful enough question. The answer is that we all have learning disabilities to one degree or another, and it is the same for an organisation. The good new is that the disablers and enablers can be identified and addressed. Forewarned is forearmed, after all. Look at these two lists:

Disablers	*Enablers*
Indifference	Interest
Reflex thinking	Critical thinking
Low expectations	High expectations
Low self-esteem	Self-belief
Low value of knowledge	Positive value of knowledge
Not-invented-here syndrome	Sharing ideas/knowledge
Negative attitude	Positive attitude
Routine	Play
Stress	Fun
Solid plans	Evolving prototypes
Secrecy	Dialogue
Bias to orthodoxy	Unorthodox
Dogma	Necessity
Autocracy	Want
Generalisations	Inquisitiveness
Assumptions	Counterintuition
Conditioning	Uncommonsense
Paradigms	Contradigms

Notice, yet again, no mention of intelligence or academic credentials. Businesses with legions of bright, highly qualified people, often behave and act quite dumb, for reasons the list above clearly shows. Yet, innovative companies, with stimulating cultures, with quite ordinary people, can achieve extraordinary intellectual and contextual breakthroughs when they embrace and develop the learning enablers.

Whether a learning bank account is in the red with regard to the enablers or not, people's values either help or greatly hinder. So values development in Chapter 8 have great favour here. However, the learning strategies themselves equally limit or empower the above enablers. In the case here, the learning strategy of *discovery*.

Learning as Discovery

The lowest, crudest strategy for learning, is learning that is imparted to the would-be student. Learning that is done to the pupil, learning that is drilled and forced upon the apprentice. In other words, *I tell, you listen, and if you don't like it, well, that's just tough*. And this is the main way people learn by today – learning as instruction (and now we know why some children simply turn off in school, and why our corporate peers nod off during strategic management seminars). Of course, there are many forms of, and theories to, learning. But there is a form of learning that is ultra-powerful and wholly germane to hyperinnovation: *learning as discovery*. And I cannot emphasise the significance of learning as discovery enough. Essentially, learning as discovery is about the empowerment of human minds, to learn spontaneously, independently and collaboratively, without coercion. The emphasis is on learning as action that is done by, not to, the student. Learning in which the student – the consumer of knowledge – owns the learning goals, processes and outcomes… Why?

First, for all the reasons exposed in the first section (paradox, unpredictable breakthrough context, rapid change, and all the rest), as scary as this sounds, there is now no one at the top that knows all, sees all, controls all. The world moves on too quickly for any deterministic mindset. Yes, we have insightful multidimensional leaders (as above), but even these wise ones are just as vulnerable to discontinuities as the rest of us. Second, learning as discovery is empowerment of the individual. And only with such empowerment will people have the capacity to thrive on paradox. Third, when people get that feeling of empowerment, grade 'A' level learning is obtainable by everyone – EVERYONE. And fourth, we have no choice here, because multidimensional knowledge and ideas are the raw material of hyperinnovation. So, it is absolutely crucial to encourage people to design their own learning strategies (knowledge, skills, thinking) as a mindset of *discovery*.

In the cultural context, and barring the technological enablers themselves (see Chapter 14), there are nine practical steps that can be applied to learning as discovery:

- *Multidimensional learning*. Coalescing a variety of knowledge bases and concepts from narrow subjects and disciplines into synthesised arenas and cross-related pools. In the real world, more and different problems need a network knowledge approach. As processes and outcome become more interrelated with other processes and outcome, we need people that can break down the lines and borders of knowledge into broad interconnected wholes. Core subjects still abound, but they are evolving at warp speed. The goal is to become hyperskilled, hyperknowledged: so an engineer need not only be studious in electronics, software and mechanics, but also become a businessman, an ecologist, a behavioural psychologist, a biologist, a chemist and physicist, all at once. A nurse, a competent medical technician, a counsellor, a social worker, a communication specialist, a computer technician, at one and the same time. And this does not mean the advent of generalists. No. The development of multidimensionalists. Furthermore, expanding towards the multidimensional in terms of knowledge and skill should not give rise to the problem of stress burn-out. What causes stress is *lack* of management support, learning productivity tools, and continuous training.

- *Just-in-time learning*. Multimedia tools and internet works enable information to be brought in, as and when, to anywhere. There is little point in spending a year in a class that teaches stuff that is out of date before it sinks in, or is available at the click of a cursor. The reality is, if you have the technology, you are seconds away from more knowledge than you could possibly absorb in a thousand lifetimes. The reality is, the world outside is changing so fast, that the only effective way to learn, is to learn the stuff you need just in time.

- *Lifetime learning*. And because the world is in constant flow, it is an imperative that we continually reskill, re-equip, rethink, redesign ourselves (a) to the tune of the demands that arise day to day, and (b) to get ahead and innovate in interconnected expanses. Because a central reality is that the realities of the next decade do not exist yet, so much of the information, knowledge and skills needed over the next 10 years do not exist yet either – they have not been invented or discovered yet. This is central, because cumulative learning drives innovation.

- *Custom learning*. Learning tailored to the interests, ambitions and direct needs of individuals and teams. Wisdom people truly relish, the team truly craves to know; since the impact on both immediate projects and future personal growth is apparent. Learning concepts and tools like edutainment, accelerated visual thinking, real-time feedback learning, knowledge network mapping, and virtual group learning are now considered very credible custom-learning methodologies.

- *Application skills*. Learning to leverage knowledge, to transfer ideas to positive ends, learning to multiply value. Becoming solutions orientated, opportunity primed, focused on outcomes rather than processes, becoming a multicultural negotiator in a global world of ideas. Learning how to seek, research and reach decision makers. First commercial, social, political, community projects must begin day one: get it in the blood.

- *Self-direction and motivation*. Professor Howard Gardner of the Harvard Graduate School of Education makes clear that the future of learning will be people bundled into self-directed 'apprenticeships, projects and technologies'. The responsibility of learning needs to be put into the hands of the individual. If knowledge is rapidly becoming ubiquitous, if information is flooding in all directions, then the first block on the road ahead, is a personal one. So people must own and drive their learning, design their own apprenticeships, seek their own projects, find the relevant mentors, and build the relevant technological competency. Further, the learner must take responsibility and measure their own performance, without this there is no ownership, and without ownership there is limited responsibility and interest.
- *Collaborative learning*. Learning as part of a group mind, to access a diversity of views and build knowledge impossible in isolation. The real world is chock-a-block with increasingly complex problems and processes that only high performance teams can solve and fulfil. Further, group learning facilitates network learning, which in turn gives compound learning. As knowledge is connected to a network in sequences, learning within the group grows exponentially.
- *Whole learning*. Building skills and knowledge that develop the whole individual, in terms of both analytical and logical reasoning, practical problem solving, creative and conceptual thinking, concept generation and manipulation, and just as important, the social and communication skills that realise all of these in the real world. All innovation is a multi-discipline process; we need people rounded and diverse in skills that go far beyond the narrow function.
- *Co-learning facilitator*. The role of leader does not disappear. The tools and principles do not deskill either. It means a transformation from custodian and purveyor of direction and knowledge, towards motivator, knowledge sherpa and co-learner. To coach how to search, build and manipulate information, and how to create new ideas to develop a reasonable quality of life in a world of increasing change and chance and interconnection. To nurture and support an atmosphere and culture of learning. Equally, to show how to be selective in focus and relevance, in a time where information comes in from all directions in massive volume and speed. This is vitally important, in a world of mix. Co-learning facilitator is yet another facet of leadership.

These nine strategies are just the beginning of a journey on the road to *discovery*. Yet are the most effective and beneficial, giving immediate returns. The great news is, once on the road of discovery, there is no stopping people. People that perhaps for years have had little or no interest in learning, people that in the past may have been told they are quite limited. Yet once engaged in a self-driven discovery programme, they open and broaden their minds to unlevelled heights. In fact, and I have witnessed this time and time again, you will find exceptionally gifted people, that without such a learning strategy would never have been exposed to all the wonderment and empowerment that comes with such a process of discovery.

Motivating Multidimensional People

High motivation, or otherwise, is another integral consequence of the culture that flows around your people. Here, I begin to highlight some of the motivational forces and factors that further kindle a culture of diverse ideas and collaboration:

- *Constantly expand world-views*. Shorter project cycles allow experience of more and different worlds, in less time. Expose your people to roles outside their usual fold. A production engineer to write a marketing plan, a sales assistant supporting a stock control improvement programme. Send your people out into the real world: exhibitions, conferences, customers, direct and indirect competition, looking for the most innovative practices, latest tools and technologies, and so on. Further, send people on a sabbatical after a long stint in a role. Encourage and support lifetime learning. Narrow perceptions and judgement are born of long stints and lack of real-world learning. Expanded world-views, even in steady-state roles, stimulate new ideas.
- *Set skyrocket learning goals and expectations*. Again, if leaders do not have high expectations, then what hope at the coal face? Encourage, inspire people to seek the best and most innovative organisations and people relevant in their field. Ask them to benchmark the best standard, then (1) beat that best standard, (2) come up with something completely different that will supersede the best standard. Remember, to be the best today, a firm has to be sustainably different. And only by constantly challenging the standard will your people effect any real distinctions.
- *Believe and let go*. Success, in anything, depends on the extent to whether people care or not. But much more than that, if you want great

people, then you had better let them be great. Constantly expanding world-views and skyrocket learning are part of the answer; the other part, I think, can be a little more difficult: true, uncompromising belief in your people. The reason being, faith in people enables the leader to truly let go, and in turn, opens the gateway to wide creative space. It allows people to learn and grow in ways that best suit them, enables them to toy and experiment with their own notions, and in the longer term, builds unlevelled confidence in their own abilities – and yes – ignites their greatness.

- *Stimulate interest through ownership of outcomes.* There are of course as many theories on the motivation of man as there are on any other subject in culture building. But just put them to one side for a moment; ask yourself this question: 'What is the common thread that's present when you excel at anything?' – I bet it is the so-called *interest* factor! Your finest subjects at school, your hobbies and your best work have all stemmed from the fact that you were keenly interested. And this is a secret key to high performance. People get interested in projects or particular knowledge if they can relate to the *outcome*, so ownership is key here. Ownership of end-results and outcomes feeds self-esteem (I did that!).
- *Effective reward systems.* In all societies, what is honoured, whatever is recognised, whatever is rewarded, is – as a rule – practised! This is another well-understood factor in culture building and motivation. Reward is simply a behaviour shaper. Reward for collaboration, and that is the result you will obtain. But I have found that most organisations build reward systems completely *back to front* in terms of motivation (especially when it comes to innovation), and in doing so, miss the point of the whole exercise. Here, all too often, the perception held by management is that *money and promotion* are the keys to motivation. A misunderstanding and missed opportunity of the first order. Because, in reality, people's emotional and motivational needs are much more immediate. People, we all know, are fickle creatures, and therefore are not sustainably motivated by longer term incentives, such as money. Yes, a pay increase will boost motivation, but it will not last for long. What people *need* most, is to be *appreciated*, given *attention*, and feel *involved* in what they are doing. And they need to *feel* this *on the spot*, without delay. The keys here, are to: appreciate through immediate recognition via tangible rewards; involve with full ownership of outcomes; and attention by simply listening to and supporting their wishes, concerns and accomplishments. Do this and you will set up a powerful motivation system. And to top all of this, the cost of doing this is shadowed in the benefits.

- *Reward for collaboration.* It is centrally important to give *team-based* rewards, as this supports the collaborative behaviour of knowledge sharing, relationships building, idea interconnections, cross-discipline problem solving, and so on. To do this, team rewards must be greater (perceived or otherwise) than the rewards for individual performance. Examples are: tie a major prize to an important team objective being completed on time, or a reward for a team-generated product concept. Without superior team-based rewards, collaborative efforts will be limited, and sometimes stopped dead.

- *Tangible symbols.* As above, recognition does not have to be in the form of financial reward or promotion. The most innovative schemes are relatively cheap, sometimes free. Contradictory to popular belief, a reward can be as easy and as cheap as a thank you note. TGI Friday, the international service excellence restaurant chain, reach unprecedented levels of real-time innovation and service responsiveness. TGI have a well-developed performance reward system. Money is part of it. But it is the recognition programme that motivates TGI's fast-paced innovative service culture. They have a hierarchy of tin badges. But these little pieces of metal mean more to the TGI people than any of the other TGI rewards. Debora Abbot told me: 'When I got my service excellence award, I was so thrilled. It meant that I was the best at what I did. It means more to me than anything…' The point is, do not get obsessed with the superficial badge issue. The badge is only a badge. It is the symbolism that is important, because it shouts 'I've been recognised for my efforts', this is the special magic that turns people on. The point is, it does not have to cost much. Be creative. Here are some ideas:

- *Reward ideas.* We had an amazing/crazy/winning idea cup, tee-shirt. We got to market in half the time printed on a tee shirt. We are 100% customer satisfiers. Certificate in demandplex analysis. Bachelor of Swarm Work. Master of Swarm Work. Member of the Time-to-Market Gold Circle. A day off, a week off, a meal out for all the family/team. Shopping vouchers. The boss cleans your car or paints your house. Cinema/theatre tickets (who does not enjoy a good night out at the cinema or theatre?). Fill up the car with petrol… Get the idea? Small innovative rewards spread equally among the team can be just as effective as larger rewards. It is the recognition that is the point. And why not ask the person closest to the job, they will already know what the standards are and what reward they would like.

- *Reward hints*. Rewards are often best given and repeated in lots of smaller doses. They are just as effective as big rewards (again, it is the recognition that counts). As above, immediacy is important, so reward within hours of recognition, this makes the reward more tangible to the action. Constant feedback on performance is also a must. There is a need to set up clear channels that communicate performance measurement. All of this goes hand in hand with the real up-to-date numbers for all of the above issues being readily available, that is, posted in the local area. Without this it does not work. So get the numbers out of the file and on to the wall.

Weave together these nine key motivational factors, and you'll set off a powerhouse of action. Because what people want, deep down, it seems, is to be appreciated, recognised, just plain given a chance to exceed. And they will rise to it all right. I have used these key factors again and again, in some of the utmost complex, turbulent innovation projects you could imagine. And the most gratifying thing of all, is that people are up for more. They come back for more, because once they actualise and engage, they never want to go back to the old ways of *I tell, you jump*.

The Hyperinnovation Culture

Culture, culture, you have a culture, after all!... And if we can actualise this, then, as I said at the beginning of this part: *whoosh, an endless stream of n-innovation...* All of this is the softest-of-soft issues, yet turns out to be the most potent, and in the end, tangible of all leadership systems. Designing a high concept vision of the future to give meaning, certitude and strategic direction for people is a major part of it. The values they build and hold are the glue to it. The leadership patterns and traits make it come alive. And the nurturing of multidimensional people make it all begin to happen. But all this takes conviction, and in the end, courage. As a hyperinnovation culture is not some easy-to-reach destination in time, it is a never-ending, often frightening, yet exciting journey of learning and discovery. A learning and discovery of hyperinnovation.

PART III

Hyperinnovation Organisation

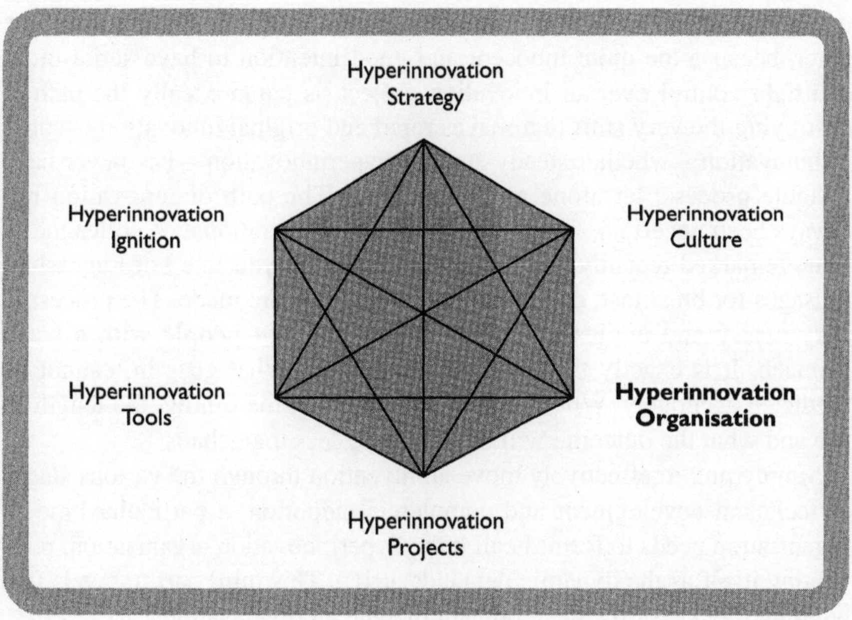

> Intelligent control appears as uncontrol or freedom. And for that reason it is intelligent control. Unintelligent control appears as external domination. And for that reason it is really unintelligent control. Intelligent control exerts influence without appearing to do so. Unintelligent control tries to influence by making a show of force.
>
> LOA TZU, 600 BC

Arthur Andersen, in one of their many investigations into the subject of innovation, concluded: *if a potential innovation is managed and organised in the very same way as a mainstream operation, then that innovation may remain only as potential.* But this conclusion has a much deeper consequence, inasmuch as it is counterintuitive. It goes against the hardened grain of traditional management style and organisation. In the traditional sense, the main way to manage innovation runs via a highly disciplined 'A-to-B' process – as one organisation I now know well gave away. On reading their message in a recruitment advert: 'We require a systems development manager to oversee our "well disciplined" design process', I could not but resist digging a little deeper. Turns out they fired the last manager because he could never get anything out the door. But was it the manager, or the 'well-disciplined design process?' My money is on the latter, because the quite innocent and good intention to have serial order and tight control over an innovation project, is paradoxically the path to destroying the very stuff that makes rapid and original innovation occur.

Innovation – whether steady-state or hyperinnovation – has never been a stable process, let alone an ordered one. The path of innovation has always been uncertain, full of the capricious and irrational. A colleague of mine remarked recently, with tongue in cheek, if you like hot Lancashire sausages for breakfast, do not be there when they are made. The process is very messy and unpleasant, and certainly not for people with a weak stomach. It is exactly the same for innovation. What goes in, cannot be predicted accurately. What resources are needed, the timing, the length of use and what the outcome will be is nothing less than chaos.

Simply put: to effectively move an invention through the various stages of technical development and commercial adoption, a particular kind of organisation needs to form: I call it the hyperinnovation organisation, reinventing itself as the dynamic demands arrive. This third part unravels five building blocks for the development of such an organisation.

Chapter 10 – Complexity, Innovation and Organisation: As we have already begun to explore, interconnected innovation is an activity where the dynamics of complexity play major influence. The result is that traditional top-down, linear organisation cannot possibly meet the often chaotic and unpredictable factors of hyperinnovation. Some of the reasons for and antidotes to this are outlined.

Chapter 11 – SwarmNets and Emergent Teams: To meet the many uncertain challenges of innovation, we can capitalise on yet more practical principles emerging from the sciences of complexity to build an agile, holistic, acutely intelligent organisation.

Chapter 12 – Project Hosting and Whole Team Building: With a facilitator-like style, leading teams towards intended results, it is possible to apply so-called systems *thinking* to build *holistic* teams.

Chapter 13 – Warehouse of Innovation: The design of physical, *fit-for-purpose* working environments that enhance multidimensional thinking, team collaboration, and quickens innovation per se.

Chapter 14 – Hypermachines: Emerging information and communications technologies, ranging from idea leverage tools, collaborative technologies, team interfaces, and virtual reality simulation tools, are enabling leaps and bounds in innovation productivity. Here, I outline a basic functional model for such hypermachines.

What you are about to discover is very different from that of the linear set. Interconnected organisations are distinct in a great many ways. Not least in their pace and collaborative nature. All told, a hyperinnovation organisation is the smartest, most responsive order yet devised for innovation. Enabling the management of the unexpected found in complex and innovative projects.

CHAPTER 10

Complexity, Innovation and Organisation

For most, the 'gap' between a seed idea and a full-blown market is more likely to resemble a canyon. Converting nebulous concepts into commercial successes sometimes takes on the appearance of the unmanageable, and some say it is best left that way. For innovation is just about the most slippery, unpredictable, chaotic process I know. For the new is not familiar, it is strange, it is about going beyond convention, current experience and best knowledge.

I have met some of the finest systems innovators – individuals, firms and alliance networks – in the world; people and organisations that have achieved sky rocket results. But even these giants succumb to the same laws as us mortals. I have seen the best at work, developing something quite similar to which they have accomplished 99 times before, with great success. Only to find that the one-hundredth time, with that little insignificant connection, bringing the whole thing crashing, melting, collapsing and blowing up in the lab; or ageing, decaying and gathering dust on the shelf… Hence, it is perhaps with little surprise that we can begin to see the dynamics of so-called *chaos*.

Butterfly Effect

Chaos theory attempts to explain the kind of dynamic systems that have overall global order, but are grossly unpredictable in detail. It is ultimately a study of uncertainty. When one thinks of chaos, it is of pictures of turbulence, of randomness and anarchy; and these ideas would not be so far off the mark. Yet chaos has a centrally important role in innovation and its organisation. One of the driving forces of chaos is something known as *sensitivity dependence on initial conditions*, often called the *butterfly effect*. The notion that the most subtle and delicate events like a butterfly flapping its wings in the Amazon rainforest (tiny input) can start a growing chain of events that cause an eventual typhoon in the South China seas (massive output). The butterfly effect begins to tell of the secrets of how simple, subtle events can ignite a cascade of discontinuous, disproportionate and unpredictable change on a quite gigantic scale.

The Butterfly Flaps at Rationality

There is a story I was told as a child. The tale of a wise man and a king. The allegory ended with the king asking the wise man to suggest a reward for the sacrifice the wise man had endured. The wise man gave the king a simple request: only that he would like to have a chessboard full of rice, beginning with one grain on the first square, two on the second, four on third, eight on the fourth and so on and so on, doubling each time until the last square. The king agreed to such a modest request and clapped his hands and the wish was the king's command. The storyteller, a teacher of mine at an infant school, then told of the king's error. That by the time the last square had been reached, there would be enough rice to cover the whole of India, two feet deep (10 million trillion grains of rice in fact). I was amazed. But at the age of seven, I was unaware that I had just had my first lesson in a fundamental principle of chaos: *exponential growth*. This is of course our tiny, but powerful friend the *butterfly effect* flapping its wings again.

To help explain the uncompromising impact of butterfly chaos on innovation and organisation, we can use a well-known experiment. Let us look at the common or garden snooker table (Figure 10.1). If we place, for example, five snooker balls in line, equispaced at 500 millimetres, what is the probability of the fourth ball hitting the fifth, if the cue ball hits the first object ball? At first, this would seem like a simple problem. But in fact we have a highly chaotic exponential grain of rice growth situation in front of us: the first ball has 10 variables to contend with, even with the omitted variables of kinetic energy, mass, friction and elasticity. The 10 variables are: the direction of the ball, variables 1 and 2; the speed, variables 3 and 4; the axis of rotation, variables 5 and 6; 7 and 8 the speed of rotation of the ball along its axis; 9, the diameter of the ball and 10, the inclined angle to the tangent of the second object ball. The same goes for the second, third, fourth and fifth snooker balls. By the time the fourth ball hits the

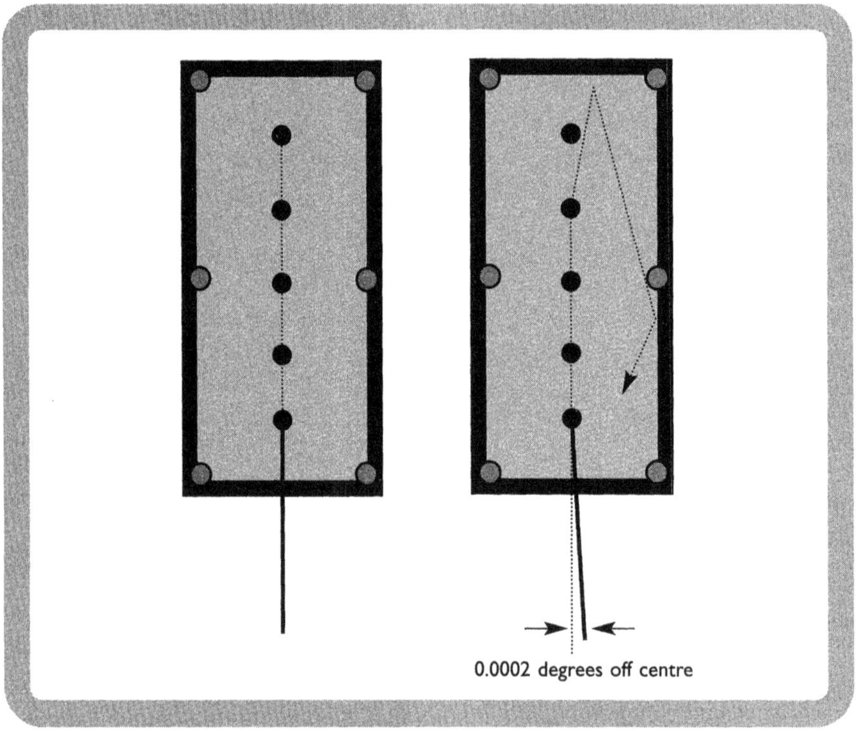

Figure 10.1 Butterfly effect of a snooker table

fifth, 40 variables would have to be contended with. But in fact, because any one of those variables can change, there are a possible 100,000 variable combinations by the time the fifth ball rolls off.

If the first ball hits the second ball only fractionally off centre, the error will grow rapidly, as each ball knocks on into the next. As the picture shows, just a slight change in one of the potential variables can exponentially cascade down the system and induce enormous changes in outcome. The further the balls are spaced, the more chance the error has to grow. This is the fundamental principle of a chaotic system. In fact, in the real world, the probability of the fourth ball hitting the fifth as intended, is a probability close to zero. *The main point here is this: like the grains of rice on the chessboard doubling up to an inordinate number within an extremely short sequence, errors within a complex system can compound to surprising and disproportionate changes in outcome, within a relatively short span.*

The reason for not commonly noting this sensitive sequence as it really is, is because we delude ourselves that the real world is rational. Made of exacts, axioms, real things; and for sure, anyone can say, 'there are five snooker balls on the table in a straight line'. But in actual fact all that we have rationalised (snooker balls) is made up of imperfect objects, events and especially concepts: size, shape, colour, position, velocity, mass, and so on, are not rational entities of whole numbers. Recall Bart Kosko's description of fuzzy systems in Chapter 2. 'No one has ever seen a circle… We have only seen approximations, imperfect greys instead of perfect black and whites. Zoom in close enough and you will see imperfection in the drawing… or assembly of subatomic particles.' In reality, the precision ground and polished snooker balls are really wobbly, uneven, fuzzy geometric shapes.

Initial Conditions Uncertainty Principle

If an infinitesimal error in input or slight difference in starting position, say 0.0002 mm, can exponentially cascade, even within a short space, into dramatic changes in output; and at the same time we can never know these irrational numbers (or errors) because they are so many and so small, we can never know enough about *state one* to predict accurately *state two*, and if we cannot predict state two, heaven knows what the outcome of state-*n* is going to be. Since we can never know the true value of any variable, we can never know the exact initial condition, and never predict accurately any outcome within a system. This is known as an uncertainty principle. We cannot know the precise input at any given time, therefore any outcome is ultimately uncertain. This is why the weather, traffic jams, a rapid river, the stock exchange, and the case here, *n*-innovation, are uncertain events. We can never know enough about the initial conditions to predict a for certain outcome.

It does not take too much reasoning to appreciate why innovations appear from obscure origins, why most innovations fall within the near success/failure curve, and why the path to market is one hell of a slippery mess. It is centrally because all innovation is subject to the dynamics of chaos. Sure we can demand outcomes and results (as I will explain), but who, what, when, where and how is not precisely knowable until it happens. One event (decision, experiment, new information, error, whatever) can completely change the next sequence of tasks. At its lowest level, just a simple change in detail on a component or technical specification or management process can set off an exponential growth sequence of (unpredicted) events. It of course may not, but the probability is that it will.

Butterfly Wings in Innovation Projects

I recall, during one particular complex systems development project, a simple feature on a prototype component acting as a thermal conductor. Extensive laboratory experiments gave lists of empirical data, that told that the *feature* was of the right proportions to dissipate the required amount of heat energy; and that it would operate precisely within the material's continuous running temperature limits. Months later, the manufactured component arrived, and was assembled for final testing… Guess what?… The thing melted like chocolate!… So, the feature needed to increase in size, and a higher continuous running temperature material needed to be specified. This was the simple initial condition that set off the cascade of events below:

I sent an e-mail to the purchasing department and told them the news. In turn, they rang the component supplier, who in turn contacted the tool designer, who then hailed the tool maker. The design engineer modified his engineering drawing, and zapped the new specifications to the purchasing department and component supplier. But the supplier called the next day and told me they did not deal with the specific material, and besides, the new size wall thickness may produce sinks in the component. 'No!' I said. 'The component has aesthetic restraints and needs to have an even surface finish.' So it was back to square one! The scenario then grew and grew, all because of one simple change. Weeks later, via a convoluted exercise involving a dozen people, the problem was solved. But you may say that I was a poor engineer (maybe), or that the supplier would not cooperate (not likely), and so on. But it is nothing to do with that. Systems innovation is chaotic and uncertain – period! This happens all of the time, everywhere in complex innovation. It is just that the best innovators expect and accept this fact, and design an organisation that can thrive on paradox.

The Unexpected: A Second Principle of Hyperinnovation

Clearly, the greater the complexity a particular innovation project exhibits, the greater the number of potential initial conditions, the more uncertain that innovation becomes, in turn, the greater potential for the *unexpected* (for want of a nail, and all that)… Surprise (as Chapter 1) is a natural consequence of the complex and chaotic, and it is a fact of life that the unexpected should be expected, and not brushed under the carpet. In short, the greater the complexity and/or novelty embedded within a given innovation, the greater the frequency of the unexpected. From this, we find a *second principle of hyperinnovation*:

$$\lambda\psi \propto \Delta Y$$

Frequency of the unexpected ($\lambda\psi$) *is proportional to uncertainty* (ΔY). Organisations need to be designed not just to live on, but take advantage of, the chaotic. The unexpected does not necessarily mean doom and gloom, it can often mean an advancement and opportunity. But it really depends on whether you can take advantage of it.

Emergence

For reasons above and beyond, I have hit my head against the restrictive and retarded functional hierarchy. I knew deep down that there must be a smarter, simpler way to organise for innovation. Not just cope, but take advantage of the capacious, the fuzzy, the unprincipled and uncertain. But like most things in life, my inspirations for a solution to such a quandary, came literally from out of the blue: the behaviour of swarming birds!

Saunter along the seafront promenade that connects my home city of Brighton and Hove in the early autumn evenings, and you will not help but be almost hypnotised by the multiple flocks of starlings swarming above the West Pier. Hundreds of thousands of them flying in unison. It's an awesome sight. Not just the scale of the roller-coasting translucent black mass, but the split-second, pinpoint synchronous flow of the flock. For many years now I have wondered how this could be. How can such a network made up of bird-brained autonomous units, work with such agility, such speed and accuracy?

Here, once again, the science of *complexity* begins to explain how such networks of very large numbers of simple entities, behave in surprising, frequently paradoxical ways. What *emerges* from a complex network of quite simple entities (masses of atoms, swarms of ants, teams of people), is often quite profound. From M. Mitchell Waldrop's must-read book *Complexity*:

> Take water, for example. There's nothing very complicated about a water molecule: it's just one big Oxygen atom with two little Hydrogen atoms stuck to it like Mickey Mouse ears. Its behaviour is governed by well-understood equations of atomic physics. But now put a few zillion of those molecules together in the same pot. Suddenly you've got substance that shimmers and gurgles and

> sloshes. Those zillions of molecules have collectively acquired, liquidity, that none of them possesses alone. In fact, unless you know precisely where and how to look for it, there's nothing in those well-understood equations of atomic physics that even hint at such a property. The liquidity is 'emergent'.

Kelvin Kelly explains further in his paradigm-smashing book, *Out of Control*. Kelly wrote:

> It has long been appreciated by science that large numbers behave differently than small numbers. Mobs breed a requisite measures of complexity for emergent entities. The total number of possible interactions between two or more members accumulates exponentially as the number of members increases. At a high level of connectivity, and a high number of members, the dynamics of mobs takes hold. More is different.

Kelly's point? The interaction of greater numbers produces a nonlinear reaction that compounds exponentially. This is a fundamental secret behind why birds can move in synchronous unison, with such speed and agility. We have evidence of this through the work of zoologists. Zoologists have used high-speed digital camera technology to capture flocks of birds in an attempt to understand how this kind of synchronous dynamic occurs. At around 600 frames a second, something quite amazing is captured. When 600/s frames are viewed at around 20/s, it can be seen that the wave motion through the flock is faster than the movement of any one single bird! The whole (flock) reaction time is faster (greater) than the sum of the individual birds! You've got synergism! You've got our friend the butterfly effect doubling up grains of rice on the chessboard again. But further, scientists have now simulated this in computer systems. What has surprised the zoologists (and me for sure) is that whenever they look at the complexity on the computer screen, the basic rules are fundamentally simple – complexity emerges from the many interactions – the complexity is in the organisation, not the rules. Craig Reynolds, a computer scientist at Symbolics began to uncover this phenomenon. He has designed a program that simulates autonomous, bird-like agents – which he calls 'boids'. On running the program, the boids instantaneously flood the computer screen and begin to flow in a dynamic, realistic looking flock… So what?… Well, the hub of all this is buried in the fact that Reynolds' computer program contains only three local, very simple rules: *(1) Match the speed of the neighbouring boids. (2) Move towards the centre of the mass of boids. (3) Maintain a minimum distance from other boids and objects.*

M. Mitchell Waldrop eloquently writes about the Craig Reynolds simulation:

> What was striking about these rules was that none of them said, 'Form a flock'. Quite the opposite: the rules were entirely local, referring only to what an individual boid could see and do in its own vicinity. If a flock was going to form at all, it would have to do so from the bottom-up, as an emergent phenomenon. And yet flocks did form, every time. Reynolds could start his simulation with boids scattered around the computer screen completely at random, and they would spontaneously collect themselves into a flock that could fly around obstacles in a very fluid and natural manner. Sometimes the flock would even break into subflocks that flowed around both sides of an obstacle, rejoin on the other side as if the boids had planned it all along. In one of the runs, in fact, a boid accidentally hit a pole, fluttered around for a moment as though stunned and lost – then darted forward to rejoin the flock as it moved on.

From these kinds of computer simulation of complex systems, scientists have found that complex patterns and behaviour do not have to come from a composite of rules. In fact, profound emergent effects – from intricate self-replicating patterns of snowflakes to the cognition of a mind – propagate from fundamentally simple elements, acting under a very simple number of rules. Waldrop again:

> Instead of writing global, top-down specifications for how the flock should behave, or telling his creatures to follow the lead of one Boss Boid, Reynolds had used only the three simple rules of local, boid-to-boid interaction. And it was precisely that locality that allowed his flock to adapt to changing conditions so organically… 'Try doing that with a single set of top-level rules… The systems would be impossibly cumbersome and complicated, with the rules telling each boid precisely what to do in every conceivable situation.' In fact, he had seen simulations like that; they usually ended up looking jerky and unnatural, more like an animated cartoon than like animated life.

Again, less and open rules is more(ness), vague and general is high resolution. Kevin Kelly adds to this:

> There are two ways to structure 'moreness'. At one extreme, you can construct a system as a long string of sequential operations, such as we do in a meandering factory assembly line. The internal logic of a clock as it measures off time by a complicated parade of movements is the archetype of a sequential system. Most mechanical systems follow the clock. At the other far extreme, we find

many systems ordered as a patchwork (network) of parallel operations. Very much as in the neural network of a brain or in a colony of ants. Action in these systems proceeds in a messy cascade of interdependent events. Instead of the discrete ticks of cause and effect that run a clock, a thousand clock springs try to simultaneously run a parallel system. Since there is no chain of command the particular action of any single spring [individual] diffuses into the whole, making it easier for the sum of the whole [network] to overwhelm the parts of the whole [network]. What emerges from the collective is not a series of critical actions but a multitude of simultaneous actions whose collective pattern is far more important. It is the swarm model.

The Net Works

While walking along Brighton beach one Sunday afternoon, an enormous flock was in full flow. Like a scene from a Hitchcock thriller, just as if they had been waiting, they took off from the quarter-mile-long perch in a vertical direction, peaked at about 1000 feet, then spiralled down towards me. What I saw outperformed any pyrotechnic display... My mind began to wonder? It occurred to me that the uncertain nature of innovation requires a match-for-match system of organisation, not unlike what was swarming above my head that day. I began to make notes of why this is the case:

- *Uncertainty.* Hyperlinked systems are indifferent to uncertainties. They can build bridges across canyons of uncertainty, even though the other side is nowhere in sight. Lack of information, knowledge or people does not stop the show, the system at large fills in the gap real time, (without) a centre to command and control. Complex systems are instantaneously self-rectifying once they are up and running.
- *Interconnectionism.* As complexity in product, service and process innovation cross-connect and compound, nonlinear adaptive systems build ever more robust foundations for managing this very growth. Multi-dimensional innovations line up nose to nose with complex adaptive organisational systems. Varied and compounded cross-functions and components in product or service innovations mate directly with complex nonlinear orientation of people and resources. Linear (clock-ware) systems cannot deliver multiple parallel solutions to complex products that need cross-discipline answers.

- *Novelty*. Unusual and unique situations and problems need unusual and unique organisations and solutions. Top-down linear organisations are crusty, homogenous, limiting regimes. Novelty is stamped out, rather than seen as an opportunity. Hyperlinked systems embrace novelty, and cannot help but build on from the unusual and the unique. Further, complex systems are the lap of innovation and creativity, they are always unfolding, reconnecting, exploring new creative spaces.
- *Knowledge*. Top-down, functional organisations stop knowledge generation in its track, and innovation with it. Nonlinear nexus of minds interlocked in unique and unusual ways generate and build unique and unusual knowledge.
- *Scale*. As current and future products and services reach unlevelled magnitude, bottom-up self-organising systems swarm around the parts that other traditional approaches cannot possibly reach. Small and simple steady-state inventions can live with simple and very slow top-down linear hierarchies. Big multidimensional innovations need lifelike and uniquely adaptive structures to: (1) keep the number of agents down, (2) bear the innovation's weight over less agents, and (3) move fast to cope with massive project inertia (big projects do not budge that easily).
- *Unexpected*. Complex systems are not shocked or stopped that easily. Unplanned tasks do not have to wait in line, they are jumped upon as and when they arrive. Highly novel and complex innovations contain a constant stream of the unexpected. Linear organisations freeze when something unexpected emerges (for example the problem-solving meeting has to be arranged). Messy, nonlinear organisations heat up into action (for example the problem is solved there and then). Self-organisation is rife even under the conditions of surprise.
- *Rate of change*. Complex adaptive systems absorb runaway trains. Changes in specification, explosions in the lab, customers moving the goalposts or plain dumb errors, do not start a runaway cascade of unplanned tasks. Initial conditions are caught in the network, before they magnify.
- *Self-organisation*. Hyperlinked systems facilitate self-organisation among agents, whether molecules in a tissue or people in a network. Consequently, interconnected organisations set up a simple closed-loop feedback system of information, which builds and energises emergent self-organising teams.

- *Prediction.* High levels of learning and adaptation allow a keen sense of smell for what is around the corner. Multiple interactions of people – that linear systems stop – allow cross-fertilisation of knowledge and experience. Collective minds outdo any one individual. A collective sixth sense soon develops. Reaction soon turns to action.
- *Speed.* Problems are solved, decisions are made, actions are taken, results are achieved faster than any one or a group of functions can muster. Complex adaptive systems break the increasing complexity/shorter-cycle paradox, by facilitating an exponential growth cascade. The flock flows faster than any one agent. Integrated and multiple parallel activities accelerate the process and deliver complexifying innovation in less time.

CHAPTER 11

SwarmNets and Emergent Teams

So what do we have?...

1. All innovation is inherently chaotic, and therefore uncertain.
2. New tasks often grow at exponential rates.
3. The spontaneous and the unexpected are the norm for *n*-innovation.
4. Large groups of interacting autonomous agents produce a whole that is greater than the sum of the parts.
5. Simple rules breed complex behaviour and profound emergent structures.
6. Bottom-up organisation is more flexible and responsive.
7. Feedback is what gives learning and adaptation, in turn, self-organisation!

To underline all of this, Kevin Kelly wrote:

> For jobs where supreme control is demanded, good old clockware is the way to go. Where supreme adaptability is required, out-of-control swarmware is what you want.

Engineers have taken many solutions to problems from nature (this will increase dramatically in the future), and there is no reason why we cannot take another leaf out of nature's book of design rules and apply it to organisation. What unfolds below is clearly in the swarmware school: the analysis and design of *swarming organisational networks and emergent multidimensional teams.*

SwarmNets

Ideo Product Design, a multiplexing product design consultancy, have won more design awards over the years than any other (over 100 at the last count, including the coveted IDEA). And what is so special about Ideo? They live by the law of the swarm! David Kelley begun the business back in the 1960s; his approach to design was nothing less than unique in those days. People at Ideo fly from one collocated project to another, working in small collocated swarms of people who live within one supernetwork. Small projects may only take a few weeks or months. Larger concept-to-customer projects can take years and will see the swarm system oscillate with different numbers of people day to day. The process is highly dynamic, chaotic. There is no attempt to expedite or organise the project from the outside, the swarm own and are accountable for their goals. Living in the network are industrial stylists, product design engineers, mechanical, software and electronic engineers. Commercial people. Support people in CAD. Prototype people, test specialists, and so on. The project is the attractor that swarms the flock together on a vigorous time-base. It is a strange model to that of the norm, often finding bosses reporting to subordinates and getting actions. That is the law of the swarm!

Chiat/Day/TBWA Inc., the hugely successful ad agency, organise to the tune of the heterarchical. When I made a visit to Chiat's panoramic-viewed, 38th-floor offices in downtown Manhattan, I found the personification for all I am trying to portray here. These people would seem quite nuts to the conventional manager. An analogy that describes this organisation is a hybrid of a highly colourful university campus/stock exchange floor/zoo of people, ideas and projects, purposefully zooming around a building, resembling the characteristics of a swarm of busy bees. Imagine this: arrive at Chiat on your first day as, say, an account executive. First thing, go get your company car keys and credit card. Walk up to a counter surrounded by a giant pair of bright red lips (it's true) and logout your laptop and radiophone for the day/week/month. Among all of this, you are given a key to a locker which is the only piece of turf you own. But where is your office? Your desk? Your PC and potted plant? – Forget it! The only territory you have is that locker! Where and who you work with depends on the demands of the project. Even more unusual, there's no 9–5! You can work from home, at the client's site, or from a restaurant downtown. Or you may choose to work from the creatively designed – for flocking people together – offices that Chiat have built. The New York office is a labyrinth of hallways, project rooms equipped with ubiquitous mobile Power Macs webbed to a large common area they call the Clubhouse. The project rooms are where you can get together, with whoever you need to for an hour/day/week/month. The decor reflects the culture of the organisation bright, colourful, some would say wild. This highly flexible, highly fluid organisation is built on the heterarchical SwarmNet model, enabling swarms of the right people, at the right time, to flock together when the real-time project demands – not when the fairytale critical path analysis says so, not when empire building managers say, but as the chaos demands.

Emergent Innovation from the Swarm of 10,000 Minds

To give another angle on the importance of networking, innovation's manifestation of chaos, and why the likes of Chiat/Day/TBWA design such emergent organisations, absorb this anecdote.

Take the design and development of a G3 mediaphone platform (the new internet video-streaming mediaphones). Marketing people work alongside product designers to conceptualise the product. Telecommunication, satellite and systems design engineers, spread across a multi-enterprise (for example Nokia, Marconi, Sony, Icon and others), are brought in, to work on the systems architecture and functional integration specifications. Marketing and product design specialists may want to target customers to come in for focus group discussions, to find out how the mediaphone may actually be used day to day. Feedback from customers is then fed into the industrial design α-models and technical specifications. Marketing, the product designers and systems people get together again. This may happen one or 10 times more until marketing are happy with the product specification. By now, layout detail designers and mechanical, electronic and acoustic development engineers are brought in to start the feasibility study. Prototype technicians are brought in. The engineers develop the mechanical, electronic and acoustic prototypes and may bring in specialist lab technicians to test the prototype. This loop may be gone around one or a dozen times (re: iterative capital, Chapter 3).

If the feasibility evaluation proves positive, product, production and market development people are brought in. CAD draughtsmen, tool designers, production and industrial plant engineers come in. Production machine equipment suppliers are brought in for discussion about how the mediaphone is going to be manufactured, assembled, tested and packaged. All of these inputs will affect the optical, mechanical, electronic, embedded software, and acoustic design. This loop may iterate one or, more likely, a dozen times.

Next, component suppliers are brought into discuss the manufacture of each component (typical mediaphones contain over 120 individual components, sourced from over 50 suppliers). Each supplier's manufacturing process capabilities need to be considered against the mediaphone's functional and assembly requirements. About 20 internal people are now involved and over 50 suppliers have been involved in specification and component price negotiation.

And do you know what? The process has not even started! To come? The engineering 3D models and drawings for each component need to be further detailed. The contract assembly machine suppliers need to get their design engineers cracking to develop the assembly machinery and test rigs. Component suppliers have to negotiate with their tool designers and toolmakers. Now there are 250 internal and external people involved. Months and often years later through one hell of a chaotic process, components and assembly machines are manufactured. A production line is built, machines start to appear, trials and adjustments occur, and more people are brought into the fold. Maintenance people and external contractors are brought in to lay new power and pneumatic lines. Production staff are brought in and start training on the new assembly machinery. There are now 350 people involved. Marketing meanwhile have been in negotiation with 400 global distributor hubs, with 3000 local retailers. There are now 10,000 people directly and indirectly involved, and not one product has yet left the enterprise.

Okay, that's enough of that. The point is, any higher-dimensional product needs the input of thousands of minds and millions of ideas, even for a pipsqueak mediaphone. Clearly, attempting to manage such an *n*-systems innovation project in the traditional top-down way is not only limiting, it is ridiculous.

MetaNets

Ameritech sits as a major US telecommunications business, with enormous geographic coverage: the north-east of North America. Ameritech used to be functionally organised, with each division focused geographically. As competition heated up, in one of the most competitively ruthless and innovative markets in the world, Ameritech decided the old way of working was fast forcing them out of the game. Today, they have moved towards the customercentric MetaNet, far away from the geographic orientation. Ameritech found that the customer no longer demanded a single service or end-product, but an integration of technologies and services. Old style functional business units stopped dead the integration of ideas. Today, through the MetaNet, they can bring together multidisciplinary teams from any of their 11 core customercentric networks, for any particular hyperinnovation project, and all in a fraction of the time. This has allowed Ameritech to enter into emerging markets, such as new learning technologies and multimedia products. Market share in terms of volume of business has dropped, but total share value has rocketed. Ameritech now operate in and create multidimensional markets, and are quite sure that they would today be lagging behind competition, without the agility the SwarmNet provides.

Rockwell-Collins, Santa Monica, California, picture this: a building filled with super-brained engineers; the hardware technology hot, the software program a feat of human endeavour, the mechanical design engineering mind-boggling, and the production operation a scene from a *Terminator* movie. The project in question, a very sophisticated *inflight entertainment system*. The level of uncertainty, huge; the customer, the prestigious and demanding American Airlines. And the deadline?... Well if Rockwell-Collins were late, the aircraft would simply take off without the multimillion dollar piece of kit! How on earth do you get such a multidimensional monster to market? Again the networks! Rockwell-Collins' amazing feat got to market because their people fluxed and flew to where and when the project demanded. Within the MetaNet lived a dozen to two dozen (depending on when one counted) sub-projects, each focusing on one particular part of the system. The total system consisted of two dozen integrated modules, each requiring focused teams, that formed, expanded, contracted and then disbanded into a new forms, as the project progressed. Each team interacted and adapted to the edge of each other team; often it was hard to distinguish who was in team X, executing Y! Small organisms (swarms of 7–15 people) working within a superorganism, dedicated to one hyperinnovation.

Unique and unusual systems innovation does indeed require unique and unusual organisation, and if this is to manifest itself, businesses and institutes must adopt the swarm system model as the basis for organisational activities. As innovation projects complexify, grow in scale, with the need to get to market faster, ultimately innovation must take place in the very organisation of agents itself. Cross-company organisational innovation is the central issue, emergent team-based networks is the platform.

Three Simple Rules for Emergent Project Teams

To equalise the extremes of the unpredictable complexity of the SwarmNet, we need a dampening mechanism. Critical points of leverage that enable self-organisation and self-direction. The lever point: large numbers of the smaller and autonomous within the bigger system. In this case, the *emergent team*. It is this kind of small team within the big swarm network that begins to facilitates bottom-up, self-organisation, giving requisite levels of idea interconnection at the speed and magnitude necessary for hyperinnovation. To effect emergent *n*-teams, we can borrow and supplant the three simple rules from the above 'boids' model:

- *Develop team values (match the speed of the neighbouring boids).* For people to gel as a we, mould as an us, swarm as one whole; team values and skills must develop. Without team empathy, trust and openness, without sharing and developing common world-views, individual members will remain as individuals, and not make the necessary deep interconnections among people and ideas (this is developed much further in next chapter).
- *Collocate the team (move towards the centre of the mass of boids).* Essentially, a collocated team brings together all the disciplines needed to meet and solve all of the issues throughout a project life cycle, in one place, and at one time. This facilitates simultaneous interaction of upstream and downstream information and local knowledge. Sometimes there are instances where innovation is difficult to define and put into words; collocation enables tacit working methods and relationships, so the undefined, the uncertain, the unprincipled can be effectively engaged. Collocated teams also remove a high percentage of waste activities, like walking distances between offices or writing memos, as communication does not rely on paperwork and e-mail/intranet systems. Information flow is simplified, making it possible to consider the whole team, not just individual specialists. Shorter cycle times are gained as a higher reliability of tasks is carried out. Strategic alliance networks are facilitated, as local teams emulate the morphology of the MetaNetwork, allowing appropriate points of contact to occur at team level. It makes definition of relationships between customer and supplier, and between the team and the wider alliance, easier to design and operate. And just as important, allows effective use of multidiscipline methods and tools (see Part V).

- *Prepare for the unexpected (maintain a distance from other boids and objects).* Systems innovation may hold emergent properties, outcomes that are greater than the sum, and with this comes much uncertainty. Clearly uncertainty goes against the grain of a hard-nosed management style. Managers want predictability, they do not want the messy, bewildering and altogether out-of-control world of the boids. Yet these managers often miss all that is desirable for innovation. Emergent properties give richer, more diverse patterns of order, giving up greater opportunities and possibilities not present in top-down planning and organisation. To effect an adaptable organisation in the face of high levels of uncertainty, managers must paradoxically learn to let go of absolute command and control, and localise autonomy, intelligence, creativity and learning in the team itself. As more unusual and curious problems arise, the greater the need for teams to be equipped with broader, smarter skills and decision-making powers. Multidimensional problems call for multidimensional roles in fact. Only, these kinds of team roles do not mean tasks and goals need not be clear. It is just that instead of a confined role – copy writer or graphic designer for example – the team role is comprehensive, a role that takes an innovation to market from beginning to end. A role that facilitates broader and total activities.

Nature Has the Answers

Nature, it seems, has the conflict between *complex* and *swift* innovation all worked out. It is the master manager of the counterintuitive and the surprising. Without any top-down set of rules, nature manages to evolve the most magnificent artefacts, products way beyond any we humans have yet to imagine. But all this, at the end of the day, is where it is all heading: greater complexity, at a faster pace. So, it seems, we have no choice but to adopt and adapt nature's ways. Hyperinnovation is the goal. SwarmNets and hyperteams are means.

CHAPTER 12

Project Hosting and Whole Team Building

As above, the innovation trek is full of the unknown; and as a result, these kinds of emergent project team need a guide, a Sherpa to negotiate the rocky innovation canyon. *Project hosts* promote live projects, recruiting staff into project teams from the network as chaotic demands arise. They promote open debate and dialogue, encourage people to put their views forward and work interactively as a *whole* team. Equally, a project host has a positive role in the nurturing of a shared psychology and development of team communication skills. All in all, the project host has a highly detailed role to play, to guide and motivate a project team through to successful results.

Roles of the Project Host

There are no absolutes in leading people, and none more so than facilitating a project team. Yet, there are a handful of key roles the host must take on wholeheartedly; I have narrowed them down to nine:

- *Focus on results over time (R/T).* Recall that, as innovation projects grow more complex, cause and effect begin to break down, where actual outcomes can go in a different direction from originally intended. Only by focusing on end-results, within specific time frames, will these kinds of complex project accomplish a short and reliable cycle time. The project host must act as a constant signal towards intended results over time (R/T). Furthermore, anything of significance within complex innovation happens when people interact. In a functional organisation, typically, team interaction is process focused, where the main attention is put on the task at hand. But this will not move the project rapidly onward, often effecting so-called wheel spinning (power and effort while merely running on the spot). Only by focusing on outcomes via real-world prototypes, set by specific dates, will results come through. Therefore, priority number one for the project host (as for the SwarmNet) must be results over time.

- *Collaboration not coordination.* To see and conduct the *whole* towards end-results, the host must facilitate collaboration. If the host breaks a project into 'bits' to hand out to individual members, the team will never gel into collaborative work. The host will only secure a co-ordained system, which like any top-down system, is jerky and awkward, full of stop–start situations. In short, *coordination is anti-collaboration.* It means the manager owns the problem, not the team.
- *Setting whole project objectives.* Results and team collaboration, are, of course, set by intended project objectives, not individual functional goals. But who truly is in the best position to set such big project objectives? The manager? The project host?... After all, surely these people have a better overall grasp of the situation? Psychologists have observed that 75 per cent of people put themselves in the top quartile for personal ability, and that most like to live up to this. If the project host sets a target in isolation, the chance of meeting that target is remote. Set a target in conjunction with the project team, and the odds for success improve dramatically. But, ask your people to set their own target, and two things will happen: (1) the goal will be of a higher standard; (2) people will bend over backwards to achieve the goal... Why? It is as I have said, we all think we are mountain movers and we have a built-in need to live up to that expectation. We can just about bear falling short of other people's expectations, but we flip if we fall short of our own. The power of this is grossly underestimated, yet it has proven itself time and time again. The project host must facilitate goal setting, but encourage teams to set project goals.
- *Communicate global pictures.* Individuals in such SwarmNets will hold local knowledge, specialist discipline, parochial language, and importantly, unique experience, collectively adding up to a spread of individual realities and single-minded models of the world. This is quite common in all walks of life, but is often amplified within innovation projects, particularly at the beginning. So, there is a succinct need for the project hosts to continually communicate the global picture

emerging from the collective of individual realities, without this, excessive tension and unnecessary conflicts will occur. The goal is to share team mental models of the global picture. This global view comes with time, but must emerge during the earlier stages of a project. Team-building skills can also help here (see below).

- *Emotional support.* Innovation teams often live on the edge of creative chaos, with charged emotional highs and lows. Confusion, uncertainty, just sheer frustration can sometimes lead to near manic, quite neurotic behaviour. Without emotional support, such as faith and reassurance of the team's abilities, without empathy towards the kind of trauma a team can experience, the dynamics of risk taking, relationships and interconnection will not occur. Team counsellor is the metaphor.
- *Performance measurement.* A key role for a project host is to measure the project team's performance, in terms of results, set against the project objectives. A description of performance metric development is outlined in Chapter 26. Equally, performance results must be displayed clearly within the immediate areas of the project team. Hiding results in a file misses the whole point: feedback for self-regulation.
- *Culture building.* Project hosts have an extremely tough role to play here, as they must actively exemplify the values necessary to promote collaborative work. Two of the most important values a team can strive for are a climate of trust and openness. Particularly within a politically motivated environment, when an inquiring, or perhaps naive, question, is put forward, it is often an opportunity for the group or another individual to show superior knowledge, or even to ridicule the inquirer. Dealing with unique issues on a daily basis calls for an open-minded climate, so the project host must ensure that an open, trust-based culture emerges. The culture-building and creativity methods outlined in other parts of this book help, and the team-building techniques below develop this aim further.
- *Real-time listening and constant feedback.* What is the leader's most sophisticated management tool in an ambiguous, fast-paced environment? Answer: his eyes and ears. One true definition of a leader is to act as mentor and inspiration. But all rests on an ability to listen, observe and provide feedback. There is a list of methods available for improving listening skills. Beyond the method, it is a question of practice. The more practised pausing, focusing and concentrating on content, tone and body language, the more one allows thought streams to happen, the better one becomes at listening – but it must be a conscious effort. Further, keeping a project team requires constant feed-

back. Feedback gives the opportunity to learn and correct as we go. It is simple to do, just four steps: (1) Devise a weekly feedback monitor, on a single chart to keep track. (2) Narrow down to key performance indicators (results focused, set by project objectives). (3) Pick and point out what results are positive and performing well, as this motivates. (4) Above all, the feedback should be team based, that is, how well an individual collaborated within the team, and how the project team in general worked as a whole.

- *Facilitate collaboration skills building*. Innovation team performance depends on many factors, not least team skills. The project host must spend considerable effort building team skills. This area of responsibility is centrally important, and is therefore expanded upon in detail now.

Project Team Building: Seeking the Whole

You may be lucky and have the most genial, tolerant and cooperative lot ever to walk this earth. But put them in a highly competitive network and closely collaborative teams, under pressure, with tight deadlines, on top of each other situation for long periods, and that nice bunch will start to sprout horns and a tail, not turn up for work on Mondays, and be on the point of a nervous breakdown at the end of a relentless systems project, when you really need them to start afresh, over again. The point here: the building of a team (swarm), not just on an organisational level, but psychologically.

When people first come together, some common things go through their minds. Basic human, even primitive, thoughts and emotions that can stop coherent interaction. The reason for this is that they are a group of individuals, not a team. A team holds something quite different. The best teams are [not] those that combine in some mysterious, positive chemistry – as often purported – but built on a *positive psychology*. A team is not a real team until they have had time to develop cognate views and models of the world, appreciate each other's technical skills and talents, and build both professional and social relationships through project experiences. In fact, to most enterprises the power of the team is not just underestimated, it is unknown, and team skills are absolutely necessary if *whole teaming* is going to work.

Psychologist B.W. Tuckman observed that whenever a small group of people are initially put together (especially people from a diverse range of backgrounds), and then work together throughout several project life cycles, the group as a whole seem to go through a common sequence of working relations development, on both human and task levels. Tuckman narrowed these sequences into four phases (my interpretation):

1. *Forming:* on a task level people establish objectives and begin to fathom how and what they need to meet those objectives. On a people level they try to understand what is suitable behaviour (key values) and look towards the stronger or more senior people in the group for guidance.
2. *Storming:* on both task and people level, this is a very emotional time, as people are trying to exert their own experiences and individuality.
3. *Norming:* cohesion, swarm spirit, standards, key values and roles begin to be accepted.
4. *Performing:* words like flexibility and collaboration spring to mind. People have found their space and now most of the emotional energy can be focused on the project.

Tuckman's model infers that people in groups must advance through the first three stages to become what is often called the *high performance work team*. Today, many team-building experts apply Tuckman's observation to give a structure for developing a specific team-building programme. And perhaps now we can see that *confusion, conflict, inflexibility* and the like, may just be a result of the earlier *forming* and *storming* stages of development.

A key, then, must be to find ways to accelerate team building through the early stages, make best use of the norming stage, then zoom to the performing stage... Mere logic!

The Psychology of Hyperinnovation Teams

But what of *n*-innovation, often the result of counterintuitive logic? Do any differences exist in the group dynamics and culture building? Does the psychology of a multidisciplined team differ? Is the nature of the environment unique?... *The one major point I must underline about a systems innovation project team, is that their needs and circumstances are unique, unlike any other collection of people I have come across.*

Most people work within rules, regulation, routine – a steady-state environment. The next day's schedule, game, format is much the same as the last. Even in the modern-day flexible service operation, where continuous improvement is vital, the change in routine is evolutionary, gradual.

To the hyperinnovation team, the notion of routine is absurd. Dealing with unique situations, solving problems that have not existed before, and literally creating something from nothing is the nearest they get to the luxury of routine. Look at the contrast between the two environments:

Mainstream environment	*Hyperinnovation environment*
Certainty	Uncertainty
Routine	Surprise
Knowns	Novelty
Symmetry	Paradox
Meditated	Spontaneity
Order	Chaos
Planning	Learning
Procedure	Induction
Experience	Naivety
Specified	Seeds/Clues
Best	Different
Continuity	Discontinuity
Causality	Acausality
Linear	Systemic
Familiar	Strange/Weird
Efficient	Creative

Clear antithesis. The issue here: *hyperinnovation environments* bring about a compounding effect on a team as a whole, namely: *anxiety*. When we do not understand and when we are working beyond the predictable, we often suffer enormous emotional stress. On top of this, we have the not so plain and simple human relationships to deal with. Personalities, experiences, knowledge, life stage, gender, creed, and so on, all come into the melting pot of people getting along. Altogether, this brings considerable work stress on top of the normal project tasks a team has to deal with.

Indeed, we all have different levels of tolerance to anxiety brought about by uncertainty and sensitivity to one anothers' feelings. It could be said that we all have a threshold to emotional survival. One important area of team building is to develop a climate that reduces the amount of mental energy we expel to protect our emotions. Okay, for those with a thick skin, this is less of an issue. But when working in a high pressure, uncertain environment, everyone must be considered. Furthermore, in an environment where surprise and paradox engulf, *counterintuition* and an *uncommon sense* must dominate thinking (recall Chapter 2). So, there is a clear need to build a supportive environment and counterintuitive mentality, thereby allowing the finite amount of emotional energy people have to funnel into the project at hand.

Mutual Reality: Building Deep Swarm Wholes

Among all the proven team-building methods, joint learning and knowledge development is by far the most potent: people who learn together, grow together (much of the time). More often than not, team learning and knowledge building happen within normal day-to-day, on-task experiences. But where on-task learning can fall short is in *breakthrough*. So there is a necessity to complement on-task learning with in-class learning and proto-playing. This gives the opportunity to look at currently unrelated areas, providing a neutral environment when needed. But, as much research has shown, the best results in learning new skills and acquiring new knowledge happen when directly related to the real work content; one true insight in the real world is worth a week in the classroom. The key is a combination of *in-class* learning coupled to *on-work* learning and review.

We have explored the notion that new ideas emerge via network patterns among team members' minds and tools. This is, after all, a benefit of the nonlinear organisation I am describing here. *However, for a project team to truly enter into novel innovation spaces, the team must at least begin to feel comfortable with interacting and debating in unique and unusual ways.* What can stop the show is for individuals to feel odd, even threatened, during this often unusual activity. *Therefore, if we are to seek and find those fundamentally original and multidimensional concepts, we must build the swarm whole.* Below is a system of team-building exercises to help build a positive synergetic total.

Whole swarm traits. First, there are some keen indicators that monitor movement towards whole team systems: holistic, playful, deep, surprising, conceptual, messy, inquisitive, reflective, friendly, complex, enlightening, neutral and productive. In the opposite direction, there are some traits that indicate a fragmented group of individuals: bias, certainty, narrow, functional, solemn, aggressive, simple, fruitless, deceptive, argumentative, divisive and emotionally painful. If you experience the latter, then I recommend that you and your people spend generous amounts of time carrying out and reviewing the results of the following exercises.

Developing shared mental models. Conflicting mental models (the simplified and highly personalised view of reality we all carry) often inhibit the building of a whole team mind. In particular, new ideas fail to make it into practice because of a discord between the different internal mental models we hold. *Mental models inform and guide what we see and pick out in any given situation, this is one reason why different people can see and prioritise quite distinct issues and facts from the very same situation.* Here, mental models can go so far as to limit creative thinking, and even the making of unfounded assumptions and generalisations. In fact, mental models can affect assumptions so much so that they grow to be a real threat to team collaboration. Harvard's Chris Argyris, who is perhaps the pre-eminent authority on the subject of building shared mental models, says that a team may function quite well within a routine environment, but when working with complex, often novel, tasks the 'teamness' seems to fly out of the window. For a multidimensional innovation team, this can be very bad news indeed. Hyperinnovation teams are often made up of multicultural, multilingual, multiethnic, multidiscipline, multidimensional people, so conflict among ideas (values, knowledge, experience, ambitions, approach, and so on) can quite easily manifest itself. Unless teams share – at some level – mutual realities and world-views, complex innovation projects will be tardy, and in extreme, never make it to market.

To assist in the building of whole team mental models, we can use three practical methods:

1. *Drawing out generalisations and assumptions.* Generalisations can force us into narrow, quite distorted perspectives. Assumptions can lead us to false conclusions about the people and tasks we have to work with. Thus, drawing out generalisations and assumptions for reflection can open single point perspectives, towards diverse, but shared world-views. Example discussion:

Kim's drawing out:	'Where do you stand on Ann's qualification as Thunderbolt project manager?'
John's assumption:	'Ann's far to young to head the Thunderbolt project.'
Ali's generalisation:	'Yeah, Green Horn.'
Kim's expansion:	'Wait a moment, didn't she write that report on Thunderbolt Topology… and wasn't she captain of the Basketball team at Princeton/Oxford/Open?'

John's open reflection:	'Got to admit I didn't realise she had those kind of talents.'
Ali's open reflection:	'Maybe a young team manager would break new ground.'

The key here is to hold up the main points, expand on the assumptions, and then reflect on those assumptions.

2. *Constructive honesty*. What we think and what we say are often two very different things. We keep our deepest thoughts private for many reasons, not least office politics. But politics, after all, is often a matter of timing. During discussions or meetings, ask team members to write down what they *actually* say, and what they *actually* think underneath. Then ask them to reconsider what they say in light of the private thoughts they have written down. The result is often quite resounding. Example discussion:

Kim's idea:	'Most of our customers are 50 years of age and over. What about bigger text size on the display?'
Ann's direct reply:	'Yes, bigger display text seems like a good idea.'
Ann's concealed thought:	'It'll never work because the 5000 series chip has only a 5k memory.'
Ann's reconsideration:	'We'll need to upgrade the 5000 series chip, to an 8000 series; this'll up the cost by $1.87 per unit.'
Kim's admission:	'At 50,000 units, that's just over $93,000, we can just about absorb that... Anything else we need to consider Ann?'

The keys to constructive honesty: Write down private thoughts and reconsider the consequences, then acknowledge those consequences. This is simple, but potent stuff.

3. *Cross-discipline tools*. The structured hyperinnovation tools in Part V are not merely about building the ultimate concept, but highlight the array of talent and competency needed. In a structured and objective way, each team member can share his/her different views and concerns in a cross-discipline manner (much more on this later).

Proto-games. Another key to building whole team minds is to facilitate accelerated team experiences. The greater the pool of team experience, the greater the recall of positive (and negative) team outcomes. This is where playing (proto-games) can stimulate and step up the *whole* mind learning and creative experience (recall Chapter 2). Here are seven exercises to speed up team mindset development:

- *Role swapping*. Working in close and continuous proximity with other, sometimes unknown people, with vastly different backgrounds and skills, can spin disorientation. For many will not have had any close contact with such diverse disciplines before. For example, I consulted on a new platform multimedia project for one of the big publishing houses. The prototype, make or break, had to be ready within six months for review at a major Far East exhibition. The ensemble of skills composed: a playwright, a crime writer, a psychologist, a systems analyst, three software programmers, two graphic designers and a book illustrator. They came together for the six months, full-time, then went on their merry way. Few had any real understanding of the other's role, and on the first day you could sense those basic instincts mentioned above – not good for the timeliness and creativity of the project at all. The first week, before conceptualisation proper began, each member swapped their various roles to experience the glamorous life of the so-called other half. Exhilarating and dumbfounding was each member's experience. An experience that accelerated breakthrough understanding at the beginning of the project, rather than via accumulation throughout the real project.
- *Team narrative building*. This is very useful for whole team building. The idea is for the group to write a meaningful story – a tragedy, comedy, whatever – spell-checked, punctuated, printed and finished in a binder, within 24 hours. The team must create a unique story, develop the concept, then each member must write a single chapter, at least one page in length. The rub: narrative alignment and continuity in each chapter requires intensive whole-mind collaboration. Quickly members see how collective wholes can build complex, highly creative, in-depth narratives, in shorter cycles, in directions that would not have emerged in isolation. You will find members physically crawling over each other, skipping lunch, staying late into the night, engaged in holistic creativity. This begins to build the team mindset further. The whole team learning experience here is real, tangible and accelerated breakthrough comprehension.
- *Whole group problem solving*. These kinds of game may only be solved by the whole team. If any one or a few individuals limit information or knowledge sharing, it will stop the problem-solving process dead. Picture puzzles are typical and good examples of whole problems. Break

the problem (puzzle) up into a dozen or so clues (pieces), then spread them about the group, even hide a few clues, with other clues leading to those clues spread around the group. Chuck in a few rules, like you cannot talk to any one if you are wearing a yellow hat, and you can only receive information if you are wearing a yellow hat. Remember, rules inhibit creativity and communication. Surprises abound here. These games can be applied in many different contexts and platforms, such as outward bounding (below) or within other in-class proto-games.

- *The synergy game*. Take a poster picture, preferably one with lots of content (say a panoramic city view), and stick it on a wall in front of the group. Give each member an identical piece of card and ask each of them to write down a description of the picture (on the card) in their own words. Give them five minutes to do so. Now gather up the cards and randomly shuffle the stack. Now read aloud each description in turn. What you will most likely receive is a diverse array of descriptions about the content and theme of the picture. Again, mental models are at play here. Each individual describes what she or he sees, guided by the distinct models of the world they hold. In the real world this happens every day, and is reason number one for the quite senseless conflicts we see between people. Now part two of the game: on a single large piece of paper ask the whole team to consider each member's thoughts and expressions about the picture. Ask them to interconnect each individual idea so that a team description of the picture emerges. Ask them to reserve judgement and listen to each comment and view (see dialogue develop, below). The outcome is quite often astounding: an expansive, yet integrated description of the picture, a narration greater than the sum of the individual descriptions. The point is that individual views can be a source of synergistic creativity, if (a) personal viewpoints and ideas are aired, and (b) the whole team reviews and looks for connections between those unique insights.

- *Context perspectives*. This game is for groups that have spent some time together. People that have some level of shared mental models. The exercise is similar to the synergy game, but has a more tangible output (use which ever is appropriate). Copy a one-page piece of text from a book (preferably text with some abstruse insights). Split the group into a set of smaller groups, give each subgroup a copy of the text, then ask each subgroup to think of an individual theme (for example computer programming, market learning, organisational theory, whatever is appropriate). Ask each subgroup to read the text from the point of their theme, and write down what they learn. What usually happens is that each subgroup picks out quite unique insights and ideas from the very same sentences. The lesson is, even though we may have shared mental models when we read from the same hymn sheet, our different context perspectives lead us to see and prioritise things differently. For example, I worked with a team made up of medical doctors, hospital administrators and systems analysts, who were involved in specifying the layout for a new teaching hospital in London. I gave them a piece of text on the *self-organisation of ant colonies*. What happened? The doctors gleaned insight into new ways for testing vaccines. The administrators saw new ways to organise bed rosters. The systems analysts saw that distributed computers throughout the hospital might be a more effective way to coordinate operations. We then brainstormed to gel these disparate insights together.

- *The egg game*. A well-proven, simple, but effective tool for team building and evaluation. Present the team with a standard box of farm eggs. Ask them to design and make a protective packaging for one egg, which will withstand a drop impact from 10 feet on to a hard floor. Set a time of two hours and modest budget. After the allotted time is up, the team submit their idea and test the design. Then evaluate the team's effort, looking for strengths and weaknesses ranging from quality and quantity of suggestions, range of thinking, focus on results over time, budgetary management, and most important, team traits such as mutuality, trust, openness, and so on. This kind of evaluation can also take place in an interpersonal learning review (ILR), discussed later in this chapter.
- *Pre-project talk shows*. One very powerful team mind amplifier, is to carry out a pre-project talk show, not unlike the inquisitive collective debates we see on TV. These are good models for the kind of pre-project debates, a chance to air views and concerns, even the content issues of the project. The picture here is a group of people in open debate sitting in a circle – not around a table or desk – following trains of thought in directions that could not be developed within isolated individuals or groups. Some of the positive traits to look for are moments, sometimes minutes, of silence. This is good because the mental cogs are turning. Sometimes several people will all talk at once. This is also good as it highlights the level of engagement and interest. The goal is not to reach conclusions or solutions, but to open up the team mind, leaving open-ended points to be solved during the project proper. In fact, the emphasis here should be fun and intrigue. There will be moments of empathy and moments when the team enters a whole-mind experience. The gains from this are immeasurable. In fact one

empathic moment can change the face of the team for ever. It is also a good idea to hold these kinds of informal project talk show throughout a project's life cycle. The idea once again is to accelerate team learning and to begin to build dialogue.

Building team dialogue. The biggest barrier to team collaboration, and the greatest restriction for teams that swarm, is the stranglehold our paradigms and disparate mental models have upon us. As in Chapter 2, the normal workaday context that is cemented by past experience and knowledge, limits breakthroughs in thinking and all the insight that comes with it.

However, and thankfully, there is one team-building mechanism that helps break this deadlock: so-called *dialogue development.* True team dialogue helps reveal and question deep-held assumptions. Dialogue facilitates free-flow thinking across minds, which leads to new, often remarkable, insights. In dialogue we can explore complex issues from many angles and views, in non-judgemental, inquiring, often naive, frames of mind. This often enters teams into a higher level of collective thinking. Peter Senge, author of the remarkable book, *The Fifth Discipline*, says: 'in dialogue people become observers of their own thought', which is central for multidimensional thinking.

However, perhaps the commentator who has contributed most to the understanding of team dialogue within the modern setting, is the late David Bohm, the quantum physicist. 'In dialogue,' he said, 'groups of people can explore individual and collective presuppositions, ideas, beliefs, and feelings that subtly control their interactions... Dialogue can expose the often mystifying patterns of inconsistency that lead the group to evade certain issues or, on the other hand, to maintain, against all reason, standings on and opinions of particular issues... What makes this position so dire is that thought generally cloaks the problems from our direct awareness and prevails in creating a sense that the way each of us perceives a situation is the only reasonable way in which that situation can be interpreted.' Clearly, dialogue development is a central mechanism within the building of whole teams.

Bohm put down guidelines that promote and help develop whole-team dialogue (my interpretation):

1. *Suspend assumptions.* This does not mean suppressing individual thinking, but offers ideas up for group questioning and examination without jumping to conclusions. The goal is to see contrasting views that enlighten each others' perspectives from multiple angles, to let ideas flow, to go down creative and unexpected thinking paths. The

outcome is true whole team ideas. It is easy to fall back to isolated mindsets and assumptions. Practice is key. Eventually the compound mind develops, members begin to see and understand the concept of *suspended assumption.*

2. See and treat each other as colleagues. Boss/subordinate or senior/junior models must be put on ice. The goal is to build an open, genial atmosphere. This enables each member to think and speak freely, and see personal views in the light of the wider context. Only then are differences in world-view held up for scrutiny. You cannot force people into this mode of thinking, they have to want to move to this orientation. I find the secret here is to get on and practise. Even if early trials fall short, in time people learn naturally how to be suspend assumptions and open the gate for collective free thinking, through reinforcing feedback.
3. Naive listening orientation. The goal is not to convince everyone that your position is right, but for everyone to learn and gain deeper insight. To recognise that collaborative input will refine an individual's ideas.
4. The project host must hold the context of the dialogue. The project host's role is to coach the process and context, bringing in different points of view, encouraging open multidimensional thinking, and generally monitoring the suspension of assumptions.

It is true to say that most people have not experienced even a moderate level of dialogue with work colleagues. We have all been conditioned into defensive, often offensive ways of communication. And this is one of the work life's great wastes, because so much potential remains untapped. So *team dialogue development* must be taken on wholeheartedly. Read and learn all you can here. Study Peter Senge's book *The Fifth Discipline*, it is a brilliant piece of work. Check out the works of David Bohm. But most of all, practise, toy and play to develop a deep team dialogue within your organisation. Because as experience of dialogue increases, an extraordinary sense of shared meaning will emerge, where people find that they are neither opposing, nor simply interacting, but beginning to build truly holistic insights and collaborative solutions.

Interpersonal learning reviews (ILRs). This is a group self-analysis and learning system, enabling individuals to review and understand their role as a greater whole. It is not intended to point out success or failure, but to evoke holistic learning and reflection. In a Machiavellian-like environment, these kinds of review are often seen as a sign of weakness and potential threat. In fact, I have seen many a review turn into a game of stealth. On the other hand, I have seen acutely political enterprises and groups move from power cultures to one of creativity, openness and rapid learning, helped via the following ILR steps:

1. Hold reviews in neutral spaces.
2. Clarify the purpose of the learning review (for example, gain new insights within a particular project, such as, was the whole team aligned with specific objectives and end-results? Which sub-team owns which part of the project? 'What's been learnt here?' is a common inquiry).
3. The *host* must hold the main context of dialogue.
4. Focus on one or two practical points to hit home (for example, what would be the benefit of giving up the latest information on smart-materials?).
5. Keep the dialogue specific and focused on real projects, asking what have we learnt?
6. Collect hard facts and data to further keep it objective, and maintain focus.
7. Individual members should be encouraged to put forward their views about the group and what has been learnt.
8. If the review begins to turn into a witch-hunt, reclarify the purpose of the learning review, and keep on clarifying until the penny drops.

Avoid a 'Tick the Box' Mentality

Pursuing and developing that team *whole* is a serious and continuous activity, driven by highly developed methodologies, borrowing concepts from social psychology and behaviour science. As a result, all of the above takes time, practice and effort. In fact, if you are not spending a significant portion of time during a project's life cycle (between 5 and 10 per cent), then you will not achieve the breakthroughs in dialogue or mental model sharing necessary for such hyperinnovation. In short, this is not a 'tick the box and we're done here' issue, it is a never-ending journey of discovery and development.

CHAPTER 13

Warehouse of Innovation

The hub of the multidimensional interconnection of ideas rests on how creative the collaboration is within the relevant teams, and across the SwarmNet. Creative collaboration, hence, is also the product of physical organisation design, not team psychology alone. In the words of Michael Schrange, 'To build effective collaboration, we must also build shared spaces'. And there is plenty to note in the construction of such spaces.

Office Ecology

Given a greenfield site, architects are now recruiting the skills of so-called *office ecologists,* people who study the effects of building design and layout on team productivity and collaboration.

Francline Becker, an organisational ecologist based at Cornell University, claims that interior facilities that grease idea interchange are something that have shot up the architect's agenda. Nike have invested heavily in this sort of thinking. Nike's headquarters in Portland, Oregon, USA, is designed to inspire and wax communication. The innovation centre has the spirit of competition built in. Called the Michael Jordan building, it contains images of top sporting stars to help inspire the conception of the new generation of intelligent sports gear. The green-glass building is a maze of concourses, atriums and open plan areas for the teams to swarm spontaneously. The environment increases the frequency of informal, on-the-fly meetings between engineers and scientists, or chemists and marketers, sparking spontaneous ideas. The environment is designed for *nose-to-nose* collaboration.

Yes, *nose-to-nose* like those *boids* in Craig Reynolds' computer simulation! Here, studies have analysed the implications of physical location and distance between people in teams, and none more so than the work by MIT's Tom Allen. Allen concludes that fragmenting people in narrow roles and departments hopelessly dampens the potential for collaboration. A separation as little as 5 metres can significantly limit communication. The work revealed that the likelihood of two people communicating at least once in a given week separated by a distance of 10 metres is only around 10 per cent of that of two people separated by 5 metres (5 m = 0.225, 10 m = 0.075, respectively). So, taking this into a complex innovation setting, people being separated by a wall, a floor, or even a building (let alone a city/country) has a devastating effects on communication.

The point is this: if people are separated by walls, let alone a building – even with the advent of e-mail and video conferencing – communication only becomes necessary when there is a reason. Because of this, two things happen: (1) team members have to go out of their way to communicate (for example, walk to the next building/room), and (2) communication becomes fragmented, a snapshot in time. A clear case of out of sight, out of mind, the very opposite of what's needed for high levels of collaboration.

Local Viewpoints

Collaboration is further encumbered by *local viewpoints.* In fragmented functional groups, concentration, and the mental models and world-views that emerge, focus on highly provincial matters. Take, for example, a production engineering department. Dominant local issues are likely to be production methodology or troubleshooting on the factory shop floor. Attempting to gain the attention of the *production engineer* (or software programmer, copywriter, broker, any functional specialist) and involve them as a committed member of a project team is near impossible. The perspective is production engineering, not *multidimensional innovation.* Loyalties, knowledge building and relationship development focus on the technical discipline of production engineering as an end in itself, not one of many means to *n*-innovation. The difference of mindset has profound consequences on collaboration and cycle time.

Collocated Executives

Honda are the fastest (cycle-time) automotive business in the world. In fact, considering the technical and commercial complexity factors in each new platform Honda bring to market, they are possibly the fastest innovators vis-à-vis everyone else. The core of Honda's fast-paced innovation strategy is set in a unique way of working, and it is claimed it was key to developing the innovative management systems Honda now have in place. They call it the 'Joint Boardroom'. Directors and executives sit on several different teams, located within one room – a big room. Allowing spontaneous action to new issues that arise out of the blue. They take positions at different tables assigned to different teams to discuss matters of mutual concern. They also assign tables for free discussion. This allows for partners, joint ventures and of course customers, to come into discuss high-level issues. The executive teams go out in groups to explore the market, competition, conferences, exhibitions, and other winning companies. They bring back new, first-hand knowledge on a regular basis and throw it into the melting pot for open discussion.

The collocated boardroom allows for strategy development in a multi-discipline manner, facilitating cross-fertilisation of local knowledge, giving opportunities to consider functional aspects that may have been neglected in the past. The open physicality promotes a free atmosphere to discuss a wide range of issues, that would be restrained by a provincial approach. Beyond this, it is about culture building. Team building not only happens on the front line, it must happen at the highest level, setting the precedent (walk the talk) for hyperteams. Senior executives cannot expect the ranks to flow as a swarm, if they do not set an example.

Environmental Management

Aesthetics are just as important as function. Working environment gives a clear message about (a) whether you care, (b) the image the organisation is trying to set, and (c) what is valued most. It is culture building again. I have consulted in firms that have an excellent environment for their key executives and a rubbish tip for the average worker, and then ask for speed and innovation to improve. Cultural values are acutely reflected in what you do, not say. Environment reflects the key values you want to make happen. One very successful toy company has developed a set of unique working environments; as soon as you walk in you can feel the creativity and openness. They have famous cartoon characters all over the design studio, tables that look as though they have come from a scene from cartoon land, the carpets are multicoloured and the lighting is clean and bright. This may not suit the needs of say a pen maker or an earth-moving machine manufacturer; simply design for purpose. In Japan, I visited one of Canon's toolmaking subcontractors. Next to a welding bay was a large open space with a lily pond, fountains and waterfalls, shrubs and trees, picnic tables, sculptures of traditional Japanese scenes. Is this the stuff that adds to competitive advantage, kudos and a multidimensional organisation? Again it is all about the ideas you want your people to work with. Grey–dull–divided environments can lead to poor–dull–divided ideas. Bright–flexible–integrated environments can lead to hyperinnovation. Chiat/Day/TBWA Advertising Inc. build awe-inspiring work environments. In their Venice, California, office, one of their conference rooms looks like a fish. A giant pair of binoculars sits over the entrance to the building. It has a labyrinth of creative work nodes designed to support and stimulate creative thinking. Most of the furniture consists of pieces of modern art, sometimes mistaken for quite odd-looking abstract sculptures. This company has won a list of awards for creativity, stimulated by so-called *environmental management*, as in all of the above and more below.

Hyperinnovation Warehousing

Thus, there is much we can do to advance communications and creativity in teams. What follows is a basic model that can be applied to the design and building of a working environment that greases hyperinnovation. There are three basic stages.

Stage One: If at all possible, move the whole of your enterprise into a warehouse! If need be, as big as the one you do your weekend shopping in, if Safeway and Toys R Us can do it – you can. British Telecom do this, they have built a mega-innovation warehouse. Foot for foot these warehouses are cheaper to lease and maintain – fact – check with any real-estate agent. For the 95 per cent, less than 500-people businesses and institutes out there, there is no excuse. Here is list of things to do:

- Flatten it. Rip out all the segregating walls and partitioning.
- Flexible services. Put in flexible, moveable services; air-conditioning, lighting, heating, water, plumbing and communications.
- Dynamic learning. Build flexible hyperlearning environments.
- Room for thinking. For sure, put in enclosed quiet thinking areas.
- Image. Paint it bright and decorate in the image you are trying to portray.
- Social. Whatever the cost, build a meeting area/club house, à la Chiat/Day/TBWA. Put in free fresh coffee, tea and cold drinks, even if

it is only in this area (yes, they will come from the far sides, that is the point). Put in a fashionable/innocuous (depending on your image) café/bar. Make it fun and friendly.

- Processes. Contain single collocated core business processes within this single warehouse.

Hyperlaboratory: Playgrounds for the Mind

Stage Two: A hyperlab is a playground for the imagination. A collocated network of diverse tools and toys for play and research into, and core development of, *hypertechnology*. Hyperlabs combine disparate research tools and techniques, so unique combinations of technology can complex in composite ways, where connections are messy, overlapping, webbed and redundant. As discussed, many breakthroughs in applied science and technology will be an effect of synergy between different domains; for example; quantum computing fuses with nanotechnology, or artificial intelligence with biotechnology. It is at the borders between these inspiring territories, where quite extraordinary, multidimensional technologies, such as hypertechnology emerge: hence the mandate for *hyperlaboratories*.

MIT's artificial intelligence laboratory, serves as a model of such hyperlabs. Not unlike a scene from *Alice in Wonderland*, presenting a cocktail of weird mechanical devices and strange gadgets, tangling mechanical insects that roam a yellow brick road leading up to a smart computer called Oz. The MIT hyperlab brings concurrently diverse areas of technology, science, arts and philosophy, interconnecting wisdom and wizards from biology, mechanics, entomology, cybernetics, athletics, mathematics, gaming and chemistry, conglomerating in extraordinary and counter-intuitive ways. A team dreamland designed for paradox and surprise:

- *Emulate a rich zoological ecology.* As in nature, the more diverse the research tools (species), the richer the experimental connection possibilities and original gateways for innovation. Surround the team with the stuff that will make them think and learn in *n*-dimension (colours, bright lights, thought-leading books and videos, strange toys to play with, video screens (see Chapter 14), music and so on. Again, we are what we eat.
- *Let the edge of chaos rule.* Do not suppress order, let order emerge. Chaos is precipitant to the new. Tight order means that the lab has found the best way of doing things, thus the lab is not doing much new. Neat

labs are a sure sign of bureaucracy. Messy (not dirty) hyperlabs are a frenzy of ideas.

- *Juxtapose tools and toys.* You might expect to see a microscope next to a musical synthesiser. Shock test machines and sewing machines juxtapose. An artificial spider web immediately next to a hydraulic piston rig. Why? Again, the more alien and convoluted the context and tools, the greater the potential of *hyperinnovation*.

Project Hives/Theatres

Stage Three: Again, we can learn from the likes of Honda and Chiat/Day/TBWA, even surgical theatres, and exhibition stand designers. They design their project environments to: (1) assist teamwork, (2) magnify and speed communication on a face-to-face level, (3) elevate employees to a high state of esteem, and (4) motivate. Physical project working environments should be thought of as a living tool:

- *Multifunctional collocation.* All of the facilities outlined below may be collocated in one open arena. Contain live projects within this single area. Hyperinnovation requires ultra-diverse teams of people, with hugely different skills and tools. The environment must be multifunctional, where the whole activity from start to finish can be managed in one zone. Consignia Research Group's Innovation Lab, near Rugby, UK, has developed a multifunctional environment that integrates an experience zone, a creativity domain, a home of the future, a play area (for adults), and a tranquil relaxation zone. The place smells of multidimensional innovation.
- *Customer analysis.* The hive must be equipped with technologies and gear that assist in customer expectations analysis (see Chapter 20 for analysis tools). Philips Electronics, for example, have developed a whole environment that integrates design engineering work with customer analysis. Instead of merely asking customers to come in for a focus group to view, say, a new home entertainment system, customers actually get to play with the new gadgets in the circumstances they will be used in the real world. The environment has everything to make the customer feel comfortable and behave as they would at home.
- *Mobility.* Workspaces are designed for a purpose. Innovation can be a fairly physical job, requiring team members to handle large quantities of sometimes heavy products, engineering samples, prototypes and

componentry of all shapes and size. These workspaces are also designed as mobile modular systems. In other words, the workstation, bench, computer, hot desk or whatever, can be moved easily from one area to another. As project teams flow dynamically around the process, the physical environment flows with it. Think of a surgical theatre, with a system of flexible, moveable tools and equipment literally integrated with the surgical procedure. Call on your local drama theatre. Ask the set designers and builders how they move those massive sets between scenes; they are experts in designing mobile systems. Talk to exhibition stand designers. You have no doubt seen what they can do, designing massive and very creative infrastructures that can be erected, stripped down and moved on to the next exhibition in less than a day.

- *Flexibility.* Improvement in productivity and speed can be enhanced if workstations are also designed for use with an increasing number of innovative work tools, information systems, documents and drawings. Decluttering and storage systems must be considered. Hot desks can very quickly pile high with gadgets and gizmos, prototypes, notes and coffee cups. Ideas that can be incorporated here are: vertical stack systems, suspended/overhanging work tools, carousel desktops, circular surround tables and superlarge wheelie bins.

- *Open spaces.* Meeting areas for team supplier meetings are situated within the environment. These include major meeting areas, and half a dozen small meeting areas. They are open plan too. No partitioning or fabricated offices. Physical openness helps promote cultural openness.

- *Visibility.* Planning and analysis areas are specifically designed in conjunction with the meeting areas. Problem-solving methodology charts are mounted on the surrounding walls. Information about customers, competition, technology and especially team performance is displayed in an open manner, on every available space. The idea is real-time, highly visible, cross-discipline information.

- *Real time.* Results measurement tools are vividly displayed in the simplest form. The idea is that everyone knows instantly where they are in terms of results over time. Not sophisticated computer PERT/CPA charts, but large, vividly coloured calendars marking where they are against where they should be, against each major objective.

- *Project information.* Up-to-date and well-managed multidiscipline physical/online library and databases (see multidimensional navigator, next chapter) containing everything from customer to technical information.

- *Real world.* Integrated design of experiments, prototype and test facilities, with appropriate expertise, are collocated in the middle of the team. Not some dank and dark workshop, downstairs. This aids real-world experiments, prototyping and test.

- *Collocate product/process prototyping.* Master prototype build area – whether a new shopfront, fast food production line, to a breakthrough helicopter rotor blade system – to build and conclusively prove prototypes, is a must. This area facilitates project-specific integrated design, build, experiment and test cycles of both product/service and the manufacturing/assembly processes. Collocating the product/process development is must. *Build the production-line prototype right next to where the core product/service technologies are being developed.* Only then do you gain the opportunity to innovate at the process level and prove those unknown quantities in shorter cycles. There will be streams of people who will tell you that it cannot be done! But the likes of Motorola, Honda, and dozens of projects I have run, do it this way, achieving order-of-magnitude breakthroughs in project cycle time and process reliability.

CHAPTER 14

Hypermachines

Productivity across the SwarmNet, can, of course, take a giant leap through the use of information technology. But this is not merely about productivity-enhancing tools per se. Information technology merely scratches the surface. The core of the issue here, is the effective collaboration and multidimensional thinking within both home teams, and wider collaborative alliances outside the fold. This last chapter in this part details a basic functional model that goes some way to achieving that goal, some-

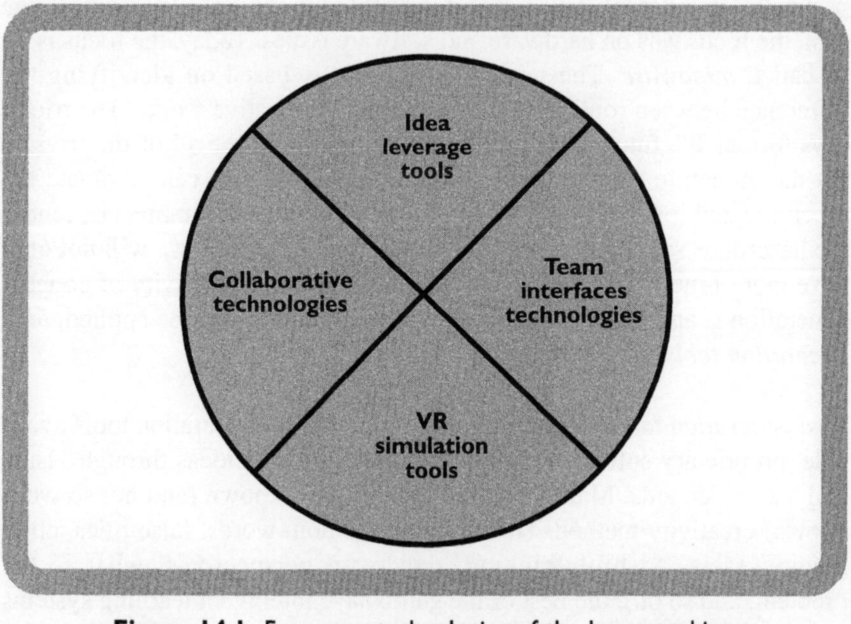

Figure 14.1 Four core technologies of the hypermachine

thing I have coined a 'hypermachine'. It covers the four cornerstones of such hypermachines, including, (1) *idea leverage tools,* (2) *collaborative technologies,* (3) *team interface technologies*, and (4) *virtual reality simulation tools.*

Idea Leverage Tools

Idea leverage tools are, as described, tools in the truest sense, like a screwdriver or power drill. But instead of a physical tool, they are what Howard Rheingold (the guru of the thinking tool) calls 'intellectual power tools' and 'thought amplifiers'. Glitzy terms, but that is what these tools are about. Idea leverage tools do not replace the team mind, but amplify creativity and intelligence. By rendering complex concepts simpler, or by increasing the rate of idea productivity, or by enabling teams to think as a whole, or indeed, by totally changing the way in which we think altogether, teams are now generating hyperconcepts beyond any achieved before. Furthermore, idea leverage tools can accelerate and deepen team experiences and insight, by simultaneously boosting the magnitude of idea interconnection, while taking the weight of idea flow in and across a team.

Recently, efforts to amplify the team mind with such idea leverage tools have shot up the corporate agenda. For Honda and British Telecom (BT) in particular, investment in this area has doubled in the last five years. In the past, the focus was on hardware and software issues. Today, the focus is on so-called *mindware*. The mindware concept is based on identifying the difference between routine work, and unique or creative work. 'The trick,' says former BT futurologist, Peter Cochrane, 'is to get rid of the trivia – get the human to do the clever stuff.' Essentially, if we can automate the repetitive and routine, speed the slow, make accurate the imprecise, render the hazardous safe, and strengthen where there is fatigue, we will not only have more time for creative endeavours, but the entire activity of concept generation is amplified. To achieve this, two key tools can be applied, *idea generation tools*, and *idea management tools.*

Idea generation tools. There are many kinds of idea generation tools available, proprietary software applications that construct ideas through visual and text-based aids. Many are coupled with well-known (and not so well-known) creativity methods (for example, random words, false rules, challenging facts, wishful thinking, daydream perspectives, what is the problem, and so on), the best of the genre have intelligent learning systems and routines built in. Some idea production tools are based on arcane principles used by some of the most innovative organisations, now and from the past. Some work as a sketch pad for visualisation and organising ideas, with user interfaces specially designed for multidimensional thinking (for example, interconnected mind maps, nonlinear checklists, counterintuitive hints, and connected problem-solving techniques).

Specifically, idea generation tools are concerned with problems and solutions, questions and answers, unknown and known facts, giving the team inspirational themes and idea springboards to create concept outlines, basic project layouts and concept diagrams. The *Innovation Toolbox*, by Infinite Innovations (UK) Ltd, is a powerful application here, incorporating a problem-solving structure which guides users through different problem-solving processes to ensure the right problems are answered, and that all ideas are properly evaluated. *BrainStormer* is mindware designed to help generate new ideas in teams, directing the team through a complete brainstorming session. It stretches the whole team's imagination, offering up idea ranking tools against specified criteria. *Simplex*, by Dr M. Basadur, is perhaps one of the most popular idea generation tools. The software can be used by individuals and teams, and is an ideal tool for managing creative collaboration. Simplex has various unique features that are easy to use, including 'Why/What's Stopping Challenge Mapping, Action Planning, Evaluation and Selection of Options, and The Basadure Creative Problem Solving Profile.' Simplex is also a very good idea management tool, as it manages both planned creative sessions and spontaneous on-the-fly information, in an easy store and access format.

Idea management tools. A kind of corporate memory system that stores both mature and early obscure scraps of information, knowledge and ideas, in both structured and unstructured ways, thus improving team recall. In fact, unstructured text-based information is often the most valuable kind of information within a company, yet is all too often lost on a scrap of paper thrown in the waste. Idea management tools collect this kind of unstructured, fuzzy information regardless of format, capturing freeform ideas for exchange, manipulation, analysis and query. Centor Software develop and market XML powered applications (CenBASE for example) to do exactly this. Some systems even allow such raw thoughts and draft ideas to be organised by metaphor, a very powerful way of breaking down the barriers between context. Furthermore, as ideas (for example, concept outlines, best practices, new lessons learned and project notes) develop and mature through their natural life cycle, idea management tools continue to augment, so they can be recalled in new projects.

Idea management tools are often driven by a *Hyperindex* (see below) which classifies, stores and locates ideas as they emerge. ACTA's *Advantage* is an easy-to-use tool for recording and organising ideas, it does not have all the features of more professional-level programs, but its relatively low price makes it an attractive tool to begin with. More advanced idea management systems have so-called group decision support systems built in, allowing groups to recall and explore the intricacies of problems and challenging situations as a whole team. This also facilitates multilocational group problem solving for teams displaced over geographic locations, providing highly effective anytime, anywhere virtual meetings. *Grouputer*, for example, is a meeting room technology that transforms the way people meet, further enabling collaboration. Designed for innovation team building and interactive learning, it allows participants to enter and compare ideas simultaneously, so that each new idea can be seen in the wider context.

Collaborative Technologies

Clearly more kinds of expertise and organisations are becoming involved in the activities of innovation, and as a result there is a distinct need to bring together people and groups that were once considered outside the fold. Essentially, *collaborative technologies* are systems that tie dispersed and remote work groups into close-knit teams, by enabling instant peer-to-peer access to information and design tools, allowing for the spontaneous sharing of ideas and data.

To give an insight to the real potential of such collaborative technology, Dr Lewis Perelman, Research Fellow at the Discovery Institute, wrote in his book *Hyperlearning*:

> If connection in hypernetworks can enable fairly dumb computer chips to perform at relative 'genius' levels, the same kind of amplification of far more powerful human brains may occur when groupware and large capacity telecosm networks link people together in a similar way. The resulting superexpertise of 'human hypercubes' may be the key to keeping human power in the lead and in control of systems marching steadily toward 'human equivalence'.

When such large crews of diverse and talented minds are connected with such enabling technologies, it can quickly lead to a synergy hugely superior and distinct from the sum of the elemental. The thought space between minds goes up exponentially for every new mind coupled to that network (re: the first principle of hyperinnovation: $1/2*\sum\alpha^2$). The greater and more diverse the number of minds, the richer the emergent patterns become.

Proctor & Gamble (P&G), for example, have a global network of associates, approaching 110,000 in number. Each associate has access to a collaborative intranet called *My Idea*. Individuals and teams put their ideas onto the network for scrutiny by the *Corporate New Ventures* (CNV) innovation committee, who in turn use web-based tools to analyse market feasibility. Once an idea gets the go-ahead, the CNV panel may call up any associate, from anywhere in the corporation, to take the product to market, including highbrow scientists and engineers based in any of their development sites worldwide. To date, P&G have launched well over 100 new products via the collaborative network. Not only cutting the time it takes to go from a seed idea to market launch in half, but enabling the conception of highly original multidimensional products that just would not have emerged via the top-down approach. Under this scheme, P&G have found detergent experts crossing boundaries with paper millers, who cross ideas with nappy designers, who talk with brand marketers. All of this, of course, is hyperinnovation in full flow.

We can see that such collaborative networks interconnect and intercreate ideas in planes and in numbers as never before. These kinds of hyperteam share knowledge, context and tasks of vast magnitude. Consequently, the kind of perspective gained from unique combinations of knowledge and ideas, create ever distinctive insights and understanding, eventually leading to fundamental innovation. Collaborative technologies, such as P&G's *My Idea*, are vital for a world of rapid mix, and thus is the precise formulation needed for extradimensional innovation.

For the purposes here, we can look to five requisite tools that actualise such collaborative technologies: intelligent webs, the digital intelligence engine, mobile tools, multidimensional navigator and hyperindex.

Intelligent webs. It is perhaps with little surprise that the intelligent web is by far the fastest-growing area of this technology. Intelligent webs have expert learning systems and neural networks built in, guiding the whole team through complex problems and concept building. The idea being, the artificial mind eventually gets to know the team so well, that it continues to build a team/machine dialogue beyond any unaided team memory and relation capacity. Creating this team/machine dialogue leads to whole team generated, highly unique concepts, that would otherwise be impossible to create and manage under conventional approaches. Specifically, dialogue is enhanced when data and ideas pass through conceptualisation, design and development, manufacture/service, sales and distribution, in a way so that data value is augmented. The best seamless web systems have two-way (full duplex and synchronous) data flows, that is, data can flow up and down an innovation activity and change at any point.

Furthermore, broadband width sending terabits across a web is not enough for the kind of collaboration needed for hyperinnovation. No. Only highly intelligent web tools can leverage and maximise knowledge productivity to a level where the interconnection of ideas research that magical point of criticality (Chapter 5). The goal is to effect a swarm of interacting, and thus *intercreating* ideas that lead to emergent *n*-concepts, beyond the conception of any single human (and I would argue the smartest stand-alone team could not create without such tools). Think of this as a spiralling swarm of virtual ideas, just like the birds above the West Pier. The pattern of ideas that emerge is often quite startling. The other powerful aspect of such intelligent web tools, is that they can have parallel thought processes, millions, even billions of thoughts, when we humans can only have one train of thought. Although many parallel thought processes can of course occur in a team, they are only limited to the number of team members, and can only be heard one at a time.

There are even web-based technologies that are actually beginning to understand a company's business as a whole, coming out of companies such as Intelligensis and Oracle. These types of intelligent web tools actually make judgements from the patterns of ideas and information flying across the enterprise. They can anticipate what may come next. The web tool's main goal is to answer more than mere singular queries, but collective or holistic questions. In fact, a few commentators argue that these systems do not merely hold an artificial kind of intelligence, but deserve to be recognised as an intelligence in their own right. These tools are designed to learn from the team, interact with the team, and develop a kind of *mutual intelligence*.

Digital intelligence engine. These are smart technologies that not only assist in complex innovation, but actually partake. Digital intelligence engines learn in heuristic ways. Yet, at first, these machines act quite dumb, but as they learn, soon begin to outpace human thinking in several areas, not least memory search and locate. These digital intelligence engines also head up higher levels of teamwork, holding the dialogue as projects progress. They can predict outcomes for certain tests, compile from massive amounts of data, that humans cannot take in. Furthermore, these kinds of digital intelligence engine eventually improve upon themselves. That is, they do a better job the next time around. *Fuzzy logic* tools, for example, learn your habits and anticipate your next move, automating the routine, eliminating tasks where fatigue and boredom can set in, allowing more time to ask 'what-if' questions. There are four basic subsystems to a digital intelligence engine:

- Neural networks. Machines that mimic the architecture of a brain. Neural nets learn without top-down control from a programmer, but by bottom-up multiple-loop information feedback. Neural networks are good at recognising patterns in complex information streams. Here the neural net learns with the team as they progress through the project activity, coaching and prompting, giving up advice where needed.
- Rule induction. A set of precepts, dictums and laws that induce on given problems or data. The induction engine is linked to the neural net and knowledge base.
- Knowledge base. The knowledge base is the heart of the hypermachine. As the team execute different problems, the knowledge base grows for future rule induction.
- Inference engine. As implied, this part of the hypermachine generates intelligent advice. The engine accesses the rules and knowledge base through the neural net, and makes the necessary interconnections and conclusions, in the many different contexts and meanings.

In non-technical terms, this area of the technology is a bit like the Google search engine. That is, they assist, stretch and monitor team creative problem solving and thinking. There are plenty of proprietary and customisable digital intelligence engines available, and abundant application examples. Go out and look for the latest kit. This stuff is evolving faster than I can write.

Mobile tools. The goal is to enable teams and individuals to work anytime, anywhere. These days, the environment may take the form of a hotel room, an airport lounge, a client site or home den. The goal, here, is to eliminate the barriers of collaboration outside the company. Individuals and teams working in the field need to access and/or share data and ideas seamlessly in real time, regardless of their location. Such virtual connection between remote teams gives instant responses, consequently increasing productivity. A key here is to arm individual team members with mobile communication and multimedia tools. W L Gore & Associates, for example, go to town when arming their associates, from the simplest tools such as personal pagers, to mobile intranets and e-mail gadgets, up to and including broadband conferencing access. Without this, outfield team dialogue will develop at a glacial pace. The good news is that there is a whole array of hardware platforms and software applications hitting the market, that are ever more reliable and affordable. Names like Toshiba, Microsoft and Nokia see so-called *mobile commerce* as the next big growth wave within their industry.

The first goal here is to actualise immediacy, for all the above reasons. The contemporary way of achieving this is via a so-called *always-on* mode. In simple terms, most data received is bursty. That is, you log on to your e-mail, type a word, and wait for it to download and then read the message. Down- and uploading data uses a lot of bandwidth, but there are gaps as the server looks up your e-mail. GPRS, or General Packet Radio Service, is beginning to allow for high-speed connection, so that millions of users can be logged on to the same network at the same time, in an always-on mode. Other mobile connection technologies such as infra-red ports or Bluetooth (short-range (25-metres), high-frequency radio transponding up to 1 Mbps) enables the interconnection of disparate tools such as personal digital assistants, printers, cameras, games consoles, and other digital tools into so-called *wire free* personal area networks (PANs) and collaborative area networks (CANs). These networks are not limited to the kinds of working environments described in the last chapter or even the home den, but in-field *on the hoof* applications, such as the car, boat, train, jet and of course the humble individual along the street/shopping mall/school/and so on. Ultra high frequency (UHF) beacons placed on roadways, city blocks, business parks, marinas, that transmit ever higher bandwidth capacity are growing in number. The service providers, ranging from traffic management to information exchanges, to entertainment, to the remote access providers themselves, are fast increasing in number, and none of this is even close to what is to come over the next five years.

Third generation universal mobile telecommunications system (3G-UMCS) technology will access *multimedia-rich* services and content, on a near global scale (North and South America, Europe and much of the Far East). These 3G devices will be smart voice activated with larger viewscreens, that learn your express needs, habits and tastes. Wherever there is a need to communicate via voice, video or data, 3G-UMCS is only going to proliferate. In fact, the Mobile Data Association (www.mda-mobiledata.org) claim that there will be at least one billion mobile units, of one kind or another, shipped by 2005. Whether it be up-front ideas during concept generation, or data within the supply chain, or customer support, hand-held multimedia devices, such as Compaq's pocket PC, with software from the likes of Parallel Graphics, to view and interact with 3D graphics in real time, are only set to grow in number. The other mobile tool that is expected to make big waves over the next few years, is the PC-Tablet, coming from the likes of Microsoft and Compaq. This device looks like an electronic book, but has all the functionality of desktop PC… Here are some guidelines for the development of such mobile tools:

- Why do you need mobile tools? It is a question every organisation now needs to ask. Are your people working more in the field? Do you need to collaborate with suppliers, and alliance partners? Do you need to learn from the customer (re: Chapter 3), do you need to collaborate with customers?
- Where is the data likely to be needed? Local, regional, global, where? The good news here, is that remote access technologies are evolving, and the number of locations are dramatically increasing. Logging on to internet service providers (ISPs) without having to set up an account in different countries, for example, is a growing necessity. Various service providers, such as Cognito and iPASS, offer such open remote access, connecting remote access nodes in modern airports, hotels, malls, and so on.
- Are there any repeatable processes that can be workflow mapped and automated? Innovation, in the most part, is not a repeatable process, as I will further explain in the next section. But there will be common subprocesses that can be captured on-line. Identify them and automate them (for example, the customer analysis tools in Part V).
- How is the data going to move? Is it synchronous, is it wireless, is it wireless on GPRS? Will it go through trunk radio, will it include emerging 3G platforms? You need to know this, as it will define the boundaries and investment costs for how far you need to go to meet your objectives.
- Scalability for growth in the future, so there is a need to identify the kind of data, the bandwidths required, and the amount of traffic growth.
- Secure remote access is obviously important, as the outfield equipment is, after all, out there. Kit gets lost and stolen, files are opened in public places, new people are coming into the fold all of the time. A layered approach to access is a good starting point. At the end of the day, who gets to access *what*, needs to be defined by company policy.

Multidimensional navigator. This tool renders colossal amounts of information in a format that is easily accessible and recognisable. For sure, in an information-dense universe this is core to any hypermachine. Multidimensional navigators that bring together vast pools of information and interconnect ideas in unique ways, are now hitting the market. The whole team can, via a puck or eye gesture, move ideas around on the media screen, and integrate information from far-flung on-line databases. The hypermachine's digital intelligence engine can look for holistic concepts in a complexity beyond any human capacity, thus giving a powerful lever between engulfing amounts of informing and understanding in complex projects. This is a vital must if teams are to manage continued upward complexity. The goal is to make often abstract or tacit ideas visible, so that formal real-world knowledge searches can be made in the form of some graphical representation, and eventual direct links to the whole team mind.

Hyperindex. Information begets more information, but only if we are in a position to access and use current *what-is* information, via creatively searching through *what-if* options. This is accomplished via a so-called *hyperindex,* which is coupled to the navigator. An *n*-index interconnects specific data, facts and figures, design techniques and tools, documents and drawings, reports, and so on, in many dimensions. The hyperindex can also assist in jogging the team mind, leveraging on tacit knowledge and approaches. The hypermachine index may be organised as follows:

- *Classification.* The *whats* of the index system, facilitating the meta-tagging, cataloguing, and indexing in themes, titles and keywords.
- *Place.* The *where* of the index. Where information, knowledge and ideas are stored. Whether in a digital database or the physical world.
- *Time.* The *when* of the index. When the information, knowledge or idea was generated. This helps keep track of the evolution and augmentation of ideas.
- *System.* The *how* of the index, how the information, knowledge or idea is stored, within a digital database, library, museum, or real-world artefacts.

Team Interfaces Technology

Perhaps the most interesting area of the hypermachine is the technology that interfaces with individuals and teams; and is also conceivably the area that has the most potential for innovation. These team/machine interfaces not only replace the keyboard and mouse, they completely redefine what it means to interact with technologies, such as idea leverage tools (above), or simulation systems (below). Team interfaces turn such activities with technology, away from a cold, detached experience, to one of fun and dynamic interactivity. The goal is to develop an environment that is not only smart, but effect relationships that are intimate and tacit. There are five emerging core technologies that can integrate as a team interface:

- *Haptic systems.* This technology integrates the sensation of motion to the positions of limbs (for example hands, fingers, feet, knees, head, eyelashes) in relation to the physical world. For example, when one casts a fishing fly into a lake, or the movement one makes while driving a car, *haptic* systems can simulate and translate such dynamic forces directly to human sensations, effecting meaningful tactile input. This technology can be applied in the manipulation of objects in a virtual simulation, say, moving a virtual chair across a virtual floor. It helps perceive the physics of such an activity (moving a chair), without the need for physical artefacts.
- *Kinaesthetic systems.* Dynamic force feedback systems that engage with our tactile senses in real time. For example, the sensation of what it would be like to wave your hand through a viscous fluid. IBM have developed such tactile systems that interface with a scanning tunnelling microscope. Scientists can now actually feel with their fingertips the surface of atoms lying in a matrix. These *kinaesthetic* models thus move away from mere computer graphical representations, to create multi-dimensional simulations that include the measures that scientists use to describe such molecule behaviour.
- *Gesture recognition.* Tools to capture body language and gesture subtleties, heading up where further suspended assumptions can be achieved. Gesture recognition technology picks up – via inbuilt sensors and motor domains – body and facial movement: point, blinking, nod, stir, frown, shrug and any mixture thereof, and the mind of the hyper-machine interprets holistic gestures. A good application for gesture recognition is for people with a physical handicap or people recovering from a major accident. It is possible, for example, to manipulate a whole virtual world via mere eye movement. And now put this in the context of a team, collectively manipulating a design simulation. You get a VR simulation of unheard of collaboration potential.

- *Visualisation technology.* There is no more powerful thought capacity than visual thinking, and this is heightened when put into the context of innovation. Visual thinking is understood to be the human mind's primary thinking mechanism. Tools that enable heightened visual thinking of the untouchable, unseeable, unthinkable are now hitting the market, and the technology now in the research labs borders on the profound. Autostereoscopic-visioning is very exciting, and by itself opens up the door for 3D holographic views of design schemes. Multiway, real-time, all-ways-on, large-scale (5 × 3 metres) digital videoscreens now link dispersed team members, allowing face-to-face collaboration with simulated models and data, instantly. The speed at which this technology is blossoming is incomprehensible.
- *Virtual immersion environments.* Three of the five senses – sight, sound and touch – are totally immersed in VR, cut off from the outside world. This technology gives almost real-world quality graphics. Sound is 3D, giving realistic acoustic source points. Technologies that improve the field of vision, such as eye-slave and 170-degree-wide vision units, are emerging. Digiscent (smell) and digiflavor (taste) technology are available now. Even deeper technologies such as retina injection, write to retina, kinaesthetic and real-time polymorphological feedback are in the VR labs. Above all, this is executed in real-time, real-world density holographics; not on screen, but projected by a laser all-round imagery.

Now thread each of these team interfaces into seamless wholes, and you begin to develop a ultra-powerful collaborative tool beyond the puny limitations of the mouse and qwerty keyboard. And this is no sci-fi dream, it all happening now.

TRW, a British design consultancy, have linked hands with SGI, the US supercomputer giant, to build an advanced immersive virtual reality design studio. It has 170-degree field of vision, giving designers that 'in there' illusion. The immersive design environment is impressive to say the least. The half-light gives a futuristic theatre-like atmosphere as soon as you step into the room. Within this environment Renault are collaborating with TWR on the design of a range of new sports vehicles. The team interface technology has shaved months off the design cycle time, and has allowed TWR and Renault to walk through design solutions in ways far beyond that possible with physical prototypes. In particular, they can blow up design assemblies 100 times real size, allowing designers to move through schemes not unlike that from the land of the giants. This perception change gives the Renault/TWR design team the confidence, and indeed the capability, to look at more radical options, while accelerating learning and therefore reducing design risks.

Perhaps the foremost leader in team interface innovation is Trimension. They design and integrate immersive work environments, giving up full-blown stereoscopic imagery, tactility and sound for application in science, design, architecture and entertainment. This allows for holistic visualisation of large data sets and complex design problems. The *interaction-kit* is most impressive. The 3D-stereoscopic eyeglasses and interactive data gloves enable users to manipulate virtual models in a more natural and direct way than the conventional mouse. Working in synch with the interaction kit, is the *ascension tracking system*. It can simultaneously track head and hand movements, while keeping the relative geometry of a virtual model absolutely true. And the *solid screen technology* provides excellent focus and calibration without loss of a single pixel. As an integrated system, Trimension's virtual reality rooms now set a new standard for collaborative team interfaces, and is only set to rapidly advance in development over the coming years.

Virtual Reality Simulation Tools

The design, build, test and verify in the mind of a hypermachine is now essential for teams to:

(a) view the consequences of designs before manufacture and/or market introduction;

(b) shrink design cycle time;

(c) reduce the cost of design cycle;

(d) reduce the cost of the actual end-product/service;

(e) improve the performance of the design;

(f) enter brand new vectors of conceptual design space.

Among the hundreds of proprietary platforms in this field, there are two kinds of design simulation power tools that will significantly up performance in all these areas: genetic algorithms, and seamless simulation suites.

Genetic algorithms. If you need to produce designs of superior performance, in significantly shorter time frames, then capitalise on genetic algorithms (GAs). GAs exploit Darwinian-like natural selection in the mind of a computer... Take, for example, perfecting the hull of a huge, transoceanic container ship for *speed* and for *cargo* capacity. If it were possible to engineer a ship to carry a standard load, but cross an ocean at twice the speed, that would indeed be a viable product. Traditionally, engineers apply engineering principles based on empirical data built up over years of engineering ship hulls. Every now and then, usually from some out-of-the-blue origin, a radically new idea will come about, and again through accumulated experience, will eventually lead to a breakthrough in design. GAs, however, can start from scratch, with no experience whatsoever. The hypermachine's neural net serves as the environment. The physical conditions of the ocean are input into the simulation knowledge base, and via the rule induction engine, the physics and technical parameters of materials and construction methods are added. Next, the design intent is input: *best speed with a 200 kiloton load over an area 500 metres by 50 metres*. The GA is then initiated, bringing into play nature's editor: *natural selection*. The computer model cycles at high speed, learning, adapting and feeding back. The weak designs die, and the strong designs are built upon. Eventually through the code's search, the ultimate performance scheme for practical design intent is reached. Nature's design rules have been simulated, but instead of natural biological evolution's time base – millions of years – the hypermachine gives intellectual evolution's time base – just a few hours... *And so it seems that evolution has itself now become a design tool!* Design simulation using GAs and other advanced tools most certainly can now:

- *Find a fundamentally original design, faster.* GAs can define their own criteria for design selection, without human input, and as a consequence are not limited to cultural conditioning or the bias of human personality (not that bias and personality are unimportant in design). Selection pressure, whether natural or artificial, breeds perpetual novelty as a result of the vector search through conceptual design space not only being acutely accelerated, but quite different from that of human bias. Different in that the next cycle of the simulation is a result of previously unknown and non-deterministic internalised artificial selection pressures. Thus GAs find unique schemes faster.
- *Find a more effective design that no human can imagine or understand.* Biological-like algorithms evolve, for example, software programs that have no direct meaning in human comprehension, yet are simpler and more reliable than any top-down design using the most advanced

methodologies. BT use nature's processes to grow software for complex distributed telecommunications systems. In one case, BT researchers have reduced a cumbersome, yet fathomable, software program from 1,600,000 lines of code to a mere 1000 lines that is ultimately incomprehensible, yet totally reliable. Again, computer-evoked counter-intuitive outcomes can outfly human intelligence. Thus GAs find more potent schemes faster.

- *Find the most efficient design with the least resource.* Lighter and stronger; longer and faster for less power; quick refinement; even complete optimisation; these are all contradictions in terms, yet engineers have for many thousands of years battled to break these kinds of performance deadlock. But now – if you have the time on your hands – go take a walk in the park. It does not take too long to notice that nature's body designs outgun any human effort on improving efficiency along any and all of these lines. Now GAs are beginning to match nature's design work, via selecting stronger, yet again, counterintuitive designs that break the more-for-less rebuttal. Electric motors designed like abdominal gut, composite substrates mimicking living cells, load-bearing structures with the strength of steel and the weight of honey-comb, fluorescent ultra-low energy lighting with 20 years' life, all now take a leap in efficiency through application of GAs. Thus GAs find fitter schemes faster.
- *Create a more beautiful and elegant design than any human.* By repeating symmetry breaks and fractal self-similarity algorithms over and over, while selecting and feeding back towards the design intent, architectural structures and domestic products begin to look like nature's garden. Who can argue that nature outguns us here too. The wonderful news is, this really is the shape of things to come. Thus GAs find more attractive and refined schemes faster.
- *Find the safest design.* Through continuous weak/strong selection cycles, noses get put on the front of human heads rather than on the back, or here, crowd control flow dynamics or car tyre tread reach safer designs in shorter time. Thus GAs find more secure schemes faster.
- *Give birth to the least expensive design in the least time.* As a result of the above, what-if simulations of conditions in the mind of hyper-machines are being used to experiment with ideas that could not be justified in terms of time and money in the real world. Even end-product direct costs are being shrunk as a result artificial selection. Thus GAs find more economical schemes faster.

The field of design simulation via genetic algorithms, along with other advanced tools, is a rapidly growing application science and technology. Proprietary application GAs are with us now, go seek them on the www; download the freeware; play, learn, adapt and feed back.

Seamless simulation suites. Clearly, as products and services become ever more diverse and interconnected in terms of their core technology and market demands, *simulation* tools must accommodate such complexity. *seamless simulation suites* are new and emerging tools that offer a window on the total cycle of complex innovation.

Take the innovation of an *inflight entertainment* system. Such a system is made up of two dozen major subsystems, each integrating a diverse spread of core technologies. The list of subsystems goes something like this: Electro-optical systems for the flat video-view screens. Interconnected cable looms with a combined length of six miles and more. A passenger control handset integrating telephonic, acoustic, text messaging, games control, and credit card reader systems. A video-on-demand juke box. A head-end central entertainment control system... and this just scratches the surface... to come, add and interconnect about 10 more complex assemblages, each with tens of thousands of lines of embedded software code. Next, all of this kit and code has to be qualified and certified to airborne equipment standards, in turn mechanically and electronically integrated to the cabin service system, and then maintained and serviced on a daily basis. And do not forget the fact that this system has to be continuously in development to keep up with a competitive context that is evolving at fast gait.

In the old days (about five years ago), all this equipment would have been designed, developed and integrated via piecemeal computer-aided design systems. Today, the so-called seamless simulation suites are sweeping in, a fleet of tools that design, develop and integrate all of the above core technologies in one seamless model. It is possible to go from basic concept right through to fully integrated systems model, all in VR. Whether electrical, electronic, software, ergonomics, styling, mechanical, optical, thermal, dynamics, statics, molecular, acoustic, animation, process, whatever the *n*-innovation is made up from, it can be designed and integrated in virtual reality. Here is a list of key functional aspects of seamless simulation suites to guide selection. This is a top-level list, and applies across the many kind of suites your enterprise may choose to develop:

- First and foremost, fully associative integrated modelling capability that uses single source data for that single model.

- Smart automation of basic design and development tasks (for example auto-assembly, or non-rational molecular build parameters, or auto-software routine validation, and so on).
- Collaborative web integration capability, for real-time meetings across internal teams and external alliances, on a global and local scale (for example MS NetMeeting).
- Smart translators that allow the sharing of data between other heterogeneous VR simulation systems.
- Flexible configuration, both logically and physically, as different innovations require different information processes and simulation tool arrangements.
- Automatic and instant live web-page creation for instant view in the real world with customers, suppliers, maintainers, partners, and so on.
- Real-time web-based system maintenance direct from the system provider.

Again, the systems are mostly proprietary these days, and can be found through any number of VR journals, and others alike.

Implementation Approach

DIY or ASP? In management consulting speak, that really means do-it-yourself, or tender a turnkey solution from a comprehensive application service provider (ASP). There are, of course, advantages and disadvantages on both sides. The easy answer is to look at your firm's technical capability, and indeed vision for such hypermachines. But at the end of the day, this is about collaborative work again. Even the largest of the ASPs such as I-Fusion and SAP, are not geared up to meet every company's needs, all of the time. What it takes is an alliance strategy among many different kinds of service and technology providers.

However, there are handful of principles I would recommend when building and implementing such hypermachines:

- *Discontinuous strategy*. You are in one of the fastest growing, rapidly developing areas of technology. This is not merely a continuous improvement game, it is an area fraught with discontinuous, disruptive technologies, that change the rules of the game overnight. It is, after all, hyperinnovation in one of its most ardent and accomplished forms. Your hypermachine will grow and evolve beyond recognition within even a very short span.

- *Work with ASPs that have a proven track record.* Always question any major investment decision in this area. Always seek more than one opinion and solution to the same problem.
- *Enjoy the ride.* At the very least, this is about further enabling and amplifying the hyperinnovation organisation. At its utmost, it is a creative endeavour, a job of discovery and adventure. Do not panic when the system crashes, do not go ballistic when data disappears into the blue. Anything and everything can be relearned and duplicated, and in my experience learned and cloned for the better the next time around. Yes, mirror all your data around the world in deep concrete bunkers. Build redundancy so the show does not stop. But most of all, enjoy the ride.

Hyperinnovation Organisation

Organisation – whether people or information, ideas or technologies, indeed entire collaborative networks and giant institutions – is the most complex task of all. Yet, remember the sagacious words of Loa Tzu, 'that intelligent control appears as uncontrol or freedom'. And nature is showing the way here. If we take on the principles emerging from the science of complexity, even the most demanding hyperinnovation projects can be managed with the speed and agility of swarming of birds... Clearly, if hyperinnovation is the end, then the hyperinnovation organisation is the means.

PART IV

Hyperinnovation Projects

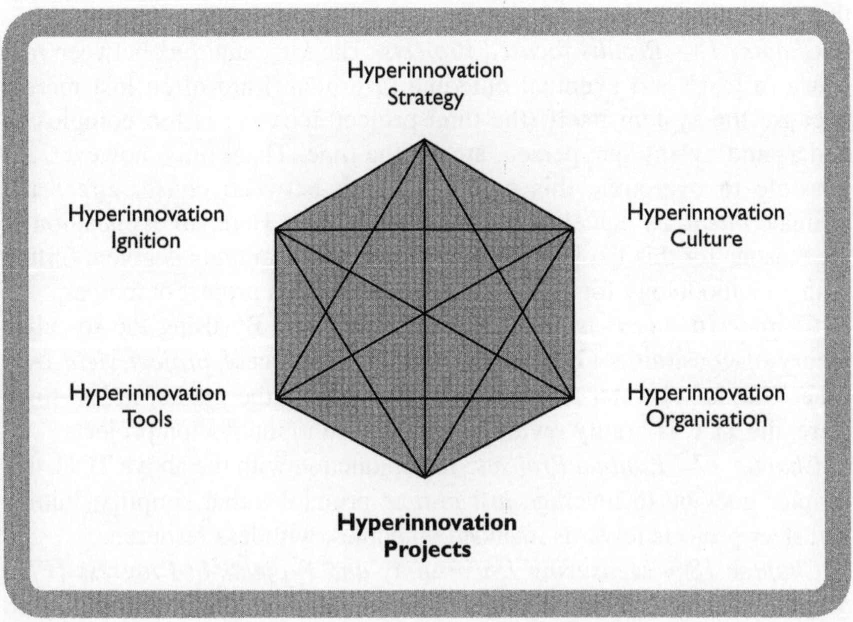

The first thing project planning does is to tell you what you didn't want to know.
ADRIAN DOOLEY, CHAIRMAN, THE PROJECTS GROUP

Countless books have been written on project management, yet few begin to address innovation. Part IV takes an in-depth look at hyperinnovation and its project management. Here, once again, the needs of multidimensional innovation differ vastly from conventional project administration for reasons we have already begun to explore. Innovation by its very nature, means going beyond current experience and knowledge pools, and way on into the unknown. As a result, *uncertainty* underlies innovation's every step. But more, we are talking multidimensional innovation – innovations that contain ideas from diverse and unique origins interconnected in novel and often complex ways. Conventional project management crumbles under these conditions, and reason number one why innovative product and services often arrive late to market, below specification, over budget, and ultimately and most importantly fail in the market. Here, *hyperinnovation projects* make use of new management concepts, outlining the necessary project principles and methodologies that further support the kind of dynamic, emergent organisation outlined in the last section; including:

Chapter 15 – Results-focused Projects: The *logic* and *link* between root cause (a task) and eventual outcome (a product) are often lost merely because the system itself (the total project activity) is too complex to understand by any one person, at any one time. Thankfully, however, it's possible to overcome this potential break between *cause*, *effect* and ultimate *intent*, by acutely focusing on outcomes. Here, an explanation of the reasons for this likely seizure amid inputs and outputs is given, further with a methodology for the delineation of intended project outcomes.

Chapter 16 – Less is More, Results over Time: By using the so-called theory-of-constraints (TOC) it is possible to increase *project yield* over time. That is, a greater number of projects hitting the market in less time. Here, the TOC is briefly reviewed and applied to innovation projects.

Chapter 17 – Kanban Projects: In conjunction with the above TOC, this chapter goes on to leverage *just-in-time* principles that simplify, initiate and steer projects towards intended outcomes, with less resource.

Chapter 18 – Measuring Uncertainty and Projects-in-Progress (PIP) Mapping: The greater the uncertainty factors in a given innovation project, the longer the relative cycle time. Consequently by quantifying specific project uncertainty it is possible to forecast a relative cycle time for any given project. Here, a methodology is outlined that does exactly this. As a follow-on, a methodology for quantifying the *combined* uncertainty of the total number of projects-in-progress (PIP) is given. Hence, it is possible to map the timing factors for each PIP as a collective. This helps gauge how many different projects a particular organisation can take on at any one time and effectively bring to market.

All told, hyperinnovation projects go dead against the grain of conventional project management wisdom. But, as all must be clearer by now, the nonlinear business world we all live in, with its growing number of interconnected innovations, calls for a complete rethink in terms of mindsets and methods to bring such complex, often counterintuitive, propositions from initial concept to market.

CHAPTER 15

Results-focused Projects

When you get to the peak of the project, and turn to look back, you will see a clear-cut path trailing down the project's mountainside. It certainly will not be a straight line; the path will have snaked around problems, crawled over obstacles, pushed through delays, and jumped intellectual crevasses. On that peak, you will wonder how you made such a mess of the journey. In the extreme you will want to purge the so-called culprits, and the mistakes and delays they made. But the next time around you will be faced by the same difficult mountain to climb. Some – almost all – never learn. Each time they approach an innovative project, they anticipate doing it absolutely *right first time*, and set off for a smooth climb. Even veterans make this same mistake – some never accept that innovation is uncertain, embedded with lists of unknowns, with often complex and chaotic tasks – and in doing so, innovation projects progress at a glacial pace, limit multidimensional thinking, and drain the coffers almost dry.

The Death of a Project Manager

What is the universal method for monitoring and controlling an innovation project? Answer: the classic style critical path plan – a capture of tasks, trailing off in a path of linear causality. But can you control an innovation project reliably using this approach?... The short answer: *no, you [cannot control] an innovation project by a schedule*, because there is no such thing as a reliable innovation project plan. *Innovation is quite different in nature when compared to a steady-state process.*

Take for example the case study of the construction and commissioning of a huge, towering offshore oil rig – a great feat of human endeavour. Project management teams use some very sophisticated planning methodologies to assess the 'who, what, why, when, where and how' of the project and their associated risks, which in turn allows for fairly sound project scheduling. But, facts are facts, projects of the 'oil rig' type, and their lesser mortals, are well-defined creatures. Designs have been proven time and time again, accumulating massive pools of knowledge and experience to aid the targeting of project threats, opportunities and associated probabilities of outcome. Many of the risks are 'knowns', allowing for worst/best case projections to be mapped with some accuracy. For example, the 'weather' is a project risk. When a rig is constructed and commissioned, the weather has great influence on project timing and eventual cost. Whether the weather will be kind or against the project, is an uncertainty. But this uncertainty has limits, the worst case could be extreme weather conditions and its effect on the project can be worked out for worst case outcome. In turn, appropriate contingencies can be put into place to overcome these uncertainties, and the project can move in an orderly fashion through its life cycle. The key point – and this is what is so different about managing innovation projects – is that the [weather] is a [known]. As unpredictable as it is, it is a [known]. But true innovations are strangers. We cannot *know* what the uncertainties are going to be until they arrive. Innovation is by definition about going beyond experience and knowledge pools. There is little or no database to indicate project threats and opportunities, and therefore uncertainties can be – under this context – absolute.

How Effect Comes Away from Intent

To further compound this, the old *Newtonian* world-view of project management says *that for every action there is an equal reaction*; that is, events are mostly predictable through a discrete set of deterministic causes. However, higher-dimensional innovations do not conform to the rational notions of Newton. The more complex a system becomes, or the more event sequence is broken down, the more effect detaches from its cause. In fact, flat causality in higher-dimensional innovation is an illusion. Tiny perturbations in event sequence cause gross shifts in downstream outcome (the butterfly effect). Further, planned intent can unhinge from effect, in innovations that contain many novel ideas. Novelty will bring with it the unexpected, and in the unexpected come contingencies. Under these conditions, Newtonian-style project management that says everything can be defined as a neat and tidy linear programme, is all but useless. The fact of the matter is, in multidimensional innovation projects

Harrisian hyperlogic takes over; that is, for every interconnection there may be an unequal and unexpected reaction.

Keep Your Eyes on Results and Outcomes

If effect comes away from its cause, and intent disappears out of sight, how is it then possible to manage such complex projects, without cause, effect and intent running astray? The simple answer is to focus on end-results. Only by keeping your eyes on end-results will you ever have any chance of hitting intended targets. Traditional project planning involved keeping an eye on the process and how the sequence of tasks maps out on paper. But in reality, the result will always be a product of an acausal set of events that can only unfold in real time (there will still be a process, but it will be of an emergent kind, not a top-down planned typology. Each innovation project will require a unique set of activities and therefore is non-repeatable in detail). By focusing on results, you will continuously calibrate the direction of the project in real time. So forget the process, and focus on intended results.

There are two questions to ask here: First define in qualitative and quantitative terms exactly the demanded end-results (what at the end of the day do you want in your hand?). If you do not know what you really want, how will you know when you get there? Second, and just as important, ask, ask and ask again, and then ask again: 'what do we need to do that will achieve the result/s?' Try to answer these questions in the simplest terms.

Defining the End-result

Focusing on results dramatically declutters the project from the start. Even for innovations containing hundreds upon hundreds of interconnected subsystems (Boeing 777, digital cash, Disney theme parks), by succinctly defining what you want, profoundly focuses the whole team mind. So define in a succinct way, exactly what you want to achieve. This is a major achievement in itself. Examples:

- All-in-one lowest cost energyplex service
- Most thrilling interactive hypermovies
- Ultra-friendly internet toothbrush system

- Affordable home dome VR centre
- Ultra-glamour class inflight cabin service
- Absolute cover insurance.

The single best means to define such an intended end-result is in the real-world prototype (physical or virtual). Michael Schrage remarks that *customers are not interested in technical specifications or sophisticated project plans, they want to see what they are going to get at the end of the day... and the best way to capture that, is in the prototype...*

How to Get What You Want: Learn to Think in Multidimensions

In simple terms, the end-result should lead each key stage of a project. Each stage is merely a reflection of that end-result. However, each key stage needs to be considered in light of each other stage. To do this you need to think in multidimensions. There can be four key stages to any innovation project:

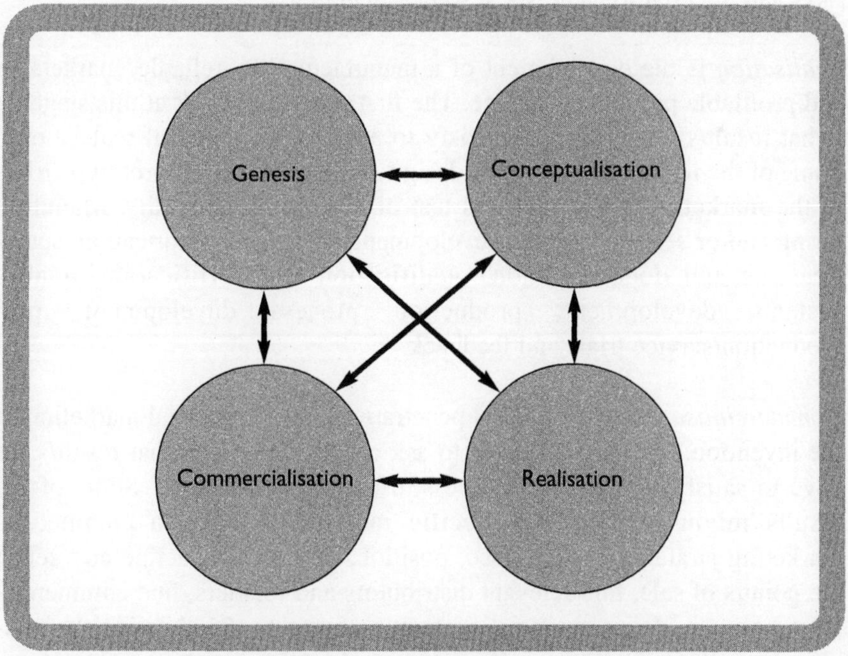

Figure 15.1 Stages of hyperinnovation projects

Genesis is the creation of a seed idea. The first question to ask at this stage is: 'what result/s does the prototype have to satisfy to achieve a successful genesis?' The rule here is that there are no rules. Genesis is not by any stretch of the imagination rational or obvious, this is primarily a creative-thinking, playing, toying process. Some of the results might be: idea synthesis with focus on design intent, gather and analyse relevant market/customer information, find the best competitors (if any) and what exactly they have achieved, build a financial model, estimates of technological feasibility, and approximate project scaling.

Conceptualisation is the objective definition of the innovation's features and characteristics in the form of robust prototype models (whether physical or virtual). The first question to ask at this stage is: 'what result/s does the prototype have to satisfy to achieve a successful conceptualisation?' This is a *what-if* stage? It is a chance to experiment with options and ideas. The *prototype* must define the 'what' but not the 'how'. This opens up creativity. The *how* must be solved during the *realisation* stage. Some of the results might be: generate a *prototype* that focuses on design intent, experimental design concepts or service layouts, core technological acquisition or development, project capital acquisition, deeper project scaling, risks and uncertainty analysis, resource planning.

Realisation is the development of a manufacturable, reliable, marketable and profitable product or service. The first question to ask at this stage is: 'what result/s do we have to satisfy to achieve a successful realisation?' Some of the results might be: the design-of-experiments, β-prototype trials in the market, development and test of system functionality. Manufacturing and/or service systems development, tooling and fabrication, specifications and documentation, qualification and certification, quality systems development, production process development, pre-production/service trials and feedback.

Commercialisation is the market penetration and commercial marketing of the invention. The first question to ask at this stage is: 'what result/s we have to satisfy to achieve a successful commercialisation?' Some of the results might be: identify specific markets, develop a commercial marketing strategy (profit, place, position, promotion), define and select the point/s of sale, find relevant distributors and retailers, find commercial sales partners, define financial accounting systems. By defining the end-objectives first, builds the key success factors into the project from the start.

Each stage will interact with each other stage. All stages *cannot* be co-ordinated by optimising and assembly of one perfect system. As in previous chapters, nature employs multiple systems that run in parallel – sometimes converging, sometimes diverging, but mostly multidimensional. Here, overlap between any sub-goal will affect each other sub-goal's progress (A=B;B=A). Product prototypes will evolve as learning through experiments and testing evolves. Marketing strategy will change to the tune of information coming in from conceptualisation prototypes. Quality systems will change as manufacturing systems prototypes develop. All of this is a highly dynamic, highly ambiguous den of activities. Only by continually focusing on end-results via real-world prototypes in the light of these dynamics, will you stand any chance of true and timely innovation.

Keep All Project Problem Solving at the Team Level

Accelerating multidimensional innovation also means not building those all too common mountains out of tiny molehills. What makes a major conundrum out of a simple issue, is when day-to-day problem solving (for example identifying a customer requirement, changing a technical specification, procuring a new component) is either interfered with or resolved up the hierarchy. The lessons here: if a project problem is solved up the chain of command it tends to gain political momentum, no matter how small the issue starts out. That is, simple issues tend to become exaggerated, just by the fact that a senior manager is involved. In the extreme, simple issues can blow up into hot potatoes, which can then be used as a political leverage point. I have seen project teams, on more than one occasion, walk out of a meeting under a cloud, just because some Machiavellian executive has made a political issue out of something that should not have even been contested in the first place. This can deeply demoralise and demotivate an innovation team.

And if you are an executive, even the chief officer, I have some tough words for you. Be very tight on results. Demand that results are achieved on time, budget and specification. But let the team take control. If you do not, you will tip the cart up, and all the apples with it.

Daily Real-time Results Focused Meeting

Furthermore, if bimonthly progress meetings are the common platform for project control and proceedings, especially if headed by senior management teams, then delays will only accumulate. Again, innovation is a real-time business, so again, *all* project problem solving has to be carried out within the team.

To keep problem solving within the team, I would recommend one formal scheduled meeting. A *daily results-focused meeting* (circa 10 to 15 minutes), held by the project host, where everybody available in the crew gets together around a real *prototype* (not a detailed schedule), each morning to discuss the day's targets and deliverables. It is a clarifying of events, set against each key stage end-result. This is not a meeting with an agenda, the dynamics of innovation will outdate the agenda as soon as the ink dries. Open, creative, intelligent, spontaneous, interactive, on the fly, are some of the words that accurately describe this kind of collaborative powwow.

Again, focus on results to build in a feedback loop that recalibrates the prototypes each morning (for a more detailed account of feedback systems and control, see Chapter 26). So tear up your formal plans. Roll up your sleeves. Go on a diet and just do it in real time. Not stodgy wait a week progress meetings carried on up and down the hierarchy – real-time action, real-time information, real-time problem solving, real-time decision making, focused on real-world end-results from within the team is a winning formula.

CHAPTER 16

Less Is More, Results Over Time

Increased project yield is partly the product of more 'results over time', by concentrating on fewer projects at any one time.

Techno had a list of 15 projects, all of them being actively worked on at one and the same time. Resources are spread equally over each of the 15 projects. Some of the projects are missing their milestones. Staff are redeployed to shore up the lagging projects. Reliability, performance, customer's needs are skipped over, and functionality is being trimmed. Costs increase, pressure heats up, tempers fuse, morale falls, the boss steps out on to the ledge, and one year later not one project has been launched into the market. What a mess!

Gemetics have similar resources and are developing products of similar levels of novelty and complexity. But Gemetics are working on fewer projects at any one time. Five in fact. Full-time teams are deployed for the whole innovation cycle, problems are solved on the spot. Six months later, two of the projects are launched to market. Six more months pass, and two more hit the market exactly when Gemetics want them to.

These simplified (maybe oversimplified) examples begin to open up the problem. A further analysis may reveal more.

Diffusion Confusion

Many commercial organisations have a *hot project list*. An inventory of unconceptualised products and/or services they wish to introduce, in line with a specific product/service innovation strategy. Techno have a roasting hot list of over 45 concepts, but have decided that they can manage no more than 15 new innovation projects at any one time. Various gaps have appeared in Techno's product range, and they intend to fill the gaps before year-end. Two opportunities have been spotted in the market. Techno are sure the competition have their eyes on these weak signal trends too; so, in fact, Techno plan to hit the market with a range of entirely new products within nine months.

For Techno, tradition has it that the engineer, technician, merchandiser, designer, marketer, and so on, should be working on an array of new projects at any one time, thereby *optimising* utilisation and flexibility. In Techno's development department, they have five engineers of differing levels of experience. The 15 projects were divided among each of the five engineers. Which means that each engineer is handling between two and four projects. Which particular project an engineer would work on in his batch, more often than not depended on outside influences, based on priorities set by management. For instance, if a component supplier was due for a visit, the engineer would drop project 'A', and pick up project 'B'. If a marketing meeting was called, project 'C' would be picked up, and so on.

Organisational Entropy and the Wait-state Trap

The danger here is that this seemingly flexible approach is very wasteful and misleading, especially on paper. Why?... In this case it is mostly down to two key factors.

First, *organisational entropy*, a multitude of people, working on multiple projects, attacking several issues, sets up high and unnecessary levels of turbulence. Person 'A' needs to communicate with person 'B' on project 'C'. But person 'B' is engrossed in project 'D'. When person 'B' is ready to address project 'C', person 'A' is focused on project 'E'. In a real situation, with tens, sometimes hundreds of people working on dozens of projects and thousands of issues, organisational entropy produces significant time delays.

Second, *wait-states*, an endless string of *stop/go* situations. The engineer jumps off project 'C', because the engineer either has to wait for someone else in the enterprise to progress their part of project 'C' or somebody else working on project 'D' is shouting louder. In reality the time between put down and pick up is wasteful and what is more, the greater the number of projects an engineer works on at any one time, the greater the time between stop/go. The point is, little actually gets done, because just as the engineer begins to achieve any level of work, he is pulled off a particular project.

But there is more to this. The engineer is not the only one working on the project. Hyperinnovation is a multidiscipline process. Many different people involved in the project, whether in marketing or operations or sales, are caught up in the same wait-state trap. Take all of the wait-states and organisational entropy situations on a company-wide basis, and it adds up to nothing less than a calamity. Encouraging people to work on several projects at once is of course possible and very tempting. But don't do it. Organisational entropy and wait-states will very quickly develop. A project in wait-state is a project on stop, no matter how one looks at it.

Compare this to the conclusions of Dr Eli Goldratt. Goldratt has developed a manufacturing methodology that is often adopted as a compliment to JIT/Kanban production systems. He calls it the *theory-of-constraints*, or TOC for short. TOC has nine golden rules, two of which may be applied here. The two rules state:

- The level of utilisation of a non-bottleneck is not determined by its own potential, but by some other constraint in the system.
- Activation and utilisation of a resource are not synonymous.

In essence, the first statement means that a resource can only work as effectively as the weakest/slowest link in the chain, and the second statement holds that there is a difference between what *should* be used and what *could* be used. In innovation project terms, these two statements can be compared.

As with JIT manufacturing, the machines and tools stand idle, not the component parts. In other words, instead of putting the project on hold for the sake of waiting for people, *people* must be put on hold for the sake of speeding the project. Counterintuitive logic. Taking the engineer, marketer, purchasing officer, and so on, in the multiproject scenario, he/she can only do as much as the slowest task allows, and that it is important for the engineer/marketer/purchasing officer to wait and do nothing, rather than work on a multitude of projects and add to the project delay themselves.

The key point here is that the good intention to work on a batch of different projects actually adds to choking the system and thereby creating more bottlenecks and in turn wait-states.

Yield: Results over Time

The whole hub of this issue is *yield*, expressed as project *results over time* (R/t). If an engineer or marketer is actively (activation) engaged in working on one project, say three-fifths of the time (60 per cent utilisation factor), while delivering the project on time and on budget, surely this is better than working on a whole spread of projects being engaged 100 per cent of the time and not getting any of the projects to market on time and most taking two or three times longer than intended!

Yet in traditional accounting terms this is hard to swallow. For example, take a prototype technician. If he/she finishes a prototype and has no work to do until the next stage, say the next day, or even next week, does that make an inefficient organisation? Equally, does putting her in a remote shop in the next building working on a multitude of prototypes from different projects make more sense? On paper it does. In reality it does not even begin to work. The amount of wait-states derived through lack of cumulative learning, information going back and forth, waiting for people to reply, departmental barriers and the like, defeat any hope of meeting deadlines. And besides, resources focused on a single project are so interactive that the chance of a prototype model maker, or anyone for that matter, having nothing to do for a while, is remote to say the least.

But it does not stop here. There is the issue of ownership (recall Chapter 12?). Giving ownership means commitment. You either believe that committing people on a full-time basis brings the level of self-control and trust to bring a continuous stream of hyperinnovation, or you do not. There is no grey area on this issue.

Apart from the greater project yield over less time issue, other gains are manifest. Development costs go down as economies of intellect go up. Technical solutions are of a higher standard. Customer demands are better answered. Trust grows and morale is heightened with the winning atmosphere and so on. In this case: yielding many more results, with much less, much faster, is truly a reality.

CHAPTER 17

Kanban Projects

Kanban is a Japanese word for card or signal. But it actually means more than that. The Kanban is an information system that describes exactly the type and number of materials required by a manufacturing process. Sitting at the heart of *just-in-time* (JIT) production systems, the Kanban is used to initiate the manufacture and withdrawal of items throughout a production process. This simple, yet powerful concept, is a key ingredient to reducing work-in-progress, eliminating bottlenecks, balancing workload and achieving faster cycle times. To help understand how Kanban does this, the anecdote below may help.

The Inventory Monster

Four students share an apartment. It is a fairly busy place, with the usual heavy through-traffic of fleeting visits and spontaneous Saturday night parties. But for the four students, even though it is nearing Christmas, the tension in the flat is mounting! You see, there is this thing called the 'Dish Monster'. Each student claims they clean their own dirty dishes, but within days of clearing a gigantic mound of slimy dishes, another Dish Monster appears heaving… living… breathing. Then, after a blazing row, the four students decide to sit down and devise a plan to kill off the Dish Monster. After some reflection, it came to them in a blinding flash: 'An ultra-planned, pan-galactic, washing-up schedule'. Surely a tight schedule would kill the Monster. But, in as little as a week, the student that suggested the schedule, returned home one evening to find several Dish Monsters; one in the sink, one on the kitchen table and one huge Dish Monster, with several heads, on the sideboard. Then, just at that moment, another of the students came rushing in. 'I've got it!' he said. 'Reduce the cutlery to one plate each, one cup each, one fork each and so on.' The result? Even after what came to be known as the 'Christmas to end all Christmases', no Dish Monster appeared!

This anecdote, although trivial, explains quite a lot. The cupboard full of cutlery and crockery, was a fat inventory, which fed a heavy load, built up washing-up work-in-progress, which in turn resulted in bottlenecks.

And the same applies for a manufacturing inventory, and below for innovation projects-in-progress: downstream outputs (dish monsters, heaps of work-in-progress) are only a result of upstream causes. The tightest and most disciplined of schedules will not stop it. But a Kanban will. If what is in the system is limited to the number of Kanban projects and to what is stated on each individual Kanban; that is exactly what is in the system – nothing more! But of course, in the case of innovation, it is not only materials and capital/expense costs that stake up; but ideas, time and lost revenues.

Kanban Project

All innovation projects have to be initiated at an exact time. Many firms lack a true *innovation project management strategy*, so most innovations come about either via an ad hoc manner, or kind of evolve over time. Obviously to 'kind of evolve over time' these days, is asking for trouble. Innovation projects must start and finish by predetermined dates, to hit those ephemeral butterfly markets.

The Kanban project system offers an acute way of achieving timeliness and responsiveness. As above, more comes from less. Too large a volume of innovation project-in-progress (PIP) results in wasteful wait-states and tardy time to market. The Kanban system is a way of balancing the PIP (see Chapter 18 below). A hot project list may still exist, but is controlled by a Kanban project system.

EXAMPLE PROJECT KANBAN

- Description of innovation intent. A written description of what you want in the hand at the end of the day (as Chapter 15). No more than just a seed idea. It is important to delay judgement and input of detailed concept characteristics during the conceptualisation stage.

Conceptualisation is a dedicated activity within a 'live' project, and must be handled by the project team.

- Rough visuals. Basic seed concepts in the form of simple outline sketches. Again no more detail than this.
- Market/customer targets. List of market sectors and types of customer. Again this does not have to be in detail.
- Production output targets. Even if you have a PhD in statistics, you will not predict accurately the year-by-year production/service output at this stage. Just indicate whether it is going to be custom batches of one or super-volume, or somewhere in between. This information gives the team an idea of what sort of animal they are dealing with.
- Financial targets. Cost targets. Capital expenditure. Best guess revenue and profit targets, month by month.
- Window of opportunity timing. Exhibition dates, seasonal targets, synchronised cross-product launches are examples. However, more and more the case, there is requirement to be first to market with new technology, trends, service, and so on.
- Statement of core competency. What skills, knowledge base, experience, tools does the project require? Again this does not have to be highly detailed.
- Quantified specific uncertainty. This is detailed below.

This simple Kanban turns out to be a very powerful way of unchoking the system, eliminating wasteful innovation inventory and speeds the whole activity. The Kanban *pulls* the innovation through the total activity. It provides the control to initiate an innovation project.

Kanban Projects and Self-organising Teams

Think of your local supermarket. The shelves are always filled to the brim with stock. Now think of every shop in your local mall? They are all chock-a-block with discount goods these days. Now think of how all this actually happens. Where is the grand master planner, who manages the total distribution system, who makes sure each shelf or rack is instantly replenished?... Of course, there is no godlike programmer that sits at the top, planning a perfect system. All the planning is local, it is distributed among the many shops and staff (the agents) who order from the bottom up, just-in-time when stock is actually needed.

The old reflex is to assume that such a complex system needs tight coordination from a central manager, and this paradigm is still pervasive in the world of project management and innovation. However, as with the retail example, not only is there no need for a central super coordinator, a centralised coordinator actually trips up and delays such complex systems. Yet a distributed system of ownership and control is instantly responsive to demands as and when they arise.

In innovation project terms, the *Project Kanban* is key here. Each member of the SwarmNet collects a *Kanban* (the stock) when they, and only they, are ready. Remember, if management coerce people, while they are currently working on other projects, it will induce a series of *wait-states*. Of course, often there will be times when a critical resource is unavailable to join the team. But it does not stop the rest of the team from getting on, and all important it does not stop the project from progressing. that is, it is not always necessary for everyone to start on the same day. Roles are multiskilled, that is, a design engineer can work on the marketing brief. The Kanban motivates people to move on to the next project fast, as it is a physical entity waiting to be worked on. It stops management pressure overloading the system, as above: more paradoxically comes from less. It stops project creep, that is, it stops ingress of those little significant tasks and mini-projects, because management and other functions cannot ask the SwarmNet to carry objectives not on the list. Lastly, all this is bottom-up SwarmNet driven, not top-down centrally scheduled driven.

Again all this motivates, as it promotes ownership. The Kanban may not look like much, but then again, as we all know so well, it is the simple things that turn out to be the most effective ideas.

Back to Our Two Enterprises

Techno are falling way behind schedule on all projects. Senior management are pulling their hair out. Middle management are pulling the hair out of their subordinates. Stress is white hot, morale is down a hole, and absenteeism averages 11 per cent. ‘Press down on the gas’, says the CEO, ‘Tighten procedures’, says the technical director, ‘Pull your finger out’ says the R&D manager.

One of Gemetics teams have just completed yet another project. Back refreshed from a long weekend, the whole team turn up on Monday and go off to get their new Kanban. *But in reality, the Kanban pulls each individual on to a new project*. However, the production and quality managers want two or three of the team to hurry just a 'swift issue' through, while they are getting organised for the new Kanban Project. But no! First, there is no Kanban, and second, the Kanban 'pulled' innovation process has already started. The team have been pulled together and are committed. The system is clean.

CHAPTER 18

Measuring Uncertainty and Project-in-Progress (PIP) Map

Clearly, distinct innovation projects take different lengths of time to stimulate *genesis*, hone *conceptualisation*, move through reliable *realisation*, and then achieve effective *commercialisation* – all depending on a great number of issues. Outlined here is a method for the quantification of *specific uncertainty* contained within different categories of innovation, enabling a relative estimation for project cycle times.

Five Categories of Hyperinnovation

Steven Wheelwright and Kim Clark in their book *Revolutionising Product Development*, identified five distinct *qualitative* categories for innovation projects, obvious after enlightenment, yet often the source of lagging results. From their work, I now begin to build a *quantitative* model to measure the levels of complexity and novelty found in the different categories of hyperinnovation projects. The five categories are as follows (my own interpretation):

- *Research.* Principally concerned with the consequence of *coupling* remote, uncommon, sometimes conflicting areas of technological research. It includes long-term research into conjoining fundamentally new technological breakthroughs such as quantum computing with nanotechnology, or say biomimetics into microprocessing. Medium-term investigation may include synthesis of proven as yet disparate technologies such as internet protocols carried over 120/240-volt mains electrical infrastructure. Shorter term research might include integration of dissimilar core technology, say an electronic transformer housed inside a new kind of substrate. Wheelwright and Clark say that research is about capturing new knowledge for application, and that it involves highly novel, highly complex work, going way beyond convention and experience.

- *Archetype.* Meaning original model, and without doubt the most difficult category of innovation to bring to market. Having little or no knowledge to build upon, where a technology or process is based on novel arrangements of new or unfamiliar core technology and competency. To conceive a truly original invention is a feat in itself, let alone the taxing realisation and commercialisation issues. Hand-held mediaphones with video streaming capability are an example archetype with no precedent. An archetype may create an entirely new market, stimulate new demand in a saturated market, or change the competitive context of established markets. Expect high uncertainty, basic blunders, acts of nature and booby traps on the road to and in the market if your innovation sits under this category – rates of experimentation and learning are key here.
- *Platform.* A major introduction, through the consolidation of often unrelated, but *proven* core technology. Examples: inflight entertainment systems, *all-in-one* energy services, and most new artefacts in the future. Uncertainty ranges from medium to fairly high. Few, if any, radically new core technologies are connected, and distribution/sales channels are defined. However, continuous low-risk adjustments and recombinations of proven core technology may be designated, requiring input from new and specialist disciplines and/or strategic alliances, to bring the platform together.
- *Divergent.* The most diverse kind of innovation project to manage, based on a platform of existing core technology and core competency, the aim is to introduce a distinct stream of innovations, either individually or in series. Intelligent spotlighting for shopfronts that senses what is being displayed and automatically adjusts the light beam intensity, is now in the labs. Each spotlight is based on the same core technology, but each spotlight is different in both form and function. Thus garden variety lighting products branch towards new designs. Virgin's Upper-Class inflight service undergoes relentless divergent improvement, trying out small distinct adjustments to menus, entertainment, seat size, limousine pick-up, gambling – you can even get yourself a manicure.
- *Custom.* Designed and produced with a single customer in mind. Often based on a platform, certain unique features or adjustments are made on

request. British Telecom is a custom innovator. Based on core telecommunication infrastructure and technology, BT mass customise integrated products and services for individual business needs.

The Third Principle of Hyperinnovation: The Uncertainty Principle

The degree of *novelty* (newness) and *complexity* (diversity of ideas) embedded within any particular invention sets a limitation on the cycle-time to market. Thus the novelty and complexity factors need to be defined before deciding whether a specific launch window can be achieved. As the qualitative categories above show, the degree of novelty and complexity is a grossly underexamined part of innovation, yet invaluable once carried out.

Here, the degree of novelty and complexity defines the degree of uncertainty; and uncertainty defines the relative timing factors involved in introduction. From this, a Third Principle of Hyperinnovation can be derived:

$$Ct \cong \Delta Y \propto N * Dn$$

Cycle time (Ct) is relative (≅) to uncertainty (ΔY) which is directly proportional to novelty (N) multiplied by complexity (Dn). The higher the degree of novelty∗complexity, the higher the uncertainty, the longer the relative cycle time. It is obvious that different enterprises have different innovations with inherently different levels of novelty and complexity with different development capabilities. But this gut feeling is where most – nearly all – stop. Beyond this lies a golden opportunity to quantify the exact novelty∗complexity, uncertainty, and then in turn calculate a relative cycle time to market.

Measuring Complexity (Dn)

Complexity in terms of the diversity of ideas in any given innovation can be represented in many forms. Below five key measures are shown:

- *Complexity of user interface.* Automobiles are completely designed around both the customer's physical and holistic demands, and therefore highly complex in terms of user-interface. The same goes for word processing packages, executive smart seats on passenger airliners, and hand-held mediaphones. Products like compact discs have little user interface. Facilitation of reliable and efficient user-interfaces ups the design complexity.

- *Complexity of core technology.* Sophistication, resolution and density of core technology that make up an innovation. Core technology also includes the level of sophistication employed in manufacturing, production, test, quality and maintenance processes. The complexity of any given core technology is on the up, which nearly always increases the complexity in the other four measures.
- *Performance of core technology.* Level of perceived quality determined by customers. Durability under extreme environmental conditions. Reliability over service lifetime. For example, a television in the 1970s had a six-month mean time between failure (MTBF), with of course back-up by a not so avid maintenance crew. In the 1980s this went up to three years, and by the turn of the millennium, five years was the standard MTBF for the TV. Performance perception like quality of feel, finish, style, aesthetics, and so on, also comes into the fold here.
- *Sum of core technology.* The number of discrete core technologies, in the form of subservice systems or subassemblies, that go to make up a given hyperinnovation.
- *Interconnection of core technology.* Level of discrete core technology interconnection with other discrete core technology.

By combining each of these five key measures through experience and with a history of innovation, it is possible to quantify the complexity of a complete innovation. First, general experience would give a subjective model of complexity through each benchmark, and a history of innovations introduced would give relativity through each benchmark. On a scale of 1–10, how complex is it? Using each benchmark: very simple technology and processes 1, or ultracomplex technology and processes 10.

Measuring Novelty (N)

Novelty is a more tangible measure than complexity. It can be compared directly to previous design work. Three key measures may be considered:

- *Novelty in core technology.* How far does a given innovation move beyond current experience and knowledge in a core technology or process? This can be measured along any of the above complexity characteristics above. That is design work potential minus the design work already done.

- *Novelty in market introduction.* How new is the market in which the intended innovation is to be introduced? Obviously the creation of a new market is the most novel situation to be in. If it is a *me-too* in a mature and well-understood market, novelty is much closer to zero.
- *Novelty in cost.* Often an advantage is obtained by introducing an innovation at a substantially lower price point. To achieve this, novel manufacturing/service processes and core technology may be incorporated to bring down cost. For example, the application of an automated assembly process or semi-custom integrated circuit design, that may stretch beyond design knowledge, but at the same time slashes the total product life-cycle cost in half.

On a scale of 1–10, how novel is your XYZ product? 1 = completely understood markets, technologies and processes; 10 = ultra-exotic markets, technology and processes going way beyond anything done before. Again, this is all relative. For one enterprise a new product/service might be highly novel, for another it might be standard stuff.

Worked Example

Take this example: two products need to hit the market within 26 weeks. They are both microprocessor based, power drive systems, housed in watertight plastic casings. Product F consists of nine subassemblies. So does product H.

(1) Watertight plastic housing
(2) Gearbox
(3) Microprocessor based PCB
(4) Drive motor unit
(5) Mechanical spindle
(6) Control panel
(7) Watertight interface panel
(8) Cantilever arm
(9) Software module

On the surface, in the rush of the day, product H looks similar to product F; and at first glance would seem to require the same levels of resource and cycle time to reach design solutions, component tooling, and the development and building of manufacturing processes. However, product H has what seem like slight differences. The control panel is of greater complexity and to make the control panel watertight, the plastic housing is

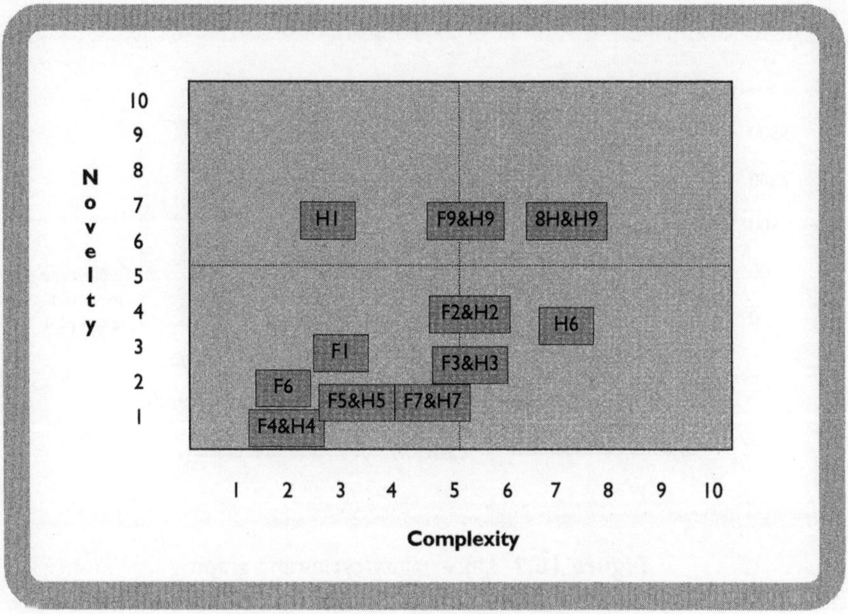

Figure 18.1 Complexity/novelty graph

highly novel. Also, the software module and cantilever arm in product H are of higher novelty and complexity than that of product F.

Each of the nine subassemblies in each product can be given a mark out of 10, in terms of both complexity and novelty, and then input to Figure 18.1. As above, 1 is very low, and 10 exotic.

Although products F and H look the same on the surface, the complexity∗novelty factor shows the difference – a 74-point difference in

Product F Novelty∗Complexity Factor	Product H Novelty∗Complexity Factor
F1 = (3 * 3) = 9	H1 = (7 * 3) = 21
F2 = (4 * 5) = 20	H2 = (4 * 5) = 20
F3 = (3 * 5) = 15	H3 = (3 * 5) = 15
F4 = (1 * 2) = 2	H4 = (1 * 2) = 2
F5 = (2 * 3) = 6	H5 = (2 * 3) = 6
F6 = (2 * 2) = 4	H6 = (4 * 7) = 28
F7 = (2 * 4) = 8	H7 = (2 * 4) = 8
F8 = (5 * 6) = 30	H8 = (7 * 7) = 49
F9 = (5 * 6) = 30	H9 = (7 * 7) = 49
Total = 124	Total = 198

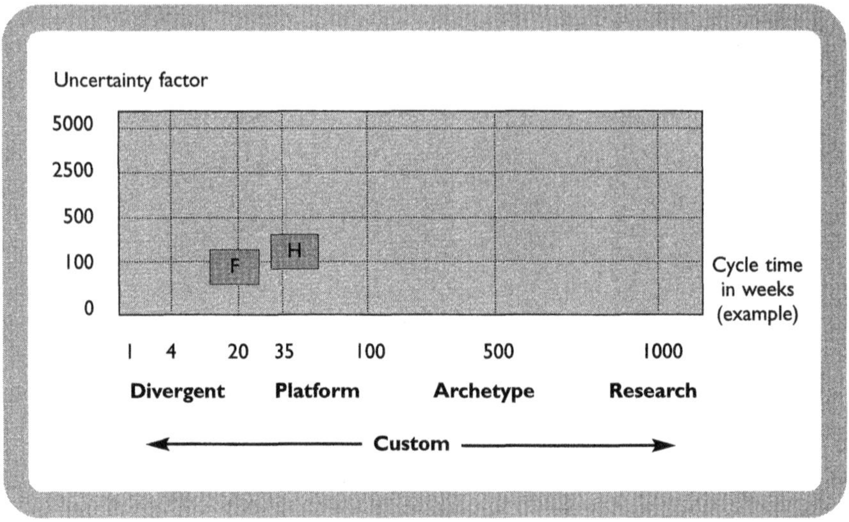

Figure 18.2 Uncertainty/cycle-time graph

fact. Figure 18.2 shows the relative difference and relationship between uncertainty and cycle time.

Figure 18.2 shows that products F and H both fall into the platform category. However, product H cycle time will be significantly longer than product F. Almost a third longer, due to the significantly higher uncertainty factors. The launch requirement for 26 weeks is probable for F, but improbable for H (35 weeks).

One enterprise I know simultaneously worked on 3 archetypes, demanding that each hit the market at the same time. Okay, this enterprise had the resources to work on three original models, but neglected to quantify specific novelty∗complexity within each archetype. After much persuasion, they too carried out this simple analysis, and were bowled over in surprise. One of the archetypes stood out like a sore thumb. Although not recognised before, the analysis quantified that this particular archetype contained *double* the complexity∗novelty than the other two. Until now, all three had been considered to be about the same generic archetype, targeted to the same launch window.

Uncertainty Benchmarking

To benchmark for relative calibration of cycle times versus uncertainty against current and/or future resources and organisation, take a sample of historic projects (archetype, platform, and so on) across the board, and carry out the above analysis. This will give you the current bank of design work done for your particular organisation, and a baseline from which to calculate future *relative* cycle times versus uncertainty.

Project-in-Progress (PIP) Map

No single innovation defines future business growth. Only the total innovation projects-in-progress (PIP) does that. Reliability of results over time across the PIP holds innovation-driven growth to ransom. One new product or service can of course, if given commitment, rush to market. The problem arrives when we consider the total PIP. That is, the many different projects an enterprise has to bring to market.

Maintaining the total enterprise portfolio, let alone expanding organically, depends greatly on managing the total PIP. Significantly, innovations set to create a new market, or attack a competitor, need to get to market as and when demanded. Again, PIP is a major factor here. The PIP must be managed via specific levels of uncertainty via the Kanban. Once the analysis across the PIP has been carried out, a PIP map can be drawn and an intelligible map of uncertainty and cycle times can be seen (see Figure 18.3).

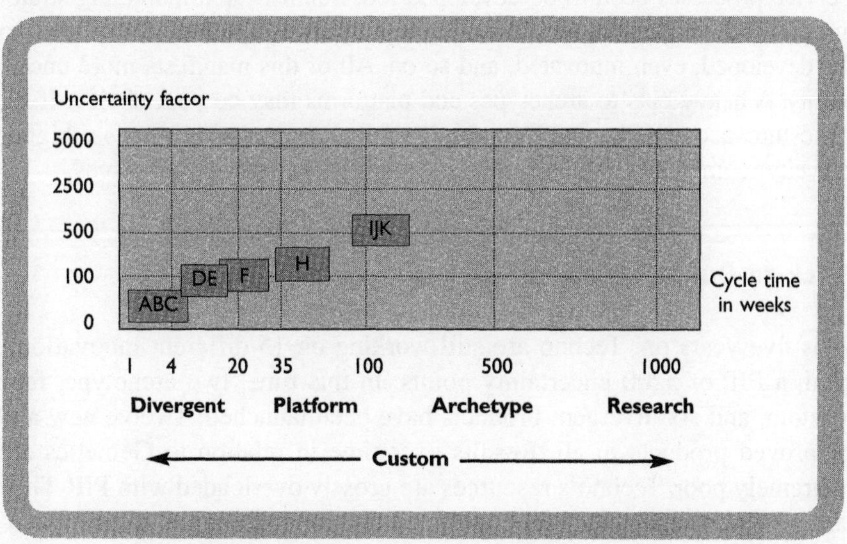

Figure 18.3 Innovation projects-in-progress (PIP) map

Tangible Bottom Line Number

This is an invaluable project decision-making tool. Management decide which Kanbans are to be made available, at different times. Now a tangible bottom line number for the potential and current PIP is available by adding together individual project uncertainties. From the above graph, projects A to K add up to a total PIP of 3415 uncertainty points. The Kanban is the valve that limits uncertainty across the PIP. Management must consider each project's uncertainty in the light of each other. A waiting project Kanban must be quantified and configured to the correct balance of effort/resource/uncertainty over a few (less is more) focused projects. Quantified PIP uncertainty helps us think about each potential project demands in relation to each other. From this, it is easier to determine the practical PIP against available resources. It adds to the evidence that a higher PIP over limited resources has a negative effect. The more projects added, the more productivity drops (re: wait-states, bottlenecks, and less results over time).

In time, it is easy to grasp the correct balance of projects over available resources, and what project Kanbans need to be set. Reliable time to market is also a product of the relative number and balance of archetypes, platforms, divergent and custom hyperinnovation. Clearly archetypes have an inherently longer time to market. There is more to consider, more to develop, more tooling to commission. Sometimes radically new manufacturing or service processes need to be developed too. Sophisticated marketing strategies have to be developed and executed. Distribution channels may need to be developed, even innovated, and so on. All of this manifests more uncertainty. A heavy bias to archetypes and platforms may be your choice. If so, take into account the third principle of hyperinnovation, that is, higher novelty∗complexity means higher uncertainty and strain on resources.

Back to Our Two Enterprises Again

It is five years on: Techno are still working on 15 different innovations, with a PIP of 5200 uncertainty points. In this time, two archetype, four custom, and six divergent products have been launched. Twelve new and improved products in all. Results over time in relation to Gemetics are extremely poor. Techno's resources are grossly overloaded with PIP. They are confused in terms of each innovation's uncertainty, and each innovation's launch date has been rescheduled several times. In the same five years, at any one time, Gemetics have set a Kanban project process. They have worked on two-thirds fewer innovation projects: one or two archetypes, two or three platforms, and two or three divergent products. A total PIP uncertainty score of 1524. But in fact, a lower PIP means that Gemetics achieve higher yield (results) over time. In any one year one or two archetypes, three to four platforms and four to eight divergent products. They have precisely quantified the novelty$*$complexity $\propto$ uncertainty $\propto$ cycle times for each project and have an extremely well-balanced PIP. In the same five years they have launched 35 hyperinnovations.

PART V

Hyperinnovation Tools

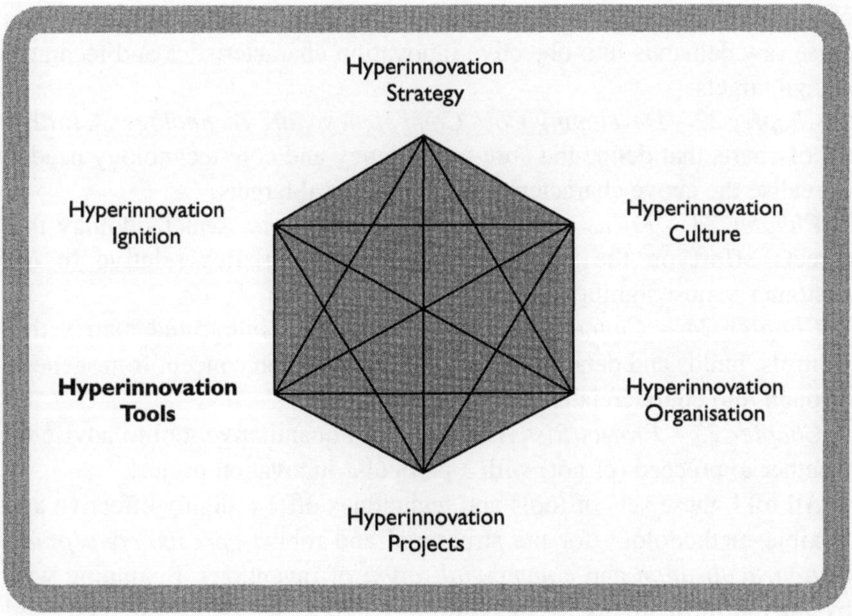

> The goal is not simply to be lead by the customer's expressed needs; responsiveness is not enough. The objective is to amaze the customer by anticipating and fulfilling their unarticulatd needs.
>
> GARY HAMMEL

All teams, involved in all kinds of innovation, need so-called structured methodologies. Methodologies are the concrete, actual doing part of innovation. These are formal intellectual tools and techniques that give rhyme and continuity to the capture of information and problem solving throughout a project cycle. Part V of the model describes and applies the following structured intellectual tools:

Chapter 19 – Searching for Seeds and Complexes of Needs: Advice and approach for the hunt of inspirational market *seeds*, and the pursuit of multidimensional customer *needs*.

Chapter 20 – Analysing Customer Demands: Practical methodology that reveals what the customer really wants deep down (even though they may not know what they want), with techniques for the precise identification and definition of so-called customer *demandplex*.

Chapter 21 – Translating Raw Customer Demands: A set of structured charts that capture customer demandplex, in turn methodically translates these raw demands into objective innovation characteristics and technical design targets.

Chapter 22 – Developing Core Competency/Core Technology: A further set of charts that define the core-competency and core-technology needed to realise the above characteristics and technical targets.

Chapter 23 – Focus on What is Most Important: A methodology that directs effort on the most important characteristics relative to the customer's most significant demands.

Chapter 24 – Conceptualisation Matrix: An integrated matrix that controls, builds and details a robust customer-driven concept from genesis through into commercialisation.

Chapter 25 – Project Risk Assessment: A quantitative tool to advise on whether to proceed (or not) with a particular innovation project.

All told, these sets of tools and techniques offer a highly effective and flexible methodology for the structured and robust *genesis*, *conceptualisation*, *realisation* and *commercialisation* of inventions. Beginning with by far the most involving methodology of all: searching for seeds and complexes of needs.

CHAPTER 19

Searching for Seeds and Complexes of Needs

Why oh why, do we try to tap new ideas by holding meetings in a sterile office, or worse, go bankdraft in hand to yet another 10 per cent royalty consultant, when there is a rich source of original ideas out there? It is beyond me. When I come back with colleagues from an exhibition or a trip to some unusual company, city and especially country, our heads are brimming with seeds for new and exciting markets. The message here: sit at your desk and that will be the scope of your view; explore the commercial jungle and a portal for innovation will open.

Delicate Seed Ideas, Powerful Concepts

A *seed idea* is exactly what it implies: the beginning of life. But instead of biological life, seed ideas are the genesis of conceptual life. This kind of thinking has enormous power, yet because these kinds of seed are conceptual they often go quite unnoticed. Seeds are delicate, fragile, untouchable creatures; in the hand, the seed does not look much, except inside is the very stuff of life. If planted and nurtured, one may find a conceptual oak tree, and from that single conceptual oak, eventually a rich market ecology. Seed ideas can start a cascade of more new ideas, which in turn can grow an entire industry, with literally dozens of new industries sprouting from that one single seed: the butterfly flapping its wings again. How any one particular seed is found, does not apply to any one rule, but you will not find it by just sitting there. The key is to get your people to make those interconnections, to expand their world-views.

This activity is vigorously encouraged in extremely successful enterprises such as Toyota, Xerox, Sony and Harley Davidson. They send waves of engineers, designers, executives, marketers and the like into the market for long periods to get fresh seeds, and to learn about the complex needs and innate desires of potential customers. The success stories are in abundance.

In Search of Empathy

During an intense brainstorm on the top floor of the Toyota headquarters, Bunkyo-ku, Tokyo, Yuki Hiroka told me the amazing story of how the concept for the original 'Lexus-AS400' emerged. Toyota sent the whole project team: designers, engineers, model makers, buyers, technicians, marketing people to California to live the lifestyle of the rich and the famous. They were given generous budgets to mix with the wealthy, sip champagne at celebrity parties, play in luxury hotels and lounge in stately houses; they ate at flambeau restaurants in Beverly Hills, drove the best cars and generally lived the life of a Hollywood superstar (now who wants to be a designer?). To hone their findings they built over 400 prototypes, instead of the usual 12, and carried out an endless amount of customer analysis to get it just right. Was all this opulence chucking money down the drain, or was it calculated strategy? Of course, they went to such lengths to acquire and develop a deep empathy for the way the rich and famous live, to get to know these people's lifestyles and what they strive for at the most subtle level.

At Honda, it is a similar narrative. Honda designers do not just sit at CAD workstations, they are sent into the market to capture the mind of the customer. They are present at the product launches and post-product analysis to gain exposure to motor pundit criticism. They analyse the subtlest of customer expectations, in sometimes obscure places and in acutely sensitive ways. They go to German autobahns to experience the psychology of driving at 200 km per hour. They watch customer behaviour and interaction with Honda and competitors' products, using techniques developed by anthropologists, social scientists, psychologists, and this just scratches the surface. Honda's whole philosophy is that their engineers are business people first, technocrats very last.

Xerox, did (and still do) something similar during the company's turnaround. Not one internal meeting was held, not one marketing brief was considered, not one designer's CAD terminal was switched on for a whole six months. Instead, a team went into the market, to the places where copiers were installed to study the needs of the customer and how the machines were really used. What they discovered was nothing less than profound. The sight of real customers, with real problems, focused the team mind to new levels. No longer was the specification for the new copier some dead list of issues, generated by some far-off expert, but real, angered, emotional customers, with genuine deadlines to meet and problems to solve. As one result, the Xerox team soon found themselves interconnecting ideas to the core, that they could simply not have imagined sitting in front of their workstations.

Hell's-Angels' icon, Harley Davidson, hold the very same learning disposition. CEO Jeffrey Bluestein lives with his customers. He attends the so-called Harley Owners Group (HOG) events every year. It gives him a chance to look for ideas for merchandise, to the very bikes themselves. Harley now recognise they are in a multidimensional business: from the biker fashion apparel, to the engine technology, to the design of the machines' image, Harley are interconnecting in *n*-dimensions. The only way to keep abreast of these kinds of biker trends, is to hang out with the 100,000 or so HOGs and mingle!

Do you remember the processions of Japanese delegates, in the 1960s and 1970s, with their cameras clicking away? No one imagined the power of this unscientific and seemingly harmless everyday occurrence. Innocently, they were given access to the inner sanctums of the best-run Western companies. And have they stopped? No way; they have developed ever more sophisticated methods to analyse the customer, competitor and pan-corporation. A colleague of mine, Debby Mills, a fashion life-cycle consultant, remembers quite vividly, about two years ago or so, when attending a fashion show at Richard Branson's Roof Garden night club in the West End of London. She told me:

> Out of the corner of my eye, I noticed a small, dark, middle-aged, oriental-looking man, standing alone at one of the bars. At first, I didn't take much notice, but after a while his manner began to interest me. He had a Palm-top Computer in one hand and a Camcorder hanging around his shoulder. He wasn't looking at the catwalk, but watching the people watching the show. Then I realised what he might have been doing. After that I couldn't resist but to go talk to him. 'I'm intrigued,' I said, 'You haven't once looked at the show, but you haven't taken your eyes off the audience.' After the initial shock of a complete stranger approaching him in such a direct way, he smiled, put his hand into his inside jacket and produced a business card. It said in English 'Joe Kaku, TOSHIBA'.

This is no extreme, I might add. Hyperinnovators go anywhere and everywhere to find interesting and workable ideas to interconnect. They might be across the other side of the globe, but equally they could be next door.

How to Connect Seeds with Needs: Study Customer Meanings

As ideas flow and interconnect, the future holds greater individualism and diversification among customers, no doubt leading to an inordinate variety of demands in and across both consumer and industrial markets. For instance, trends reveal a transformation in traditional roles of men and women; men are spending more time at home, and of course, women now dominate the workplace; thus shifting products away from housewife-orientated designs towards a family panorama; and work tools from bland functional boxes towards feminine, almost ornate looking designs. Another trend shows that customers increasingly aspire to improved performance at work, and greater fulfilment at home and away, thus *time* becomes an ever more scarce resource. As work flexibility increases, and rest and play combine, so the dynamics of the way customers integrate their lives becomes a major theme in the connection of *seeds with needs*.

A key dynamic to seed/need union, is to study the *meanings* in people's lives. Meaning is the critical dynamic in all cultural (technological) evolution. What has meaning has value, what has great meaning has great value, what we hold as sacred meaning… and so on. Music seems to have meaning in all cultures, yet each culture has evolved very different types of music, which represent the different meanings and values people hold. As ideas flow, the meanings of music transform, and in many cases begin to multidimension. We see the so-called lines and boundaries of music fuse and boost because the meanings of music flow with the multivergence of global values. What was once the exclusive domain of classical opera, now crosses commercial boundaries with hip-hop, to create op-pop. The meanings we associate with hip-hop have changed, because the proportions and distributions of knowledge and affluence are changing. Opera was once the exclusive art of the wealthy and the well educated; not so any more. As the world of ideas flows, and the current of change itself accelerates, expect the meanings in people's lives to rush, crash and mix in synch. *As ideas flow, meanings flow too.*

Sony are masters of tracking the flow of meanings. They call it 'human sciences' and employ specialists to facilitate such research. Sony's origin began just after the Second World War, in professional recording equipment. Sony's move into consumer electronics in the late 1950s took them on a slow, laborious climb. Only, it was not until Sony began to look at the market in a quite different way, that they started to break new ground. They began to look at the *meanings* of the consumer, and how they are manifest in their lifestyles, values, motives, habits and the like. For instance, they noticed that young college students would hump huge, sometimes expensive phonographic equipment around in their cars. Portable music, they noticed, could be a highly profitable market, and so the transistor radio was born. Sony's competitor, AT&T, at the time, concluded that the consumer was not ready for the transistor. Indeed today the consumer is still not ready. Remember it is not the technology that is important to consumers, but how it is shaped. AT&T missed the point. Sony, knew then, as they do now, that if you understand the way people live, what people aspire to, the values, the meanings, you will build a bridge for innovation.

General Electric made the same expensive mistake as AT&T. In the late 1970s, Sony launched an 8-inch miniature TV set into the US. This was at the same time when General Electric concluded, after a 'comprehensive study', that there was no sizeable demand for small TV sets. That year, Sony sold over a million units! Was Sony's bet based on a hunch? No. Sony looked at the needs of the customer, their meanings, and *not* merely the cold surface of market statistics. They study the way people live and consider ways of making life easier and more pleasurable. Traditional market sector analysis of demography and segmentation looks only at the surface, and the number one reason why most marketing plans fail. Sony do indeed carry out market research studies, but most of all, they love to get their feet on the street and search for seeds and complexes of needs.

The Anthropology of the Market and Multitribes

In part, this is a play on *anthropology*: the study of human groups and their ideas in the natural environment. In this case the marketplace. For the *tribes* a particular customer belongs to is one very powerful analysis orientation. A tribe is a social group with recognisable patterns of behaviour and meanings: such as status, protocols, rituals, values, symbols and local language. Technologies like tools, hunting and gathering methods all go into defining a tribe. Drag-race enthusiasts are a tribe made up of many families, not too unlike the patterns of organisation observed in the native Indians of the old Americas. Drag-car metatribes are a rich ecology of ideas, having detailed local languages and complex symbol systems. The technologies, of course, are modern-day; hunter-gathering methods focus towards information about engine design, race events and the drag-car memorabilia. One key to remember, is that the moment the so-called drag-car enthusiast crosses over to another type of tribe – his family, say father; or professional day job, say nurse or chief engineer – behaviour will dramatically and suddenly change. Status, protocols, values, language, technology, and so on, will instantaneously transform. *It seems that we have all become multitribal creatures.* This is a strength of viewing customers in multiple clans, it highlights the often subtle differences between state of mind, and the needs, meanings, wishes and expectations we express and aspire to at any give time. Consequently, consumers are many different people at many different times, and because the number of social tribes is on the up, so the customers will become ever more multi-dimensional in their behaviour and demands.

Multiprocessing Consumers and their Demandplex

Barring the technology and markets meanings themselves, this concept symbiosis begins to make even more sense when we look at the behaviour patterns and profiles of modern-day consumers.

Marketing guru Philip Kotler believes that markets are now swarming with so-called *multiprocessing consumers*: people who use two or more products interactively (yours truly is now using a HP palmtop, plus Microsoft CE, interconnected to my Ericsson digital mobile, plus drinking Kenco decaf, while watching the Discovery channel on my Mitsubishi wide-screen Internet TV, while exercising on my Cyclotronic, which is monitoring my heart rate...). Multiprocessing consumers now desire simultaneous delivery of service and product: bundled gas, electric, water and related information in one package; family banking, car maintenance, family maintenance, the kids' new shoes, an exercise work-out, and all before breakfast. This is so-called *multiprovision*, achieving much more in much less time, with much less effort.

Think of how many ways we can now communicate over long distance. The terrestrial phone, the satellite phone, the fax, the pager, e-mail, video conference, your TV; and on the way telepresence and synthetic telepathy – a manifold mix of platforms that is drawing the ordinary consumer away from passive linear observer, towards the act of *prosuming*: the simultaneous consumption and production of information, knowledge, services and ideas. For example, the internet is enabling prosumers to simultaneously consume outputs and produce inputs to the world wide web. As a custom news narrowcast is piped directly to specific prosumers, that discrete piece of news is instantaneously augmented, then rebound back into the web. Live, online radio shows access e-jockeys in home-made studios, pumping out real-time e-music and commentary. The multi-processing prosumer opens up mammoth scope for *n*-innovation.

By far the fastest growing sector of customers is the multicultural consumer: international, multilingual, well travelled, constantly on the fly, money rich but time poor, buyers and influencers. Have you met an *Hinglishman* (Hindi-English), a *Euroam* (Euro-American), an *Ozzanese* (Australian-Asian) or a *Latrabic* (Spanish-Arab)? Increasingly affluent, their tastes and preferences do not gravitate to provincial fashions or trends, but pursue an eclectic mix of ideas, food, media, music, moves and grooves that fuse cultural-identity borders. High-street shops that coalesce Asian and Western fashion, night clubs that fuse on the dance floor, TV channels that integrate ethnic programming, magazines that blend in language, gadgets with cosmopolitan flavour, and restaurants that fuse menus are just the beginning. Canada's CityTV, for example, present a mosaic of cross-cultural news from around Toronto, reflecting the huge diversity of life events, ethnic anecdotes, styles and activities that glue this city together. CityTV's goal is to hold up a mirror to Toronto, reporting on this integrated multicultural metropolis. As a result, CityTV achieve record viewing. Thus, from the world of media to the blockbuster brands, to the online e-tailer, through to domestic appliances and fashion apparel, we are seeing interculturalisation of the local marketplace as the multicultural consumer grows in number and value.

In industrial and commercial markets, hyperinnovation is in great demand. Large-scale infrastructure programmes, such as power plants or city traffic control systems, increasingly demand integrated and ever more complex functional specifications. Town planners want drop-in boxes that deliver a variety of civic tasks: digital cameras, pedestrian sensors, jumbo video screens, information systems, intelligent traffic autorouting, public address systems, all maintainable by wire and replaceable within minutes. And if this was not enough, civic planners also demand *all-in-one* packaging of insurance, financing, maintenance, energy and service management.

In the commercial lighting world, hotels, airports, galleries, museums, and all manner of shopping malls, now demand customised integrated intelligent, low-energy lighting systems. A mix of spotlights, downlights and floodlights that automatically beam with a light intensity to the tune of an ambience defined by a neural network. The technology and service systems that deliver such illuminations expand beyond the realms of the lone spotlight enterprise.

In sum, industrial and commercial customers – like the multiprocessing prosumers above – increasingly hold complexes of demand, so-called *demandplex*, that may only be effectively satisfied by hyperinnovation.

Demandplex: Complexes of Customer Demand

As ideas flow and interconnect, the average prosumer becomes thoroughly informed, *n*-learned, multicultured, more discerning, and therefore far less tolerant than ever before. As ideas flow faster, the industrial customer's scope of demand broadens and complexifies, now not satisfied with steady-state technology. As ideas flow even faster, commercial customers turn to the value-multiplied; again the fixed, the regular, the commoditised function does not satisfy. All customer types now live in ever more liberalised and deregulated global markets, so the rush and interconnection of ideas have yet to take off.

As one result of this flow, the naked marketplace begins to hit a phase transition: once isolated needs and wants coalesce to form complexes of demand. These so-called demandplex emerge via a synergy of wants and expectations emanating from a single customer base.

From this perspective, it is quite possible to lock-in customers by continually interconnecting/disconnecting concepts to meet new demandplex as and when they arise. Here, once again, for every new type of demand, new type of tribe, new meanings within the complex, so the number of new possibilities for innovation multiplies. The goal, then, becomes to multiply value by interconnecting these kinds of demandplex into single coherent hyperinnovations.

Customer Questions

To begin the search for seeds and complexes of needs, teams will need some probing questions. Here's a cluster to get you going:

- Who are my customers? Who are my most important customers? Who will influence the purchase decision most? Who are the thought leaders, lead users and early adopters that we can learn from (re: Chapter 3)? Which customers have driving problems and demands? Where do they buy, use, dispose of my product or services (the answers will roll out as a complex of demands, but that is the whole point of inquiry). Now go there – live there for a while!

- What is my customer's detailed profile? Where do my customers live, work, rest and play? What is their mindset? What do they read, write, think? What are they into? Who do they network with? What are their fears, dreams, aspirations in life? What are the meanings in their lives? What tribes and communities of interest do they belong to?
- To extract and connect a diverse and original range of ideas you will need to explore the commercial ecology far, deep and wide. Diversity is the goal. What interesting, exciting, amazing places, cities, ecologies, research labs, cultures, events can we visit to grasp that panoramic stimulus? What other relevant industries with similar customer demandplex can we explore and interconnect in unique ways? What are they up to? Who is in front and what do we need to do to jump ahead?
- What future panoramic markets – comprehensive and coherent in all their dimension – can we imagine just by observing what is going on in front of us today? What breakthrough pan-enterprise, that may spawn an entirely new industry, can we deduce, simply by interconnecting now discrete, but related demandplex, technologies and business concepts? What is the full potential magnitude – financial, technological, infrastructure – of these fresh opportunities?
- What unexpressed, latent, emerging demand complexes can we identify? What will these customers' demand complexes be 5, 10 and 20 years from now? How will their isolated needs interconnect in the future? How will the customer complex we are now observing change over the next 5, 10 and 20 years? What affiliation can we make from these exclusive observations? How can we integrate customer demandplex into a brand new *n*-business concept?
- Who will be our customers tomorrow? Who and where are our future customers now, and how will they change? How fast are they going to change and in what fashion?
- Who is leading the market now? What competitors are tinkering at the edges of tradition and the radical? Can we learn from them? Who and how will they be leading/redefining/creating new markets in the future? Anita Roddick, founder of the Body Shop advises: 'Go to where your competitors can't or won't go!' So go study places where your competitors are lacking or weak. Ask your customers – current, emerging and future – where and in what your competitors are behind or limited or have all but forgotten to do?

CHAPTER 20

Analysing Customer Demand

Customers do not know what they want until you put something in front of them, is a common concern expressed by marketing people. This may be the case; but it is more likely that customers are unable to articulate their wants in the local or technical language of the marketer or technician. Reasons, from technical ignorance to confusion about what is possible, are in abundance. It is the job of the inventor to listen, learn and empathise with the customer. The deeper the empathy with customer meanings, motives, demands and expectations, the greater the opportunity to innovate. Take, for example, the parallel of zoologists. They have accumulated an overwhelming volume of facts about behaviour of species in the natural world. By observing and studying each species, a database of knowledge has been built up about habitats, breeding cycles, mating habits, diet, roles in the ecology and so on. All of this without a single verbal conversation between the zoologist and the creature. Of course, the point in studying and listening to the customer – rather curious creatures in themselves – is to identify those emerging and unsatisfied demandplexes and look for opportunities to innovate.

Sony, again, know this well. They lead the market by understanding the extensive innate and nurtured desires, habits, and so on of their customers. Sony's playstation stemmed from this. Sony's leaders and teams spend inordinate amounts of time with customers, listening and learning the subtleties of their demandplex. To be clear, this is not mere analysis of market demography or statistics, but acute understanding of the broad complexes of meanings, habits, lifestyles, idiosyncrasies, routines, protocols, values, politics, and so on, of the species of animal we call the customer.

Customer Demandplex Analysis Tool Kit

To examine broad demands, we can look towards a bevy of practical, easy to use methods. Tools that uncover the customer's deepest secrets, even though customers may not know in their mind what they want, the techniques will deduce the black and white facts. As above, some of the tools have been adapted from the anthropologist's and ethologist's toolkit to study human behaviour. Together, they turn out to be a powerful way to get inside your customer's head.

Deep customer web analysis. It is a rare situation for only one customer to be involved in the decision to purchase/engage, and thereafter interact/use the product/service. Even if dealing with one centralised purchasing manager or end-consumer, you will probably find a whole *web* of hidden customers involved.

Pioneer, for example, found out that many families take their young children into consideration when buying a home-entertainment system. Pioneer now deliberately design these systems with the child in mind. But end-consumers are only the beginning; retailers are increasingly demanding. Wal-Mart want highly styled, *buy-me* message products, that fit neatly into 14×14 inch shelf units. And if it has a $20 price tag, you are likely to go way up on their customer satisfaction metric.

Take another example: good old washing powder, a commodity if ever there was one, where strong branding and pricing play a key role in differentiation. The likes of Proctor & Gamble spend big budgets on advertising the latest new and improved formulation. But do they go far enough? What if washing powder corporations were to look much deeper, wider? Would they see a whole web of different customers, each with a detailed demandplex? Well, good restaurants want a constant and instant supply of clean, bright white tea towels. Football clubs want to get ground-in mud, blood and dirt off their kit quick. Fishermen want to get smelly fish oil and gunk off their coveralls. All of these demanding demands are not specifically met by the big brand washing powders.

But these kinds of finicky whims and difficult wants are found in all buying decisions. It is absolutely crucial, whether the customer is an industrial, commercial, retail or consumer, that you map as near as possible the whole user/decision web.

Special systems create and make custom electronic test rigs used in a diverse range of industries with similar needs. The key, they say, is close consideration of both, the 'intrinsic customer', end-users like engineers, production line operators, and so on; and equal attention to 'extrinsic

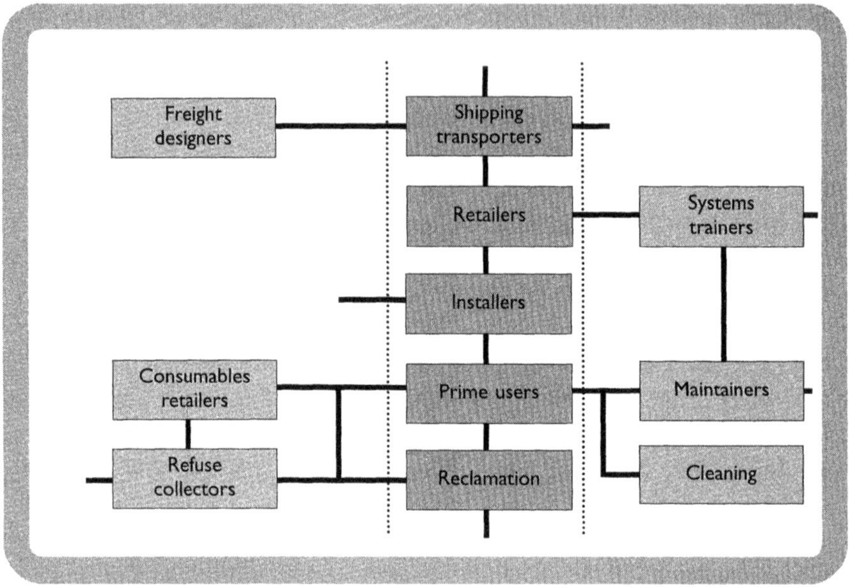

Figure 20.1 A customer web for a digital photocopier

customers', such as support, purchasing managers, maintenance people including the janitor! Each intrinsic and extrinsic specific need is an opportunity to value multiply.

Mapping the customer web. This tool identifies each direct and indirect customer in the web. It is important to map all custom throughout the web, from material supply, through end-customers, right through to reclamation. Figure 20.1 shows an example customer web, divided into direct and indirect customers.

Demandplex. As a consequence of a thoughtfully mapped customer-web, it is possible to begin to clearly and creatively analyse the needs and wants of each direct and indirect customer in the form of demandplex. This is a complete structured look at what is important to each particular intrinsic (direct) and extrinsic (indirect) customer at each node in the web. Taking each customer in isolation and starting at the very first step–interface–contact with your enterprise, it is seen that each customer will have a distinct complex of demands and priorities, covering a mix of physical and conceptual product and/or service aspects.

Take 'transporters' from the customer web in Figure 20.1: what demandplex do they express? What subtle, latent demands do they have?

What emerging demands can be anticipated? Examples range from shipment packaging size, weight, shape. Shipment packaging environmental constraints such as waterproofing, drop and bump packaging. Manoeuvrability, stacking/unstacking, and so on. What about the installers or consumables retailers or maintainers? All of these different customers will have broad demands that need to be answered and integrated into single comprehensive and coherent innovations.

Values questions: why, what, how? It is vital to understand the why, what and how the customer demands a particular characteristic, or indeed the whole invention. The answers may seem obvious, but questioning this opens a deeper understanding of customer demands and the relationships with the invention itself. The simple sample of why, what, and how questions below, may be asked either directly, or just in one's own mind through listening and observing:

- What disparate customer demands can be identified and coupled?
- What as yet unrelated areas of lifestyle or life process can be united to produce brand new demandplex?
- What deeper values, motives and meanings are flowing and linking?
- How will these once disparate demands evolve as a demandplex over the next 5, 10, 20 years?
- What technology/competency/resource can be integrated to answer these multifold demands?
- What restrictions does the customer have immediately, what about the future? How can we further conjoin demands to eliminate or meet these restrictions?
- Why does the customer do that particular activity? Can activities be enhanced as an integrated task? What real-time technology could informate or improve communications between us and the customer?
- Why would the customer want to use/interact with the potential innovation?
- How will the customer actually use the product or service? How will the use evolve over the longer term?

Allen & Hanbury's (A&H), a division of GlaxoWellcome, the pharmaceutical company, live by these kinds of value questions. For example

A&H have a diverse set of asthma research programmes, as this respiratory disease is recognised as a growth market (as unfortunate as it is), as statistics indicate asthma as an increasingly common disease. This *values* disposition has given them a world lead in inventing and developing new drugs to relieve the symptoms. Their attention is not only in understanding the disease (the purity), but focuses on how they can help the asthmatic live a normal life (the practicality). In other words, the focus begins with the why of asthma, and then the what and how can A&H actually do to help the asthmatic (customer) live a normal life.

Focus groups. Focus groups are a powerful way of revealing, and to help understanding of, the customer's conception of what is important. Focus groups primarily consist of a panel of 12 or less, emerging and advanced customers from the above web, interviewed by team members about all, and specific, areas of demands. The questions can be scientific and informal. Questions like 'what do you consider to be the critical aspects of service/product that sway your buying decision', seem to be the ones asked early on. Customer values questions above may be asked too. But, most revealing, are the questions and issues raised by the customers themselves. Recording, and reviewing after a session, can add to the overall result, as it gives an opportunity to consider behavioural aspects. The power of the focus group comes through its directness. It is undiluted, focused at the people who need the information, and there is plenty of room for open, spontaneous debate, as opposed to the traditional snapshot, clinically driven survey. Here is a list of useful guidelines for running a focus group session:

- The longer the focus group goes on, the more honest and revealing the session becomes. Once relaxed and less self-conscious after an hour or two, you will end up getting the unvarnished truth. Sometimes to the point where it hurts. No pain, no gain!
- Spend time with each customer at his/her particular point in the web. This allows focus.
- Hold the session either in a specially designed environment, where specific communication tools have been installed, and/or at the point of user interface with the product/service.
- Invite front-line people (sales force, service staff) to attend on a regular basis.
- Invite external influencers like distributors, retailers, consultants, specifiers, contractors. Add their views, needs and wishes.

- Ask above values questions in the light of the competitive context.
- Give plenty of scope (50 per cent) for the customers to ask questions and towards the end let them lead the session. This allows exploration of what has been brewing in their minds during the session. It usually turns out to be the most informative.
- Set some objective problems for the customer to solve.
- And most importantly, we all have two eyes, two ears and one mouth, and I suggest that the host uses them in exactly those proportions.

Customer lectures. You do not lecture to the customer, the customer lectures to your team. After much persuasion, a large manufacturer of paper pressing machinery, decided it give this a go. The marketing director asked one of their more fastidious customers, whether they would be interested in coming in for a day to present a seminar to the design department, at the machine maker's site. A short while after, a convoy of cars arrived. Instead of executives stepping out, it was a maintenance crew. What happened next? A flood of issues not brought up before came about. The day was strenuous to say the least, heated at some points (not the customer, the machine design engineers), but at the day's end a large notepad had been filled. At the time of writing, a new platform is being designed. A range of easy to maintain machines from the customer's (maintenance crew) point of view, not the machine maker's guesses.

Actual place, actual product analysis (APAPA). One of the more powerful techniques is APAPA. Originally, it was the idea of the late Soichiro Honda, the co-founder of Honda Motor Co. He called it 'Genba Genbutsu', meaning 'actual place, actual item'. It is a powerful tool for finding the whats, and Honda swear by it. The technique is as it is described. Instead of speculation, the design team actually go to the place, either to see how a potential product is used or how a problem is actually occurring. You will find Honda engineers and marketing people in all sorts of practical, even smilingly odd places: multistorey carparks watching people park in confined spaces; Wal-Mart shopping centres studying families loading shopping into their car; outside schools surveying parents picking up and dropping off their kids; observing young mothers with their babies; at the beach watching families picnicking and sunbathing; the list goes on. It is this microscopic attention to real-world lifestyle detail, that has given Honda their innovation edge.

Visual imagery profiling (VIP). This tool captures live action on video, giving the opportunity to capture interactions of the customer with current and/or prototype innovations straight the way through the customer web/user life cycle. More importantly, VIP can capture the subtle, latent interaction and reactions of the customer. Sony is currently using VIP with a whole range of families watching TV together, analysing their lifestyles and interaction in their viewing. One subtlety they have noticed, is while half a typical family watch TV, the other half are engaged in other activities like reading, playing or household chores. They have come up with the idea of 'personal volume control'. But not only that, they have now found a killer application for their new '3D focus sound' technology. Ever sat down in your lounge and thought that the TV volume was up too high? Well, it may have been due to the shape of the room, focusing the sound in your area. So now Sony is working on a badge, with a personal volume control. The TV has a sensor detecting – via the badge – your position in the room, taking care of the room acoustics at the same time. The prototype I viewed has a clear crystal sound. This smart TV will also consist of many other features still under cover. Like the difference between Sony and AT&T's orientation to the transistor in the 1950s, all of this technology would just be technology if it was not for the power of VIP.

Customer reaction analysis. Analysing customer reactions to an innovation in a real situation, is an extremely reliable way of obtaining and classifying latent desires and intangible preferences. This is best executed just after a customer has experienced a service or has used a product for a defined period, for example, when checking out of a hotel or after one-year's ownership of a hi-fi system. This is carried out through interviews or a questionnaire on paper or over the telephone. Simple questions are asked about what could be coupled to the core. The immediacy of questioning often reveals some real home truths, as the situation is alive with fresh memories of use.

High concept invisible and intangible desires. There is strong evidence that customers aspire towards higher intangibles. Latent or subliminal demands that may not be directly related to the core product/service, sometimes with no tangible relationship. For example, it is now recognised that the noise a car door makes when slammed closed, is a significant physiological factor to the feeling of being secure and safe while in the car. All that effort that went into creating the right sound when a 'Lexus' door is closed, is not just to make it acoustically pleasing, but premeditated attention to invisible needs. It is clear that we must become much more sensitive to invisible demands, as these are areas of potential value multiplied. Higher concept values such as aesthetics, not just visual, but all the senses, smell, touch, taste and sound, must be considered.

On-line analysis. Internet technology is reshaping customer analysis methodology. It is now possible to hold online focus groups, customer lectures, imagery profiling, and so on; for real-time learning. Electrolux are ahead here, developing extensive interactive websites for data collection, facilitating live interviews with real-world customers. Mats Ola Palm, Executive VP, says, 'Now it is the customer that drives product development', and results have shown the internet only amplifies the voice of the customer. Online analysis is not only cheap, fast (for feedback) and provides easy to obtain customer lists, it gives a better reflection of real-world customer expectations in real time. Further and most important here, the internet is designed for the association of ideas, so maximising this opportunity. It is possible to capture the total customer demandplex and customer web online. Online customer analysis is at an embryonic stage, so innovation in the very analysis methods is yet to take off.

Hyperlinking the Analysis Tools

Individually, each customer demands analysis tool offers a powerful window through which to see into the customer mind, and a robust platform upon which to hyperinnovate. And, in network interaction, they only tend to augment each other's effect: VIP can be used with APAPA, to uncover the most subtle of demands. Customer reaction analysis can be enhanced with online focus groups, to get ultra-quick feedback. Value questions, such as why, what and how, can be utilised in customer lectures to focus the minds of all involved. And so on. The key is to get creative, hyperlink their usage. Experiment, play and tinker.

CHAPTER 21

Translating Raw Customer Demands

It is quite possible to translate raw customer demandplex into meaningful product/service/process characteristics, through the use of technical design targets. Three related charts assist this activity. Each chart is a development from the previous chart. The charts are not only a way of objectively stating what is important to the customer, they are also a team-building tool, requiring cross-discipline input from the *whole* team.

Raw Demandplex Inventory

Compiling raw customer information (complex or otherwise) can be accomplished via an inventory system. Remember, it is the raw customer demandplex that needs capture at this stage. From the customer analysis tools above, it is possible to gather both positive requirements (these come through just about all the above techniques); and the latent, emerging, subconscious expectations not yet expressed.

Table 21.1 is a *very simple* (for reasons of clarity) example demandplex inventory chart for a hot drinks cup holder, the kind found in public trans-

Table 21.1 Simplified customer demandplex inventory chart

No	Raw demandplex inventory (hot drinks cup holder used on commercial transport)
1	'My coffee spills and slops everywhere when the plane bumps and vibrates.'
2	'My little angels (children) always knock their drinks over on long trips... bless 'em.'
3	'I want my black coffee steaming, darn it. I can't keep it hot for half long enough.'
4	'Add as required.................!'

port (for example passenger seats on commercial airliners, buses, trains, taxis). The raw demands came from real (irritated) customers.

Translating Raw Customer Demandplex

Until now, this kind of data will either be in the customer's coded language, or in simple form, such as raw observations and notes. To make any sense from a technical/commercial prospective, we must translate these raw observations and demands into meaningful product/service characteristics. Table 21.2 translates the raw customer demands and observations inventory into the language of your own particular enterprise (all organisations have their own unique local language).

Translating raw expectations into a particular enterprise's technical language is indeed a subjective task, and if there is any frailty in the methodology, here it lies. But this is where effort spent out and about in the market is recouped. Building that sixth sense, that smell of the customer, competition and nature of the market. This real-world comprehension will give a team intimate interpretation powers of what the customer is attempting to express and aspire to (conscious or otherwise). The parallel of learning a foreign language in class, and then after to live in the actual country, not only to improve diction and comprehension, but to understand the deeper culture, fits here. *So a gap exists between what the customer thinks is important, and how the enterprise interprets what the customer thinks is important*. And the narrowing of that gap is – in part – down to the getting your people out into the market.

Table 21.2 Meaningful details translation chart

Raw observation translation chart (hot drinks cup holder for commercial transport)	
Raw demandplex	**Meaningful description**
'My coffee spills and slops everywhere when the plane bumps and vibrates.'	Anti/spill/splash cup holder, even when cup is 9/10 full
'My little angels (children) always knock their drinks over on long trips… bless 'em.'	Surround or position cup holder so it cannot be knocked/kicked over
'I want my black coffee steaming, darn it. I can't keep it hot for half long enough.'	Thermally insulated cup holder
'Add as required.................!'	Add as required.................!

Table 21.3 Detailed design translation chart

Detailed design translation		
Meaningful descriptions	**Creative design characteristics**	**Design targets**
Anti-spill/splash cup holder, even when cup is 9/10 full	Damped centre-of-gravity gimbal	Pivot 30 deg in X and Z axis Root-locus 50 deg
	Shock/vibration absorbing suspension	Viscous damping to excited harmonic random amplitude
		90 per cent attenuation
Surround or position cup holder so it cannot be knocked/kicked over	Sink cup holder inside arm rest	Trench 150 mm deep
	Easy access for cup insertion and extraction	Hand anthropometric study
Thermally insulated cup holder	Airtight/thermal surround cup holder	Rate of Q exchange less than 0.5 j/kg Cal/minute
Add as required.........!	Add as required.........!	Add as required.........!

From Table 21.1 a second raw observations translation, Table 21.2, may be used to decipher each observation into meaningful descriptions in the local language of your own enterprise.

Translations into Creative Design Characteristics and Design Targets

This next stage involves translating meaningful descriptions into creative design characteristics and design targets (Table 21.3). There can be many levels to this; each characteristic can dissect to a point of obscurity. For practical purposes, two or three levels are quite adequate for even the most sophisticated innovation. This is very much a hyperthinking exercise: the tools above will enable teams to answer customer demandplex in unique ways. This is the epicentre of the methodology.

CHAPTER 22

Developing Core Competency/ Core Technology

To realise the design characteristics and targets, the relevant core competency and core technology must be identified and developed. Without appropriate core competency and core technology in place, quite literally all inventions have little to no chance of effective commercialisation. Core competency must reach some level of maturation, and core technology must be significantly developed, before transfer to an invention. It is an impetuous move to transfer unproved technology into the market, as underdeveloped technology always bites back, and in the extreme leads to wholesale market failure.

What is Core Development?

The clear definition of both core competency and core technology, is also important: vague interpretations often lead to confusion during specification. The definition of what is core development follows:

- *Core competency.* The collection of explicit knowledge base, skills, tools, processes and focus of effort, that enable the development of core technology. Without core competency, core technology will lag in development, and often not meet technical targets defined in the customer charts above.
- *Core technology.* Essentially, subassembly and/or subservice infrastructure that go towards building a particular systems innovation. These include technology such as a computer database, a power supply, elec-

trical connectors and cables, microprocessors, restriction enzymes, chemical assemblers, software engines, subservice systems, production processes, and so on.

The Five Building Blocks of Core Competency

The goal for core competency development is to nurture the deeper *intellectual* essence that makes core technology possible. Here, the metaphor of the *building block* can be applied to the construction of core competency. Think about your own particular competency. They are made up of blocks ranging from explicit and tacit knowledge, skills and tools, to experience, processes and focus of content itself. Not unlike the different types of brick one would use to build a house, one can configure different skills, knowledge, and so on, to build a particular core competency. Below lies a description of five such building blocks:

- *Building block one – explicit knowledge base.* The most basic type of block is your explicit knowledge base. There are four issues here:

  1. Fundamental principles of current and emerging technology, such as engineering science, direction of evolution (chance and intended) and application and market potential.
  2. Explicit knowledge of market-ecology dynamics such as segmentation, regulations, standards, trends, and most importantly how and what will influence discontinuities within a market ecology.
  3. Explicit knowledge of competition, such as their particular competencies, end-product and services, strengths, weaknesses, opportunities that the competition have not yet addressed, and the threats they represent.
  4. Explicit knowledge of customer demandplex such as latent wishes or needs, most likely future demands and preferences, who the current customer base is now, and how the future customer base is likely to change.

- *Building block two – skills.* One popular definition of skill is knowledge plus experience in application. One can learn conceptual structures to improve problem solving. Skills can also be physical. Learned physical techniques in application is a skill. So a skill can be defined as the application of mental and physical knowledge, experience and learned conceptual processes that give rise to a potential outcome. When we say highly skilled we mean that these processes have been honed to the point of effectivity.

- *Building block three – tools.* This block is made up of direct application and conceptual technological resources that assist and amplify innovation. These range from communication infrastructure such as machine-tool centres, to design aids, to specialist test equipment, to the very buildings one works within. Tools are fundamental to competence building.
- *Building block four – processes.* This fourth block builds relevant cross-discipline processes that take a technological research programme from inception to application, or take a seed from inception through to end of commercialisation. Processes also include functional issues like management and project accounting, information systems, operations, distribution, even management of strategic alliances and supplier development. Even the very process of managing competency development.
- *Building block five – focus.* The gist of the core competency: when all is said and done is the essence of a proficiency. Examples range from, say, Sony and their microminiaturisation talents. The focus of difference between, say, an electronic engineer and mechanical engineer. Even the whole locus of a business context like steel or communications.

Core Competency Chart

One effective and visible way to build core competency is to generate a core competency chart. The chart lists desired building blocks that need assemblage and interconnection to yield a specific core competency. Table 22.1

Table 22.1 Core competency chart

Core competency: Thermal insulation materials	Explicit knowledge base	Skills	Tools	Processes	Focus
Notes: Typical technical specifications: $Q=mcDq$	Heat mass transfer analysis and calculation	Materials science	CAD solid modelling	Statistical design of experiments	Efficient thermal insulation materials
Rate of Q exchange less than 0.5 j/kg cal/minute	Material heat energy conduction	Mechanical engineering	Finite element analysis Design engineering methodology	Work-flow mapping	

lists the necessary knowledge base, skills, tools, processes and focus to manifest *thermal insulation materials*. Take 'tools' for instance; it is possible to list the desired applied tools one by one and classify technique types. These can be physical tools like machine tools or specialist equipment, even warehousing facilities. Tools can be software programs like manufacturing planning systems or CAD packages. Equally tools can be intellectual tools such as the methodologies here.

In many respects, here, we are using tools to build core tools to build even more complex innovations. As the depth and range of core competency are developed and/or acquired, the greater the development possibilities for core technology.

Core Technology Development Chart

For example, what particular core technology makes up the hot drinks cup holder for commercial transport in Chapter 21? Thermal insulation mate-

Table 22.2 Core technology chart

Thermal insulation materials characteristics					
Component technology	**Process technology**	**In-house or alliance**	**Start/ finish**	**Technical specification**	**Uncertainty factor**
Thermal insulation polymers	Expanded foam injection moulding	Memetics engineering	2/2003 to 7/2005	Continuous running temperature 180'C	**47**
Die-cast aluminium alloys	High pressure die-casting	XYZ Co	2/2003 to 7/2005	Strain hardened 500 MPa (Al-Zn-Mg)	**23**
Vibration damping bearings	Viscous damping systems	Liquid Plasma Co	2/2003 to 7/2005		**18**
Coiled springs	Continuous wire drawing/ winding M/C	Coil machines	2/2003 to 7/2005	Hard draw carbon steel 1700 MPa (18Ni-8Co-5Mo-Al-Ti)	**21**
Technology characteristics total uncertainty factor					**Σ 109**

NB: These simple examples are for illustration purposes only; the method here can equally be applied in multiservice provision, complex electronics and software development, systems architecture design, any artefact or process hyperinnovation.

rials, die-cast aluminium alloys, vibration/bump damping bearings, coil springs, and so on. Again, another chart is built to guide the development of the necessary core technology for such a thermal insulated cup holder. The table can include: a description of component technology, process technology, whether the technology is developed in-house or outsourced or through strategic alliances, the start/finish dates for development and the technical characteristics of the component technology. These characteristics are detailed in Table 22.2.

CHAPTER 23

Focus on What is Important

One critical double point issues for all innovation, is to:

1. Select the most important customers at each point in the web (see Chapter 21) for analysis.
2. Focus on what these customers perceive (whether articulated or not) as their most important demands.

Which Class of Customers?

Typically, selection criteria are defined by the development of specific areas of a *current* customer base. But this will not help here. Innovation requires focus on speedy and maximised market impact through the targeting of new customers to develop future markets and revenues. Six criteria are relevant here:

- *Highest potential growth.* Which customers potentially contribute most to, (a) immediate revenues for a new innovation, (b) long-term market growth? Focus groups help here, and market data such as value segmentation levers here too. Of course this information is hard to come by when creating or entering new ground. Lack of historic data can limit accuracy. The only way to get hold of this data is to start collecting.
- *Customers with driving problems.* Plain and simple, which customers have real and immediate driving problems? Demands that need satisfying right now? This can jump-start a revenue stream.
- *Highest value customers.* Exceeding the demands of all potential customers, every time, would indeed be a remarkable achievement. This

is in fact incredibly wasteful, and I would say, from experience, limiting. Many, maybe most enterprises find a potential customer base where 70–90 per cent of revenues is ultimately acquired from 30, 20, sometimes 10 per cent of that potential customer base. This is the law of the Pareto ratio. Focus on the highest value demandplex and revenue Pareto style.

- *Influence on market development.* Thinking in the future tense requires that you consider proliferation in the market. So what customers influence your growth in the market as a whole (see Chapter 3, innovative customers and early adopters, and so on)?
- *Higher expectations.* George Stalk of the Boston Consulting Group recommends that organisations should choose their most demanding customers, determine their needs and expectations, then serve them better than the competition. Obviously, if you are meeting your most demanding customers' expectations, less demanding customers will probably follow in line.
- *Ethical reasons.* In other types of market there may be ethical reasons for selection and focus, especially in the public sector, such as medicare.

Figuring out who your most important customers are, turns out to be a complex process, with a tangled web of criteria (yet again). Once decided, you will find that each customer has his/her own particular preferences: one particular demand is going to be more important than another. Rank what the customer thinks is important, then focus on those most important demands. Pareto may help again: a *small* percentage of all possible demandplex may be skyrocket high on the customer's personal agenda. It is possible to analyse what is important by first benchmarking what your competitors have to offer, then ask the customer to weight the importance.

Comparative Competitive Benchmarking

To a point, I agree with the notion that benchmarking against a backdrop of competitors is looking to yesterday's news, when innovation is the core of today's competitive strategy. In fact, when an enterprise looks to the future it needs to be aware of the best and most innovative standards and practices of the day. This gives a stake in the ground, and relative position on the future. Even with an archetype innovation, it is possible to look for *comparative* competition. Products and systems that already reflect and/or contain similar characteristics. The levels of analysis go from indicators of competitors' strengths, like growth, market share and market position, on to deeper analysis of competitors' competency in technology, service infrastructure, rates of learning, how they are organised, how they get to market, and so on. But, just as important, analysis of feature-to-feature measurement is useful when benchmarking. By analysing competitors' products and services against your own, you can look for areas of potential innovation relative to your own customer requirements.

Which Competitors?

Who are your competitors and who is the most threatening? It is just as important to look at the new, niche competitor. New, small competitors may look harmless now, but inherently take bigger risks, produce the surprises, and come up with unique seeds. Their culture is based on the unorthodox, and if successful, go on to create and define new markets. Many new competitors will simply be me-too types. So it is important to dig deep for the more unusual ones. Do not forget the traditional competitor, they have the developed competency. Also benchmark against best competitors and companies relevant to your business outside your industry too.

Customer Demandplex Competitive Benchmarking

From the charts above, the next stage in the translation gives a competitive context. Remember that perceived value held by the customer depends partly on the alternatives, whether by direct competition or the wider context. The competition sets the waterline. Obviously, in the case of creating new markets, this would not be possible, as at present there is no competition. Again, the customer must determine whether an innovation is up to scratch. Asking internal people alone will not give a balanced view. Whether by focus group or questionnaire, customer conception must act as calibration.

Detailed Translation Benchmarking

Table 23.1 expands still further on the demandplex translation charts above, this time building objective characteristics within a competitive framework. Four more columns are added:

Table 23.1 Customer expectations competitive benchmarking			
1. Company performance level	**2. Influence on purchase decision**	**3. Comparative benchmarking reference**	**4. Overall importance weighting**
1 3 5 10	1 5 8 10	1 5 6 10	**56**
1 4 5 10	1 2 5 10	1 4 5 10	
1 2 5 10	1 5 6 10	1 5 6 10	**42**
1 5 7 10	1 4 5 10	1 2 5 10	
Competitor B			

1. Ask customers how the innovation is performing on particular characteristics.
2. The characteristics' influence on purchase decision.
3. How the next best three competitors' (if any) product/service characteristics match up.
4. A characteristic importance weighting. All qualification comes from the customer, so seemingly uncodable demandplex become coded into objective and competitive reference.

Comparative benchmarking changes subjective customer demandplex into measurable targets. Suddenly the XYZ feature has a competitive meaning, and not just another characteristic. Take the first (row) feature (Table 23.1); the customer has given a 3 on the company performance, and an 8 on influence on purchase decision, but has given a 6 in favour of competitor B. This highlights a significant sales point and focus for effort. In this case the new performance target must be a 7 to exceed customer expectations.

What is Most Important? – Influence on Purchase Decision!

New competitive targets must be set against the influence on the purchase decision. Further, the most important influence on the purchase decision must be given priority above all else. Mere logic. *By multiplying the new target by the influence on purchase decision, it is possible to weight the importance of each new target*, for example the first (row) characteristic importance weighting is 56. Once the list is completed, the chart gives a very clear competitive, thus objective, view of what is important to the most important customers. Enabling a response to the highest demandplex.

The chart format can be laid out on the wall for all the team to work around. However, charted information needs to be stored for future reference, say in the form of a spreadsheet, so a digital overhead video screen, or better still, a hypermachine (see Chapter 14) is needed. By regularly updating this information, it is possible to keep track of customer trends, time factors and the overall customer demands dynamic. This competitive/customer database over time can turn out to be a wealth of strategic information, clearly giving the speed of flow and interconnection in the market ecology.

CHAPTER 24

Conceptualisation Matrix

Conceptualisation is a medium, not only for ontime introduction, but also potential success in the market. In the same vein, the single most important reason for increased cost-to-market also derives from lack of definition at the beginning. Mostly, definition is lacking due to the absence of methodology. Below I detail a method for turning the above customer-driven technical characteristics into a total *conceptualisation matrix.*

Voice of the Customer

All that has been developed above shows how to:

1. Dig deep into customer demandplex;
2. Translate findings into meaningful design characteristics and design targets;
3. Identify the necessary core technology and competency to realise such characteristics and targets;
4. Compare design targets against the (comparative) competitive framework.

But none of this is of value unless a team can integrate and build these demandplex into an innovation. This is the task of translating further into a structured conceptualisation matrix. A further three chart stages are now added and outlined (Table 24.1).

- *Component/service characteristic.* Defining the precise technical details of each component characteristic or service infrastructure characteristic

Table 24.1 Hyperinnovation conceptualisation matrix for a hot drinks cup holder

Customer analysis				Core		Comparative benchmarking				Process controls		
Raw observation	**Meaningful translation**	**Creative translation**	**Technology design target**	**Competence**	**Technology**	**Own performance**	**Influence on purchase**	**Bench-mark**	**Weight**	**Component characteristic**	**Component process**	**Process controls**
'My coffee spills and slops everywhere when the plane bumps and jumps'	Anti-spill/splash cup holder, even when cup is 9/10 full	Damped centre-of-gravity gimbal Shock/ vibration absorbing suspension	Pivot 30 deg in X and Z axis Root-locus 50 deg Viscous damping harmonic random amplitude			1 3 10	1 8 10	1 6 10	**56**	High tolerance injection moulding and die-casting	4 tonne injection moulding machine and high-pressure die-caster	Statistical process control capability studies
'My little angels (children) always knock their drinks over on long trips… bless 'em'	Surround or position cup holder so it cannot be knocked/ kicked over	Sink cup holder inside arm rest Easy access for cup insertion and extraction	Trench 150 mm deep Hand anthropometric study			1 4 10	1 2 10	1 4 10		High tolerance injection moulding	4 tonne injection moulding machine	Statistical process control
'I want my black coffee steaming, darn it… I can't keep it hot for half long enough'	Thermally insulated cup holder	Airtight/ thermal surround cupholder	Rate of *Q* exchange less than 0.5 j/kg cal/minute	See Table 22.1 for example chart that fits here	See Table 22.2 for example chart that fits here	1 2 10	1 6 10	1 6 10	**42**	High tolerance injection moulding	Expanded foam injection moulding machine	Statistical process control

(for example infrastructure specifications, engineering models and drawings, shopfloor schemes, material specification sheets).

- *Component process/service process characteristics.* How components and sub-assemblies are manufactured and assembled, or how the service is provided (for example, process plans, capability studies, CNC machine programmes, tool lists, metrology).
- *Process/service controls.* How the specific manufacturing and assembly process parameters, or service provisions elements, are controlled to this overall specification (for example basic work flow maps, critical process point charts, statistical analysis charts, defect feedback reports, problem analysis, solving and corrective action charts).

CHAPTER 25

Project Risk Assessment

Embedded project risks need quantification when selecting a particular innovation to bring to market. Risks are project probabilities of outcome along a range of factors; the logic being, if at the earliest stages we can detect and quantify the critical project risks we can save considerable heartache as the project moves through its life cycle. Risks ranging from strategic fit, market timing, pricing, competition, technological evolution, legislation, feasibility, and above all, customer demands, all go into the melting pot of deciding whether to throw a concept in the waste basket (*Cull*), wait for a particular situation to arise (*Hold*), carry out more technological and/or customer research (*Develop*), or begin realisation or commercialisation (*Go*). Set below are 10 common project risk criteria:

- *Strategic fit.* Creating multidimensional markets requires a cross-indexing of often unrelated ideas. Several strategic project questions arise here: (a) Does the potential innovation complement the overall strategic fit? (b) Does it add to the future? (c) Does it give synergy among the product portfolio?
- *Market potential.* Without doubt this is speculation at this stage; even within well-established markets, you will not know if you will hit gold until after launch. Does the concept hold significant differentiation and/or offer stepped improvement over alternatives? What is the potential market size and rate of growth potential? Customer research and conceptualisation activity will give an indication here.
- *End-price.* The most innovative organisations set an end-price first, then attempt to achieve that price via design intent. Can end-price points be met with appropriate profitability and cash flow?

- *Cost of development.* Can the cost of development be met? That is (a) capital expenditure (infrastructure, tooling, production equipment), (b) project expenditure (prototypes, testing and qualification), and (c) overhead expenditure (staffing levels, training, materials, tools and equipment, services).
- *Product life cycle.* The two most important questions here are: How quickly is the invention likely to be copied or superseded by a competitor? What of the potential to increase the dimensionality throughout the life cycle?
- *Core competency.* Does the required knowledge, tools, skills, experience and resources exist to develop and commercialise the invention successfully? How well developed is your core competency?
- *Core technology.* Has intended applied core technology reached a sufficient level of development? One common drag on time-to-market, is that unproved or exotic technologies are incorporated in inventions. Basic weaknesses soon rear their head during development and possibly in the market. Core technology research and development must take place outside live projects, instead of being treated as a project in itself. What objective empirical evidence is available to prove that core technology (for example protocols, systems architecture, integration, safety, materials) has reached a stage where it can be transferred into real products/service invention? Compile the evidence and objectively prove it. This is key.
- *On time to market.* Lead time relates to uncertainty, which is a product of *complexity* multiplied by *novelty*. Has specific uncertainty been calculated? From the uncertainty calculation, is the launch date realistic relative to your organisational competency and reserve?
- *Conceptualisation.* Lack of definition from the outset can cause delays on the road to market. Often late changes are a result of this. Conceptualisation is key here. So is the potential invention defined in enough detail? Have extensive experiments and prototypes been evaluated in both the laboratory and with real customers?
- *Reliability.* Product reliability in the market ecology is a result of design methodology, in particular within the *strife experiments* (recall Chapter 3). Can sufficient mean time to failure be achieved at both end-product and service process levels?

Table 25.1 Risk assessment

Risk criteria	Score									
Strategic fit	1	2	3	4	5	6	7	**8**	9	10
Market potential	1	2	3	4	**5**	6	7	8	9	10
End-price	1	2	3	4	5	6	7	**8**	9	10
Development	1	2	3	4	**5**	6	7	8	9	10
On time to market	1	2	3	4	5	6	**7**	8	9	10
Conceptualisation	1	2	3	4	5	6	**7**	8	9	10
Product life cycle	1	2	3	4	5	**6**	7	8	9	10
Competence	1	2	3	4	5	6	7	8	**9**	10
Technology proven	1	2	3	4	5	6	7	8	**9**	10
Reliability	1	2	3	4	5	**6**	7	8	9	10
Total	**70**									

Risk Assessment Table

Each risk assessment criterion can be given a mark from 1 to10, tabulated as shown, with 1 being high-perceived risk and 10 being little-perceived risk. A maximum of 100 is possible (as Table 25.1). Once tabulated, an objective number will help decision making: 1–20 Cull, 20–70 Develop, 70–100 Go. If one or a few of the criteria are weak – 4 and under, further development may be required.

Put your people out there. Sitting around a table, in a sterile office environment, will destroy the whole point of the exercise. Go to customer sites with the prototype, carry out the evaluation table in front of your highest future value and most demanding customers. As much as possible refrain from professional judgement. All internal judgement is subjective to the point of conjecture. Ask, ask, ask the customer, and look for the best competition in and outside your industry. If a concept remains borderline (develop) after several (three or four) cycles, it is best culled. Detecting a weak project and aborting at the earliest stages is, of course, a positive outcome; scrapping of a project in the latter stages because of some undetected or underestimated risk is, of course, a high opportunity cost.

The Overall Philosophy and Total Practice

The overall philosophy, here, is to design in and control what is important to the customer all the way through the genesis and conceptualisation activities. The total practice, here, shown in Table 24.1 integrates each chart and embedded characteristics into one total practice.

PART VI

Hyperinnovation Ignition

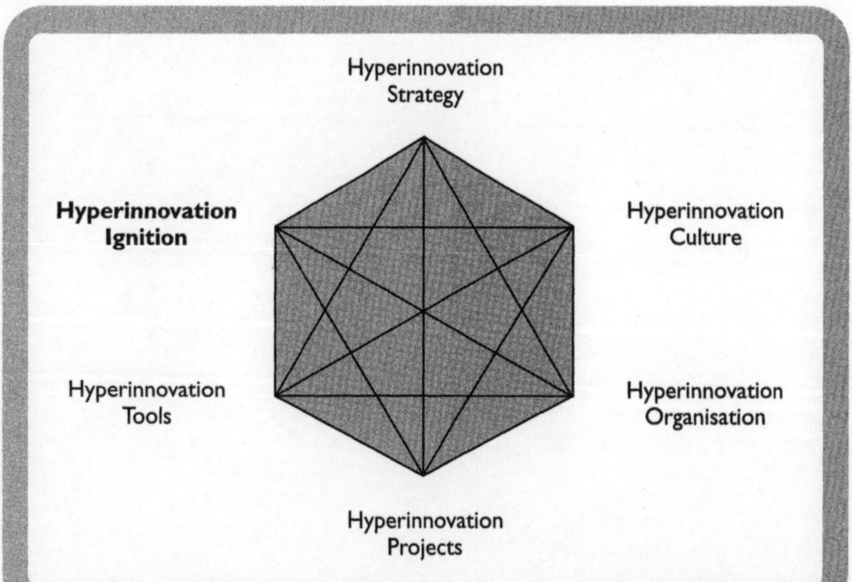

> Feedback is how a complex system governs itself.
>
> NORBET WEINER, MIT, 1949

In this final part, I describe a framework for orchestrating the necessary move towards multidimensional innovation. I call the framework *hyper-innovation ignition*! The concluding two chapters in this section consist of:

Chapter 26 – *Control Theory and the Design of Performance Metrics:* borrowing key concepts from the *control theory* of complex systems, and their impact on the design of key performance metrics.

Chapter 27 – *3...2...1...Ignition:* lastly, we move through a systematic step-by-step trigger to *ignition*; an interconnected programme of instructions that ignites hyperinnovation.

CHAPTER 26

Control Theory and the Design of Performance Metrics

We have all heard the sound of the screeching banshee over the public address system. Out flies a voice in the form of vibrating air, then at around 740 mph, impinges back on the microphone which the original voice struck. And so starts an amplifying feedback loop. More positive feedback builds more feedback to a pitch that breaks up beyond the range of human hearing.

Control Theory: Cybernetics

Astonishingly, we find feedback everywhere – feedback is nature's governor it seems. Feedback is what brings order out of chaos. It charms ultra-complex biological ecologies between total equilibrium and utter pandemonium. It regulates active brain functions and nervous systems. Feedback governs the climate from south to north poles. There is no central command and control in nature. No top-down set of rules. Only complex nonlinear feedback.

The very same mechanics found in nature can be applied to the autonomous control of highly sophisticated machines; software code, traffic systems, large crowds; even in the meditated actions of rumour mongering and propaganda. The science of autonomous control is known as *cybernetics*, deriving from a Greek word *kubernetes*, or steersman. Cybernetics dates as far back as the third century BC, evolving into a highly developed application science. Today we are surrounded with devices endowed with autonomous control. Flush the common or garden toilet and you activate a cybersystem – a system that returns to a defined state automatically.

Here, cybernetics can be applied to the ignition of hyperinnovation. In fact, as an aside, I am surprised that the many schools of change management, for that matter any human system that needs altering, do not apply the theories and tools of cybernetics. Applied in just the right way, cybernetics will destroy, transform, grip or ignite the most perennial and stubborn of man-made systems.

Seven Cybernetic Principles

Cybernetic text would fill a small library, accumulating stacks of ideas for the governance of complex systems over the last 2000 years or so. Out of this bastion of knowledge, I have borrowed seven related principles that can be applied in the ignition and autonomous control of multidimensional innovation:

- *Positive feedback.* Positive feedback amplifies the gap between what is expected and actual outcome. It ramps up small changes in the system, thus forcing the system to open up and fly in the opposite direction of the centre, average or intent. Positive feedback can be used to an advantage in systems that need amplification, such as TV reception or an advertising campaign, but if left untamed positive feedback can be very disruptive. Virtuous circles, chain reactions, the spread of a virus, economic increasing returns are all the result of positive feedback.
- *Negative feedback.* Negative feedback has a tendency to shrink the gap between what is expected and the system's actual outcome. It ramps down small changes in the system, thus closing the system towards the centre, average or intent. Negative feedback can be used to an advantage when a system has a target or objective to achieve. By comparing the system's output against the target, and feeding the comparison back into the system in a way that removes any deviation, the outcome becomes more and more predictable. The system adjusts to the consequences of the gap between the result and target. Here we can see that negative feedback is used when accuracy is required, stamping out change and securing stability. It pulls the system ever tighter to intended end-results, it sharply cuts away at surprise and novelty. Tighter and tougher management control such as ultra-communism, a compass needle pointing north, steering a vehicle or physical pain, are all the result of negative feedback.

- *Single-dimensional learning.* The application of negative feedback where behaviour is modified if the outcome is not favourable is called single-dimensional learning. Lower or single-dimensional learning occurs when a system applies the same rules over and over to seek improvements towards specific targets and end-results. Single-dimensional learning continually hones the system towards more efficiency, building a simple orderly system, with simple orderly outputs. In lower-dimensional or simple systems causality is either highly predictable or completely random. They either have tight links between cause and effect or no links at all. A piston and wheel is a lower-dimensional system, the conrod is the tight link between the piston and the wheel. A stony beach is a simple system, the stones on the beach have no links and are completely random. Single-dimensional learning is very useful for solving givens. That is, problems or goals that we know well or have come across before, solving steady-state issues very efficiently.
- *Multidimensional learning.* The application of positive feedback where causes are modified within the system before output, is called multi-dimensional learning. Recall that in a complex system, causal relationships often get lost within the system's many interactions, so making outcomes unpredictable. Novelty within the system's configuration emerges spontaneously and unexpectedly. We can see that the stock exchange holds these traits; rallies and crashes happen suddenly without warning. The weather, traffic jams and earthquakes happen in the very same way. However, this can be used to an advantage; multidimensional learning is disruptive and therefore creative, often resulting in new ways and ideas. Further, multidimensional learning solves unknown problems creatively by adjusting its internal structure in novel ways, spontaneously, without cohesion from outside the system.
- *Coevolving feedback.* When negative and positive feedback impinge upon, or work about each other, coevolving feedback emerges. When positive feedback destabilises the system, you get pandemonium. Negative feedback freezes the system, ultimately you get death. Combine both negative and positive feedback and you get dynamic self-organisation, you get non-deterministic order out of chaos.
- *Feedforward:* When a system behaves in a feedforward mode it is focused on a future tense. Here, the systems agents are indirectly hooked to an objective and unfold in line with that future goal. The human mind works – in part – like this, it can imagine a future action,

and work towards that mental action, even though the path towards that future is unknown. Indeed, the setting of a high concept vision, is an example of a feedforward system.

- *Single agent auto-governance.* If you can grasp hold of any one agent within a complex adaptive system, and control it in all its dimensions, you will have indirect control over the total system, because all agents will indirectly adapt to that controlled variable. In other words, by controlling any single agent within a richly interconnected system, and regulating that variable with the systems output, you get emergent auto-governance. No matter what state the other agents find themselves in, the system results in predictable outcomes. You get auto-governance of an unfathomable complex adaptive system.

Hyperinnovation at the Border of Yin and Yang

The Chinese recognised these cyberprinciples, albeit in a less scientific mode, some 2500 years ago – the *yin–yang* of dynamic balance (Figure 26.1), bringing order out of chaos.

What the ancient Chinese in fact recognised was the ubiquity and necessity of *opposites* within natural systems to bring about dynamic order. Equally, within man-made systems, without opposites there is no dynamic order. Specifically, without dynamic disequilibrium a system either goes anarchic or settles down towards death. This is key here: the so-called yin–yang (the positive and the negative, the light and the dark, the creative and the efficient) within a system brings about this dynamic disequilibrium. A disequilibrium that seeks greater disorder on the one side, and greater order on the other.

Figure 26.1 Yin–yang symbol

We can look at this disequilibrium effect of opposites to understand the diametric relationship between efficiency (optimisation) and creativity (novelty) within complex systems. As we have explored, a complex system has a near limitless number of interconnection possibilities (re: $\frac{1}{2}*\Sigma\alpha^2$, Chapter 1), that is, an inordinate scale of innovation possibilities within its domain. Therefore the space for novelty, and therefore creative interaction, is quite unimaginable. On the other hand, an adaptive system that is highly ordered or approaching a frozen state exerts *simple* outputs, and therefore becomes a very efficient (optimised) system. So what does this tell us?

- *The yin says:* the very notion of creativity is the new and the unique. If an adaptive system shows creative properties, it is exploring novel innovation spaces, and therefore always unfolding and learning in higher-dimensional, but unpredictable ways. But if this continues, the system overwhelms itself, and eventually begins to particalise.
- *The yang says:* the very premise of efficiency means that a system has high levels of order and optimisation. It says, if an adaptive system is efficient the system has found the best possible way of doing things, but once it does this, the system is not doing anything new, it has stopped learning, and the system begins to freeze.

Clearly, *efficiency* and *creativity* are opposites (in fact, we can now see why it is so difficult to optimise for efficiency while adapting to new opportunities), but as these opposites play against each other, battling for dominance, you get higher-dimensional innovation. *In fact, all innovation is ultimately a paradox. It is the successful embodiment of opposites.* We can see here the role of positive and negative feedback.

- *Positive feedback* amplifies effects and so gives disorder, and therefore creativity within a system.
- *Negative feedback* reduces effects and so gives order, and therefore efficiency within a system.

However, it is through the coevolution (A=B;B=A) of positive and negative feedback that the paradox of innovation emerges. You want positive feedback pushing the system out towards creativity, and negative feedback pulling the system towards greater efficiency, thereby creating innovation in a phase transition at the border of yin (creativity) and yang (optimisation).

When to Focus on Causes (Yin)

We know that *cause* breaks from *effect* in complex systems. Therefore a focus on causes forces perturbulations within a system, thereby making sure that the system is always exploring novel innovation space. In exact terms, if you want to build a creative culture, develop a novel strategy or form a highly adaptable organisation, you need positive feedback, so you need to design and focus performance measures on upstream causes. For example, focus on issues such as team building or time spent learning creative thinking techniques, increases the gap between expectation and outcome. This is the application of positive feedback, it amplifies small effects within the system, thereby delivering creative solutions and ideas, spontaneously.

When to Focus on Results (Yang)

We know that *effect* can veer away from *intent* in complex systems. In exact terms, if the mandate is to have innovation projects completed on time, to specification, to budget – negative feedback is needed, so performance metrics need to focus on end-results and key objectives. By focusing on key objectives, results follow (re: Chapter 15). The result is unconcerned with causality. By focusing on end-results – a single variable – you regulate the total system. Each subsystem adapts to the needs of each other subsystem, in line with that single control variable. By focusing on results, you will continuously calibrate the direction of the project in real time. For example, by focusing on a single end-date or customer expectation, the system adapts to that single end-date or customer expectation. This of course is the application of single-variable auto-governance and negative feedback; it shrinks any deviation from an imagined key objective towards its actual real intent.

Dynamic Disequilibrium

A secret of innovation is in the dynamic disequilibrium of opposites. Focus on end-results, and an organisation will eventually become a lean, mean, R&D machine, but will not be doing anything spectacularly innovative. Focus on upstream causes, and that organisation eventually becomes a maze of creativity, but will not be getting much to market on time, if at all. But focus on the yin–yang of cause and effect, on the right application of

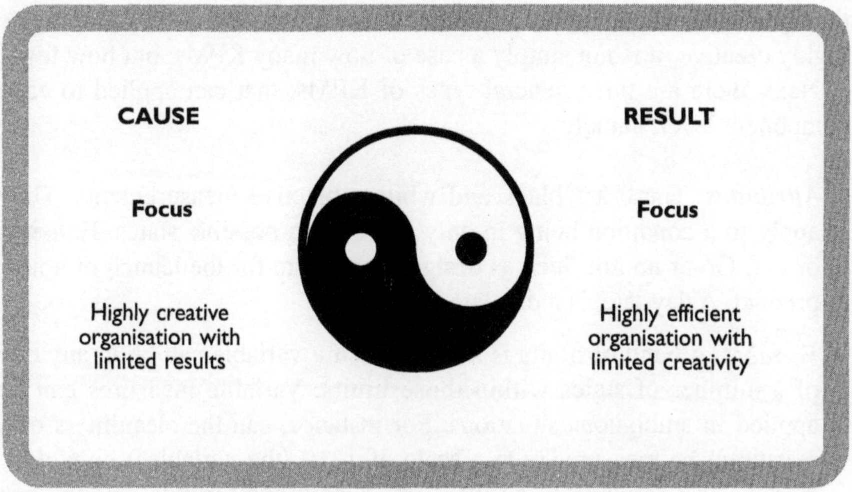

Figure 26.2 Yin–yang as cause versus result

coevolving feedback and auto-governance, and a cascade of innovation may emerge (Figure 26.2).

The design of key performance metrics has a central role to play here. By identifying what performance is required and appropriately focusing key performance metrics on either cause or effect, it is possible to govern a complex system to mediated ends.

The Design of Key Performance Metrics (KPMs)

The most important step in the design of KPMs is to define exactly what performance is required for hyperinnovation.

First, I have found – as throughout this text – that multidimensional thinking, accelerating the interconnections among ideas, and exceeding the customers' unarticulated demands are the three key areas of performance that ignite hyperinnovation.

Second the design of actual KPMs. As above, define the key performance, then begin to break each definition down into its constituents. For example: multidimensional thinking is a product of thinking strategy (for example contradigms), culture, organisation, working methods, and so on.

Third, these can be broken down further into multiple *components*. For example: multidimensional culture is a product of various behaviours, such as risk taking, integrity, trust, openness and sharing of knowledge that gives the capacity to interconnect ideas. At this level it becomes highly creative, it is not simply a case of how many KPMs, but how few.

Next, there are three general types of KPMs, that can applied to each component level, namely:

- *Attributes.* These are black and white, objective measurements. They apply to a condition being in only one of two possible states. Either in or out. Go or no go! Such as designating a date for the launch of a new product. A day late, is a day late.
- *Variable.* A band of limits is set, to which a variable can be in any one of a number of states within those limits. Variable measures can be applied in ambiguous situations. For instance, can the cleanliness of a restaurant be measured? On a scale of 1–10 (the variables) how clean was the last restaurant you went into? How comfortable was the last hotel you stayed at? Excellent, good, average, poor or terrible? These are examples of variable scales being used in ambiguous situations. Carefully thought-out variable measures can be a very powerful way of quantifying subjective issues, like cleanliness and comfort.
- *Factors.* These are ratios, rates, indices and percentages of a unit of measure. For instance, the down time as a percentage of total daily machining time for a particular machine or the rate of customer throughput on a particular service in a given hour.

You now have the basic concepts and methodologies to design and target key performance metrics in the ignition of *n*-innovation. The rest of this section uses and builds upon such concepts and methodologies (note: NFB = negative feedback, PFB = positive feedback, and CFB = coevolving feedback).

CHAPTER 27

3... 2... 1... Ignition

What lies below is a cybernetic ignition system: a step-by-step algorithm that feedforwards towards the future. There are five distinct stages to this ignition system, each in turn flowing out from the previous stage:

1. Setting a high concept picture and key values to set a coherent point in the future and compatible pattern of behaviour in times of uncertainty.
2. Benchmark the comparative competitive context.
3. Know yourself, so-called *what*-is.
4. Start the bottom-up ignition of multiple targets.
5. Repeat 1 to 5 to start the infinite regress through design space.

(1) Setting the High Concept Vision and Key Value Set

The overarching big picture should be the same in both the minds of the customer and the employee. Tom Peters says, if your people cannot capture the aim of the enterprise in less than 25 words, they ain't going to be working in the same direction. In the same light, without consistent key values, your people will be confused about the way they are supposed to act and think about the future. Now is a good a time to start development (re: Part II).

(2) Benchmark the Comparative Competitive Context

Remember if you are innovating radical breakthroughs you will probably not have any direct competitors at present. Yet, it is vitally important to benchmark the *comparative* competitive context. Indirect or ambient competition that set best and most innovative standards and practices of the day. This gives a stake in the ground and relative position. Even with archetype innovations, it is possible to look for comparative products and systems that already reflect or contain similar characteristics to your innovation. Go out and find – through customers, trade fairs, journals, suppliers and other sources – comparative competitors; whether educational institutes, pan-enterprises, the arts, the sciences, whoever and whatever. Now benchmark using the methodology below.

- *Hyperinnovation strategy.* Measure competitors management of paradox. Find out and measure how much context breakthrough they are achieving. Measure their multidimensional market learning and iterative capital equity. Measure how far comparative competitors push market panorama, in terms of multidimensional design, pan-technology, trend setting, and so on. Rate them between 1 and 10. Talk to the most innovative practices about what they think pushing the market panoramic means, or what multidimensional innovation should be about. What percentage of comparative competitors' efforts are spent laying the foundations for the creation of new markets? How many dimensions have the most entrepreneurial competitors connected to the core, and marketed in the last six months/year/three years as a whole? Individually/collectively do they dwarf your show? What will they be doing in five years' time? Are they moving towards value multiplied as standard? The most hyperinnovative practice I know is Boeing. Each carrier requires different cabin layouts and seat configuration, galleys and decor, let alone the different demand for landing gear and flight control systems; and the systems integration is ultrahyperdimensional. Boeing are in a custom-hyperinnovation based business! How do the best competitors categorise their knowledge base? What do the best practices do to engineer core competency? Strategos, the consulting firm are pioneering core competency development. Measure competitors' volume of strange alliances. Measure competitors' percentage time to market, in terms of hypertechnology and concept breakthrough, or first to a window of opportunity. Best practices are usually entrepreneurial start-ups in this case. Find out who they are, relevant to your industry. How fast is your innovation portfolio cycle vis-à-vis (a) your best three competitors, (b) the best relevant practice, (c) what could exist in five years' time?
- *Hyperinnovation culture.* Measure competitors' risk taking. Measure their failure to success ratio. Study Virgin for inventive cultural prac-

tices! Measure a relevant comparative competitor's culture. Measure their people's attitude to playfulness, openness, trust, change, new ideas, the crazy stuff on a scale of 1–10. Just as important, measure their leaders' attitude to all this as well. Chiat/Day/TBWA can show an innovative practice trick or two. Measure the leaders' transformational and multidimensional qualities. Measure comparative competitors' orientation to multidimensional thinking. Measure comparative competitors' intellectual diversity. One of the best practices you will find is the military. Cooks are crack troops, mechanics are dead shots, clerks are bomb-disposal experts.

- *Hyperinnovation organisation.* Measure competitors' orientation to teamwork. What team-building programmes do they have up and running? Measure them for effectiveness in collaborative work, innovation and creativity. Best practice are honey bees! Study them if you want to understand swarm work! What of the working environment? Is it open plan, and designed for innovation tasks? Measure it. What of the information technology initiative? Is it focus on the technology or greasing multidimensional thinking and collaboration? Measure it.
- *Hyperinnovation projects.* How fast is your most innovative competitor's time to market, from idea to commercialisation? Canon think six months for a new platform digicam is tardy! What ratios of uncertainty do they carry? What is the number of projects/team ratio? Are they achieving effective results over time?
- *Hyperinnovation tools.* How do the most innovative practices go about courting the customer? What might the best and most inventive practice be in five years' time? Measure competitors' people time spent in the market. Their engineers, designers, backroom people talking with/about customers. If your competitors do not do this, you are in luck, you have a tremendous opportunity to advance. If your best comparative competitors are doing this, what might the benchmark be in five years' time? Measure how many ideas comparative competitors have swiped from you. What kind of thinking tools and methodologies are they using now?

(3) What-Is Metrics

Knowing yourself (what-is) is central. It sets the *baseline* from where you are, to where you want to be. It reveals how far you have to go in both the direct and wider comparative context. Here we can look towards a handful of metrics related to previous sections, namely: strategy, culture, organisation, projects and tools.

As an example, hyperinnovation strategy shows that as markets and technology begin to mimic the network-like structure of complexity, we become increasingly open to the paradoxical behaviours of perpetual novelty, constant surprise, acausality, uncertainty and discontinuity. Hence, firms must not only accept this, firms must attempt to thrive on paradox. So, some example measures here. How novel is your business? Mostly old, mostly new, mostly 'what on earth is that?' (it is a great metric). How much time do you spend on innovation issues? Are you developing a learning disposition to seize on surprise? Have you accepted uncertainty as fact of innovation life, are you managing it? Are you focusing beyond cause and effect? Are you developing an unlearning organisation? Are you aligned for all of this? Out of a score of 10, how do you fare here?... Use the design of KPMs in Chapter 26 as a guide for effort. Relook at each chapter in turn, and build the appropriate KPMs to actualise them.

(4) Start the Bottom-up Ignition of Multiple Targets

Big targets have great mass, and thus huge inertia. Big optimum targets are often difficult to meet because the system itself needs to be up and running to overcome that great inertia. Set alone: 'we are going to reduce time to market by 80 per cent in the next two years', either does not work or is not sustainable over the longer term. Therefore the one big radical or optimal target may only end in frustration and possible failure.

Thankfully, the butterfly effect sees that multiple, local, small-scale targets quickly cause amplifying feedback towards the larger scale. Thus multiple short-term targets of modest measure are a more effective way to ignite transformation and achieve breakthrough. A key, here, is to ask your people, as individuals, as networks, to set multiform local targets from the bottom up. Ask for dozens of acutely focused targets.

Set out below is an example network of such targets. But I would warn, the targets are arbitrary, and only set for clarity. Your people must fix their own goals relative to the particular comparative context (stages 2 and 3):

- *Hyperinnovation strategy.* Start by devising a learning programme on the philosophy of hyperinnovation strategy, culture, organisation, projects, tools and ignition, for your top management, then ask each of your top managers to pass on the knowledge to their people. Do this through a cascade to the far reaches of the enterprise. Set up a weekend retreat for senior managers to cover hyperinnovation. Invite key people downstream. Do this within two weeks, whether you are 100 or 10,000 strong. Select a chief innovation officer (CIO) within 30 days, start at least three hyperinnovations within 60 days. Set up a collaborative commerce top team, start the search for *n*-market concepts, value multiplication, and collaborative partners. Spread the *HI* word.

- *Hyperinnovation culture.* Do the same for culture building. Set up a gathering for the whole enterprise/network/team within the next 30 days. Design a *key-point* booklet on hyperinnovation. Set the company vision and values with your senior management. Include this in the programme. Set up a continuous learning, skills development programme for each of your people. Make sure they own and measure their programme. Encourage people through incentives to engage in multidimensional thinking, customer analysis and speedy execution, in line with the high-concept vision. Set this up within 20 days. Budget and time are important, but again with some thought this can be very economical. Ask each of your people to search for the five most inventive practice people and organisations in their field of custom interest, within the next 30 days.
- *Hyperinnovation organisation.* Seek *project hosts* who take to hyperinnovation straight away. Ask them to spend 50 per cent of their time on team building. Ask them to set up flexible project hives for each focused team within the next 90 days (get facilities management involved too). Stick a full-blown basketball court slap bang in the middle of the hive. Set the pace and tone, make it exciting and energetic. Remember we are not talking capital investment here, this stuff is cheap. Ask the hosts to recruit (internally/externally) people into teams and begin building swarm skills. Again, expect and accept chaos. Build a hypermachine within the next 190 days.
- *Hyperinnovation projects.* Do not plan in any detail, focus on end-results. Stop working on a spread of projects now. Reduce the number of projects by a ratio of 5:1, via a Kanban method, do this overnight. Ask hosts and teams to focus on the Kanban. Get all of the remaining focused projects to market within the next 120 days. Expect and accept chaos. Finish one lagging technology research programme within the next 90 days to the point of a reliable working concept. Commercialise it within 210 days. Get the results coming in less time.

- *Hyperinnovation tools*. Carry out an *actual place actual product analysis* and/or *VIP*; arrange the venue/s with the targeted customers, carrying out the analysis, do all of this within seven days. Expect chaos. Do it again to the tune of different customers. Gather 20 new/raw customer demands (expressed, emerging and latent) within the next 14 days. Now translate the raw demandplex into meaningful concepts within the next 48 hours. Get the best three concepts prototyped and out with early majority/lead customers within the next 30 working days. It does not matter if they look a mess, input from real customers is the aim. Ask your people to develop core competency, in line with conceptualisation methodologies. Ask them to be radically different – avoid the orthodox. Ask each of them to become expert in one or a set of skills that go to achieving most innovative practice competency. Set a target of achieving a superior knowledge base, skills set, tools and processes relative to the comparative competitive context within 90 days. Ask your people to become competent in all the tools in this book.

(5) Repeat 1 to 5: We Have Ignition

The logic of the ignition programme, is, once again, a feedforward system, moving towards that magical point of criticality. The first cycle gives a feedback signal of current status. The second cycle is based on first-cycle results. What happens here, at the second cycle at stage 3, the metrics will show precise changes, from which recalibration of the performance targets at stage 4 can take place. From this, the third cycle will show yet more results. Then the fourth, fifth, sixth and so on and on feeding forward towards that point of criticality. It may be the twenty-first cycle, or the twenty-one-hundredth cycle that hits that critical point; yet the only chance of ever reaching that potential point of criticality will be to press the ignition button now – good luck.

Bibliography

Adair, J. *Leadership: A Modern Guide to Developing Leadership Skills*. Gower, London, 1983.

Adair, J. *Effective Team-Building*. Gower, London, 1987.

Akao, Y. (ed.) *QFD: Quality Function Deployment: Integrating Customer Requirements into Product Design*. Productivity Press, Chicago, 1990.

Allen, T.F.H. and Starr, T.B. *Hierarchy: Perspectives for Ecological Complexity*. University of Chicago Press, Chicago, 1982.

Anderson, P.W., Arrow, K.J and Pines, D. *The Economy as an Evolving Complex System*. Addison-Wesley, New Mexico, 1988.

Andrews, K.R. *The Concept of Corporate Strategy*. Irwin, Homewood, IL, 1971.

Argyris, C. *Reasoning, Learning and Action: Individual and Organisational*. Jossey-Bass, San Francisco, 1982.

Arthur, W.B. 'Positive Feedback in the Economy'. *Scientific American*, February 1990.

Bak, P. 'Self-organised Criticality'. *Scientific American*, January, 1991.

Band, W.A. *Creating Value for Customers: Designing a Total Corporate Strategy*. John Wiley & Sons, Canada, 1991.

Bartlett, C. and Ghoshal, S. *Managing Across Borders: The Transitional Solution*. Harvard Business School Press, Boston, 1989.

Basalla, G. *The Evolution of Technology*. Cambridge University Press, 1988.

Bernstein, A.J. and Craft Rozen, S. *Dinosaur Brains: Dealing with all those Impossible People at Work*. Arrow Books, London, 1990.

Bettleheim, B. *On Uses of Enchantment*. Thames and Hudson, 1979.

Bohm, D. *On Dialogue*. Taylor and Francis, Hampshire, 1996.

Boot, R.L, Cowling, A.G. and Stanworth, J.K. *Behavioural Sciences for Managers*. Edward Arnold, London, 1982.

Bottomore, T.B. and Rubel, M. *Karl Marx: Selected Writings in Sociology and Social Philosophy*. Penguin, 1963.

Briggs, J. *Fractals: The Patterns of Chaos*. Touchstone, New York, 1992.

Brooks, F.P, *The Mythical Man-Month: Essays in Software Engineering*. Addison-Wesley, Reading, MA, 1975.

Brown, P.B. *Marketing Masters: Lessons in the Art of Marketing*. Harper & Row, New York, 1988.

Bryant, N. *Managing Expert Systems*. John Wiley & Sons, Guildford, 1988.

Buzzell, R.D. and Gale, B.T. *The PIMS Principles: Linking Strategy to Performance*. Free Press, New York, 1987.

Capra, F. *The Turning Point: Science, Society and the Rising Culture*. Penguin, New York, 1988.

Carley, M. and Christie, I. *Managing Sustainable Development*. Earthscan, London, 1992.

Carroll, L. *Through the Looking Glass*. Macmillan – now Palgrave Macmillan, London, republished 1978.

Casti, J.L. *Complexification: Explaining the Paradoxical World through the Science of Surprise*. Abacus, London, 1994.

Clark, K.B. and Fujimoto, I. *Product Development Performance: Strategy, Organisation and Management in the World Auto Industry*. Harvard Business School Press, Boston, MA, 1991.

Cochrane, P. *Tip for the Time Traveller: Your Essential Guide for Technology and the Future*. Orion, London, 1997.

Cohen, J. and Stewart, I. *The Collapse of Chaos: Discovering Simplicity in a Complex World*. Viking, New York, 1994.

Copper, J. *Louis Agassiz as Teacher*. Comstock, New York, 1945.

Cosumano, M. and Selby, M. *The Secrets of Microsoft: How the World's Most Powerful Software Company Creates Technologies, Shapes Markets and Manages People*. HarperCollins, London, 1996.

Crofts, A. *Hyper: The Essential Guide to Marketing Yourself*. Hutchinson Business Books, London, 1990.

D'Aveni, R.A. *Hypercompetition: Managing the Dynamics of Strategic Manoeuvring*. Free Press, 1994.

Davidow, W.H and Uttal, B. *Total Customer Service: The Ultimate Weapon, A Six-Point Plan for Giving Your Business the Competitive Edge in the 1990s*. Harper & Row, New York, 1989.

Davis, P.C.W. *The New Physics*. Cambridge University Press, 1989.

Dawkins, R. *The Selfish Gene*. Oxford University Press, 1976.

Deal, T. and Kennedy, A. *Corporate Cultures: The Rites and Rituals of Corporate Life*. Penguin, London, 1982.

De Bono, E. *Tactics: Art and Science of Success*. William Collins, London, 1985.

De Bono, E. *How Children Learn*. HarperCollins, New York, 1986.

De Bono, E. *Sur-petition*. HarperCollins, New York, 1992.

De Bono, E. *Serious Creativity*. HarperCollins, London, 1996.

Dennett, D.C. *Darwin's Dangerous Idea: Evolution and the Meanings of Life*. Penguin, London, 1995.

Drucker, P.F. *Management: Tasks, Responsibilities, Practice*. Butterworth Heinemann, Oxford, 1988.

Evans J.R., Anderson, D.R., Sweeney, D.J. and Williams, T.A. *Applied Production and Operations Management*. West Publishing Company, St Paul, 1987.

Ferry, J. *The British Renaissance: Learn the Secrets of how Six British Companies are Conquering the World*. William Heinemann, London, 1993.

Gates, W. *The Road Ahead*. Penguin, London, 1995.

Gelentlar, D. *Mirror Worlds: Or, The Day Software Put the Universe in a Shoebox... How it will Happen and What it will Mean?* Oxford University Press, 1991.

Gibson, R. *Rethinking the Future: Rethinking Business, Principles, Competition, Control and Complexity, Leadership, Markets and the World*. Nicholas Brealey, London, 1996.

Glass, L. and Mackay, M.C. *From Clocks to Chaos: The Rhythm of Life*. Princeton University Press, Princeton, NJ, 1988.

Gliek, J. *Chaos: The Making of a New Science*. Heinemann, London, 1988.

Goldratt, E. and Cox, J. *The Goal: A Process of Ongoing Improvement*. Gower, North River, 1992.

Goman, C.K. *Creative Thinking in Business: A Practical Guide*. Kogan Page, New York, 1989.

Gould, S.J. *Bully for Brontosaurus*. Novel, New York, 1991.

Grove, A.S. *Only the Paranoid Survive: How to Exploit the Crisis Point that Challenges Every Company and Career*. HarperCollins, London, 1997.

Halberstam, D. *The Next Century*. William Morrow and Company, New York, 1993.

Halkin. S. *A Brief History of Time: From the Big Bang to Black Holes*. Bantam, London, 1988.

Hall, N. (ed.) *The New Scientist Guide to Chaos*. Penguin, London, 1992.

Hamel, G. and Prahalad, C.K. *Competing for the Future*. Harvard Business School Press, MA, 1994.

Hammer, M. and Champy, J. *Reengineering the Corporation: A Manifesto for Business Revolution*. Harperbusiness, New York, 1993.

Handy, C. *The Age of Unreason*. Arrow Business Books, London, 1991.

Handy, C. *The Age of Paradox*. Harvard Business School Press, MA, 1995.

Haralambos, M. *Sociology: Themes and Perspectives*. Bell & Hyman, London, 1985.

Harris, J. *Wonderwoman/Superman: Ethics of Human Biotechnology*. Oxford University Press, 1992.

Heller, R. *The Super-Marketers: Marketing for Success, Rules of the Master Marketers, The Naked Marketplace*. Sidgwick & Jackson, London, 1987.

Henry, J. and Walker, D. (eds) *Managing Innovation*. Sage, London, 1991.

Heyne, P. *The Economic Way of Thinking*. Science Research Associates Inc, Chicago, 1983.

Hofstadter, R.D. *Godal, Escher, Bach: An Eternal Golden Braid.* Harvester, London, 1979.

Holland, J.H. *Genetic Algorithms and Adaptation.* Technical Report no. 34, Department of Cognitive Sciences, University of Michigan, Ann Arbor, 1981.

Homans, C.G. *The Human Group.* Harcourt, Brace and World, New York, 1950.

Howard, W.G. Jr and Guile, B.R. *Profiting from Innovation: The Report of the Three-Year Study from the National Academy of Engineering.* The Free Press, New York, 1992.

Hunt, D.V. *Reengineering: Levering the Power of Integrated Product Development.* Omneo, Oliver Wight Publications, Essex Junction, VT, 1993.

Ishihara, S. *The Japan that Can Say No: Why Japan will be First Among Equals.* Simon & Schuster, New York, 1991.

Ishikawa, K. *Guide to Quality Control.* Unipub, New York, 1988.

Jelinek, M.C.B.S. *Innovation Marathon.* Blackwell, Oxford, 1990.

Kaku, M. *Hyperspace: A Scientific Odyssey Through Parallel Universes, Time Warps, and the 10th Dimension.* Oxford University Press, Oxford, 1994.

Kaodama, F. 'Technological Fusion and the New R&D'. *Harvard Business Review,* July–August, 1992.

Kauffman, A.S. *The Origins of Order: Self-Organisation and Selection in Evolution.* Oxford University Press, New York, 1993.

Kauffman, A.S. 'Anti-chaos and Adaptation'. *Scientific American,* **265**: 78, 1991.

Kauffman, A.S. *Whispers of Canot, Integrative Themes*: A Proceedings Volume in the Santa Fe Institute Studies into the Sciences of Complexity, Vol. 19. Addison-Wesley, Redwood City, CA, 1998.

Kelly, K. *Out of Control: The New Biology of Machines.* Addison Wesley, London, 1994.

Kelly, K. 'New Rules for the New Economy'. *Wired Magazine,* September, 1977.

Kosko, B. *Fuzzy Thinking: The New Science of Fuzzy Logic.* Flamingo, New York, 1994.

Kotler, P. *Marketing Management: Analysis, Planning, Implementation and Control.* Prentice-Hall, London, 1996.

Langton, C.G. *Artificial Life II,* Santa Fe Institute Studies into the Sciences of Complexity. Addison-Wesley, Redwood City, CA, 1992.

Levy, P.L. *Intelligence Collective: Pour une anthropologie du cyberspace.* La Decouverte, France, 1995.

Levitt, T. *The Marketing Imagination.* Free Press, New York, 1983.

Lipnack, J. and Stamps, J. *The TeamNet Factor: Bringing the Power of Boundary Crossing into the Heart of Your Business.* Oliver Wight Publications, Essex Junction, VT, 1993.

Lovelock, J. *The Ages of Gaia: A Biography of Our Living Earth.* W.W. Norton, London, 1988.

Maynard Smith, J. *Evolution and the Theory of Games.* Cambridge University Press, 1982.

Minsky, M. *Society of Mind*. Simon & Schuster, New York, 1985.

Mito, S. *The Honda Book of Management: A Leadership Philosophy for High Industrial Success*. Kogan Page, London, 1990.

Morris, D.C. and Brandon, J.S. *Re-Engineering Your Business*. McGraw-Hill, London, 1993.

Moss Kanter, R. *When Giants Learn to Dance: Mastering the Changes of Strategy, Management and Careers in the 1990s*. Unwin Hyman, London, 1990.

Moss Kanter, R. *The Change Masters: Innovation and Entrepreneurship in American Corporations*, Simon & Schuster, New York, 1993.

Moss Kanter, R. Essay in Chaloduis, C.K. (ed.) *Management 21C*, Pearson Education, London, 2000.

Naisbitt, J. *Global Paradox*. Nicholas Brealey, London, 1994.

Nelson, T.T. *Value-added Marketing*. McGraw-Hill, New York, 1992.

Nolan, N. *The Innovators Hand Book: The Skills of Innovative Management: Problem Solving, Communication and Teamwork*. Sphere Books, London, 1990.

Ohmae, K. *Mind of the Strategist: The Art of Japanese Business*. McGraw-Hill, New York, 1982.

Patterson, M.L. *Accelerating Innovation: Improving the Process of Product Development*. Van Nostrand Reinhold, New York, 1993.

Perelman, J.L. *School's Out: Hyperlearning, the New Technology, and the End of Education*. Avon Books, New York, 1992.

Perry, L.T., Stott, R.G. and Smallwood, W.N. *Real-time Strategy: Improvising Team-based Planning for a Fast-changing World*. John Wiley & Sons, Inc, Canada, 1993.

Peters, T.J. *Liberation Management: The Necessary Disorganisation for the Nanosecond 90s*. Pan Macmillan – now Palgrave Macmillan, London, 1992.

Peters, T.J. *The Tom Peters Seminar: Crazy Organisations for Crazy Times*. Macmillan – now Palgrave Macmillan, London, 1994.

Peters, T.J. *Thriving on Chaos: Hand Book for a Management Revolution*. Pan Books, London, 1997.

Peters, T.J and Austin, N.K.A. *Passion for Excellence: The Leadership Difference*. Random House, Glasgow, 1985.

Peters, T.J. and Waterman, R.H. *In Search of Excellence: Lessons from America's Best-Run Companies*. Harper & Row, Guernsey, 1989.

Pilditch, J. *Winning Ways: How Companies Create the Products we all want to Buy*. Mercury Business Books, London, 1989.

Plant, R. *Managing Change and Making it Stick*. Fontana, London, 1987.

Porter, M.E. *Competitive Advantage: Creating and Sustaining Superior Performance*. Free Press, New York, 1998.

Poundstone, W. *The Recursive Universe: Cosmic Complexity and the Limits of Scientific Knowledge*. Oxford University Press, 1985.

Reynolds, C. *Flocks, Herds and Schools: A Distributed Behaviour Model*. Computer Graphics, Los Alamos, 1987.

Rheingold, H. *Virtual Reality: The Revolutionary Technology of Computer-Generated Artificial Worlds – and How it Promises to Transform Society*. Touchstone, New York, 1992.

Rich, E. and Knight, K. *Artificial Intelligence*. McGraw-Hill, New York, 1991.

Robbins, A. *Awaken the Giant Within*. Fireside, New York, 1991.

Rogers, B. *Creating Product Strategies*. Thompson Business Press, London, 1996.

Russell, P. *The White Hole in Time: Our Future Evolution and the Meaning of Now*. Aquarium Press, London, 1992.

Ruelle, D. *Chance and Chaos*. Princeton University Press, CA, 1991.

Sakiya, T. *Honda Motor: The Men, the Management, the Machines*. Kodansha International, Tokyo, 1992.

Schaffer, R. and Thomson, H. 'Successful Change Begins with Results'. *Harvard Business Review*, January–February 1992.

Senge, P.M. *The Fifth Discipline: The Art and Practice of the Learning Organisation*. Random House, London, 1993.

Sewell, C. and Brown, P.B. *The Golden Rules of Customer Care: How to Turn that One-time Buyer into a Superloyal Lifelong Customer*. Business Books, London, 1991.

Sheff, D. *Game Over: How Nintendo Zapped an American Industry, Captures Your Dollars and Enslaved Your Children*. Random House, New York, 1990.

Smith, D.K. and Alexander, R.C. *Fumbling the Future*. William Morrow, New York, 1988.

Smith, P.G. and Reinertsen, D.G. *Developing Product in Half the Time*. Van Nostrand Reinhold, New York, 1991.

Simon, J. and Kahn, H. *The Resourceful Earth*. Blackwell, Oxford, 1994.

Stalk, G. Jr. and Hout, T.M. *Competing Against Time: How Time-Based Competition is Reshaping Global Markets*. The Free Press, New York, 1990.

Stapleton, J. *How to Prepare a Marketing Plan*. Gower Press, Westmead, 1979.

Stark, J. *Managing CADCAM: Implementation, Organisation and Integration*. McGraw-Hill, New York, 1988.

Thurow, L. *The Future of Capitalism: How Today's Economic Forces will Shape Tomorrow's World*. Nicholas Brealey, London, 1996.

Tucker, R. *Managing the Future: 10 Driving Forces of Change for the 90s*. G.P. Putnams Sons, New York, 1991.

Utterback, J. *Mastering the Dynamics of Innovation: How Companies can Seize Opportunities in the Face of Technological Change*. Harvard Business School Press, Boston, 1994.

Vision, G. *Modern Anti-realism and Manufacture Truth*. Routledge, London, 1988.

Wacker, W. and Taylor, J. (with Meaus, H.) *The 500 Year Delta: What Happens After What Comes Next*. HarperCollins, New York, 1997.

Wacker, W. and Taylor, J. (with Meaus, H.) *The Visionary's Handbook: Nine Paradoxes that will Shape the Future of your Business*. Copstone Publishing, Oxford, 2000.

Waldrop, M.M. *Complexity: The Emerging Science at the Edge of Order and Chaos*. Penguin, London, 1992.

Wheelwright, S.C. and Clark, K.B. *Revolutionising Product Development: Quantum Leaps in Speed, Efficiency and Quality*. The Free Press, New York, 1992.

Whiteley, R.C. *The Customer Driven Company: Moving from Talk to Action*. Business Books, London, 1990.

Wolfman, S. 'Computer Software in Science and Mathematics'. *Scientific American*, September, 1986.

Wood, L.E. *Thinking Strategies: Exercises for Mental Fitness*. Prentice-Hall, New Jersey, 1986.

Yourcenar, M. *Memoirs of Hadrian*. Penguin, London, 1989.

INDEX

www.ingramcontent.com/pod-product-compliance
Ingram Content Group UK Ltd.
Pitfield, Milton Keynes, MK11 3LW, UK
UKHW041913040925
462611UK00003B/231
* 9 7 8 1 3 4 9 4 3 2 3 8 7 *